This is the
Henry Holt Walks Series,
which originated with
PARISWALKS, *by Alison and Sonia Landes.*
Other titles in this series include:

Romewalks

ROMEWALKS

REVISED EDITION

Anya M. Shetterly

Photographs by
Anya M. Shetterly

An Owl Book

Henry Holt and Company • New York

Henry Holt and Company, Inc.
Publishers since 1866
115 West 18th Street
New York, New York 10011

Henry Holt® is a registered
trademark of Henry Holt and Company, Inc.

Published in Canada by Fitzhenry & Whiteside Ltd.,
195 Allstate Parkway, Markham, Ontario L3R 4T8.

Library of Congress Cataloging-in-Publication Data
Shetterly, Anya M.
Romewalks/Anya M. Shetterly; photographs by Anya M. Shetterly.
—Rev. ed.
p.   cm.—(Henry Holt walks series)
"An Owl book."
Includes index.
1. Rome (Italy)—Tours. I. Title. II. Title: Rome walks.
III. Series.
DG804.S45   1994   93-28432
914.5′63204929—dc20   CIP

ISBN 0-8050-2054-3

Henry Holt books are available for special promotions and premiums.
For details contact: Director, Special Markets.

First Owl Book Edition—1984
Revised Edition—1994
Designed by Claire Naylon Vaccaro
Maps by David Lindroth

Printed in the United States of America
All first editions are printed on acid-free paper. ∞

1   3   5   7   9   10   8   6   4   2

Grateful acknowledgment is made for use of portions
of "My Rome" by Muriel Spark.
Copyright © 1983 by The New York Times Company.
Reprinted by permission.

To Andrew, Alexander, and Christopher,
my favorite travel companions

Contents

Acknowledgments
xiii

Introduction
1

Information and Advice 6

Before You Go 6 • General Information 11
Entertainment 13 • Museums and Sites 15
Accommodations 18 • Transportation 19
Food and Drink 23 • Tipping 27
Telephone, Telegraph, Post Office 27
Money and Banking 29 • Shopping 29
Emergencies 31 • A Word of Warning 32
Glossary of Architectural Terms 33
A Brief History of Rome 35

Walk 1
Streets of the Papacy:
The Neighborhood of the Campo dei Fiori
45

Walk 2
The Empire and the Church:
At the Foot of the Capitoline Hill
107

Walk 3

The Artisans and the Bourgeoisie:
Around the Piazza Navona
151

Walk 4

A Village Within the City:
The Island and Southern Trastevere
201

Walk 5

The Church and the Jews:
The Old Jewish Ghetto
243

Restaurants, Hotels, and Shops
270

Index
283

Acknowledgments

This book would not have been written without the assistance and stories of many Romans: friends, acquaintances, and passersby. I owe a special thanks to those friends who have kept me abreast of most of the changes in Rome over the last ten years and whose suggestions for restaurants and shops have kept me both satiated and familiar. Readers of the first edition of *Romewalks* have also contributed with their suggestions and enthusiasm.

Working on this book would not have been such a pleasure without the inspiration of three important studies of Rome: Georgina Masson's *The Companion Guide to Rome*; Richard Krautheimer's *Rome, Profile of a City*; and Christopher Hibbert's *Rome, the Biography of a City*. I am deeply indebted to Professor Arthur Szathmary of Princeton University for both his careful reading of my manuscript and his encouragement. I also wish to thank the staffs of the American Academy Library, the Ernesto Besso Foundation, and the Jewish Museum.

Finally, I am most grateful for the opportunity to revise *Romewalks*. I thank my agent, Fifi Oscard, for her enthusiasm; Theresa Burns, editor of the Henry Holt Walks Series, for keeping it in print; and Tracy Sherrod, editor of this book, for her patience and good humor.

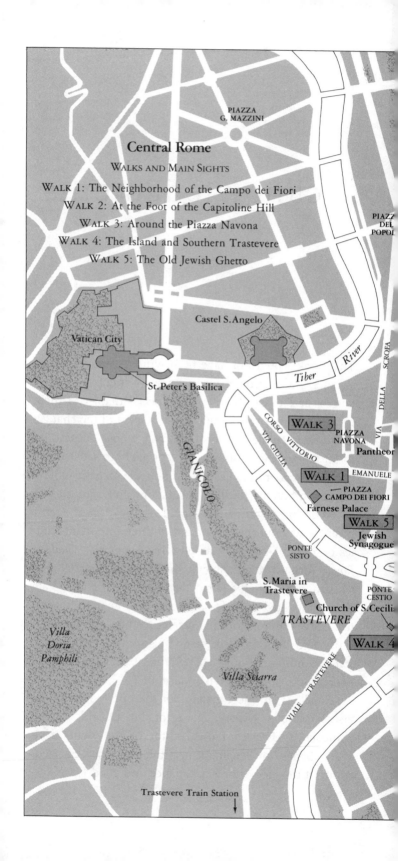

Central Rome

WALKS AND MAIN SIGHTS

WALK 1: The Neighborhood of the Campo dei Fiori
WALK 2: At the Foot of the Capitoline Hill
WALK 3: Around the Piazza Navona
WALK 4: The Island and Southern Trastevere
WALK 5: The Old Jewish Ghetto

PIAZZA
G. MAZZINI

PIAZZ
DEL
POPOI

Castel S. Angelo

Vatican City

St. Peter's Basilica

Tiber   River

VIA DELLA SCROFA

CORSO VITTORIO

VIA GIULIA

WALK 3

PIAZZA
NAVONA

Pantheor

EMANUELE

WALK 1

PIAZZA
CAMPO DEI FIORI

Farnese Palace

WALK 5
Jewish
Synagogue

GIANICOLO

PONTE
SISTO

S. Maria in
Trastevere

PONTE
CESTIO

Church of S. Cecili

TRASTEVERE

WALK 4

Villa
Doria
Pamphili

Villa Sciarra

VIALE TRASTEVERE

Trastevere Train Station

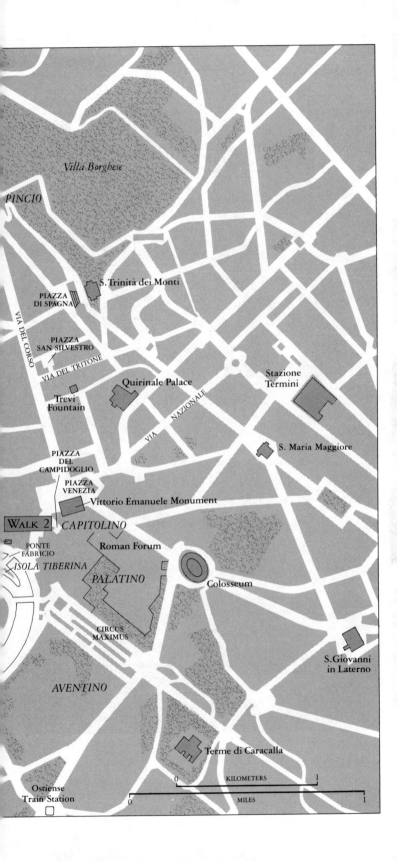

Villa Borghese

PINCIO

S. Trinità dei Monti

PIAZZA
DI SPAGNA

VIA DEL CORSO

PIAZZA
SAN SILVESTRO

VIA DEL TRITONE

Quirinale Palace

Stazione
Termini

VIA NAZIONALE

Trevi
Fountain

S. Maria Maggiore

PIAZZA
DEL
CAMPIDOGLIO

PIAZZA
VENEZIA

Vittorio Emanuele Monument

WALK 2 CAPITOLINO

PONTE
FABRICIO

ISOLA TIBERINA

Roman Forum

PALATINO

Colosseum

CIRCUS
MAXIMUS

S. Giovanni
in Laterno

AVENTINO

Terme di Caracalla

0   KILOMETERS   1

0   MILES   1

Ostiense
Train Station

La Bocca della Verità, the Mouth of Truth

Introduction

Henry James's reaction was: "It beats everything: it leaves the Rome of your fancy—your education—nowhere . . . I went reeling and moaning through the streets in a fever of enjoyment . . . the effect is something indescribable." Rome indeed provokes this kind of excitement. One of the reasons is that there is so much more in Rome than you could ever imagine—but this is also very confusing. Scattered throughout the city's historic center are layers of images associated with two and a half millennia of history. Even when something appears to belong to a definite period, a second glance often betrays a bewildering span of centuries. Nowhere in central Rome is there a sense of a well-planned city; instead, it is fragmented and untidy and has been that way since the days of the Roman republic. While the urban plans of the sixteenth and seventeenth centuries placed a great value on organization, they were ultimately exuberant and far from comprehensive. Especially today, after the spotty additions of the republicans at the turn of the century and the Fascists in the 1920s and 1930s, the effect is one of a careless blend of contrasting plans, styles, and ideas. This collage, so dominant in the visual landscape, is the key to Rome's fascination. It bespeaks the very spirit of the city, for Rome is not just a monument to history, art, architecture, or Western civilization; it is a city of people who have used and reused their monuments and buildings to live in, to do business, to worship, and to govern. Romans are always described as adaptable and their city certainly reflects that.

While not a comprehensive guide, this book presents a broad yet intimate view of Rome—one that is very much the result of my own experience of the city. Walking the streets described in this book is how I began learning the complex history of Rome and its architecture, how I absorbed the patterns and character of its people, and where I always seek this city's particular charm and beauty. Now that I no longer live in Rome, it is these walks that I always come back to when I visit.

Aside from covering some of the most historically rich and beautiful sections of the city, the five walks in this book are presented as a way to understand the many transitions in the city's growth and to give historical depth to the numerous visual images. I take pleasure in being neither architect nor historian, archeologist nor art critic, but an enthusiast of Rome who has learned a great deal about all these fields through my studies of this very special place. But Rome has even more than that to offer and these walks will satisfy your desire to shop, take pictures, watch people, or just wander. The streets themselves are like display cases, inviting you to, above all, enjoy.

I have chosen five areas to explore: around the Campo dei Fiori, at the foot of the Capitoline Hill, around the Piazza Navona, the southern end of Trastevere, and the Jewish Ghetto. Each of these walks offers a different perspective on the life and history of this city and each is as visually stimulating as it is rich in tradition. In this new edition I have separated the Jewish Ghetto and made a new walk focused on that area and subject. The second chapter, at the foot of the Capitoline Hill, includes the

Velabro, the Piazza Bocca della Verità, and a discussion of some of Rome's earliest history. As Goethe warned, "Rome . . . is like the sea of which the depth increases as one proceeds," and each walk has benefited from my further studies of all things Roman.

More than other Roman neighborhoods, the Campo dei Fiori has been carefully shaped by the Catholic Church. Located directly across the river from the Vatican, this area always provided primary access for pilgrims. Some roads were built to steer the crowds in certain directions, others to create monumental entrances. Palaces were erected to house the cardinals and relatives of the popes. In fact, Renaissance Rome was created and fully orchestrated by the Catholic Church. Today, the piazza of Inquisition fame accommodates central Rome's largest outdoor market and all the activity and color inherent in a market adds vitality to some of the most graceful architecture in Rome.

In her book *Rome and a Villa*, Eleanor Clark says of the area at the foot of the Capitoline Hill toward the Tiber River that "nowhere in Rome is one so acutely aware of the ancient city that lies buried beneath." This is a part of town where the ruins of the Roman Empire blend dramatically and unpretentiously with the multifaceted cityscape of modern and baroque Rome. During the Roman Empire it was crowned with important buildings: the Circus of Flaminius, used for horse races and triumphal court; the Portico d'Ottavia, a meeting place that included temples, libraries, and exhibition halls; the Teatro di Marcello, said to be the model for the Colosseum; and the Republican temples adjoining the Forum Boarium and the Forum Olitorium, the cattle and vegetable markets. Except for the Circus of Flaminius, the ruins of this period are not only visible, but many of them have been recycled at various points in time for other purposes and do not stand merely as museum pieces. In this ancient area, close to the city's birthplace and later the seat of its secular power, there are also vestiges of the earliest days of Christianity. During this walk we can see the important role played by the Church in Rome's design and development since the fourth century.

The neighborhood of the Piazza Navona forms a semicircle around one of Rome's most important and beautiful landmarks. Located in the heart of the ancient Roman Campus Martius, this neighborhood of baroque churches and intimate, narrow streets packed with small houses reflects the area's status as a prosperous bourgeois and artisan quarter dating from the late sixteenth century. Today it is still considered an artisan district and one of the most elegant sections of central Rome. For the last two centuries this neighborhood has been famous for its antique trade; the main streets are filled with fancy antique shops, and on the smaller side streets are numerous artisan shops specializing in copying or restoring antique furniture and art and the crafting of fine jewelry. It is an education to pass these studios, which during the summer expand onto the cobblestone streets.

Trastevere means "across the Tiber" and refers to a long stretch of the city along the river on the same side as the Vatican. The section near the Church of S. Maria in Trastevere is well known as the chic counterculture center of Rome. There is also a quieter, less trafficked Trastevere just across from the island in the Tiber. In contrast to the other walks, a good half of this neighborhood's buildings are made up of public institutions: walled-in monasteries and convents with gardens, schools, and a home for the aged. The little remaining space is packed in closely around winding, narrow streets. Once you know which doors to knock on, the gardens with their cloisters are like no others in Rome and the unassuming shops give one a special sense of community. This is a walk that presents a simpler, though no less charming side of Rome. If possible, it should be planned for Tuesday, Thursday, or Sunday morning so that you can see the rare and beautiful Cavallini fresco in the Church of S. Cecilia, which is open to the public from 10:00–11:30 A.M. on Tuesday and Thursday and after mass on Sunday between 11:00 A.M. and noon. The cloister at S. Giovanni dei Genovesi is also open during the early afternoon on Tuesdays and Thursdays.

The final walk is through a small area where walls once enclosed the Jewish population of Rome. In this predominantly Jewish neighborhood the synagogue dominates the banks of the Tiber, the restaurants specialize in Roman Jewish cuisine, and only three shops are owned by non-Jews. Nowhere else in Rome is the *passeggiata*, the traditional evening walk, taken so seriously. The entire community gathers on one street; they create such a boisterous scene that a Roman friend of mine, unfamiliar with the neighborhood, was sure a demonstration was taking place. You should plan this walk for either late afternoon, if you want to see the street life, or in the morning, if you wish to visit the Jewish Museum.

At every turn, during these approximately two- to three-hour walks, there is some detail that recalls Rome's varied history and the life of its people, be it the graceful baroque line added to an early Christian church or an ancient Roman ruin used to house the local fish market; the delightful fountains that spurt water from sources originally discovered by the ancient Romans, or a house that once belonged to a famous sixteenth-century courtesan. These are all vivid images typical of Rome's charm, and each has a story. Hopefully *Romewalks* will encourage you to undertake a protracted exploration of Rome's historic streets and neighborhoods—you may even fall in love with this city as I have!

Information
and Advice

*Hee that would see Rome may doe it in a fort-
night, walking about from Morning to Evening,
he that would make it his study to understand
it, can hardly perfect it in lesse than a yeare. A
man may spend many Moneths at Rome, and
yet have something of Note to see every day.*

John Raymond, 1648

BEFORE YOU GO

Getting to know Rome can be a life's work, or at least
one of many years. She has many faces—classical, medieval, Renaissance, baroque, modern, religious—and within
each there is a rich collection of history, folklore, and art.
The experience can be overwhelming, especially considering all the inconveniences of a modern, overcrowded
city with a cultural propensity to be casual about details
such as visiting hours or restoration schedules. It will be
an enormous help to you if you think about what you
want to see and plan for it before you arrive.

Well in advance of your departure call or write the

Italian Government Travel Office at any of the following locations:

630 Fifth Avenue
New York, N.Y. 10111
(212)245-4822

500 North Michigan Avenue
Chicago, Ill. 60611
(312)644-0990

360 Post Street, Suite 801
San Francisco, Calif. 94108
(415)392-6206

Ask for information about Rome and specify your interest in brochures on sightseeing, hotels, restaurants, museums, and, most important, a map. You will be doing a lot of walking because that is the kind of city Rome is and your map may be your most precious guide. It will also help you in your choice of a hotel.

Book your hotel room as soon as you have decided on your schedule and make sure you receive a confirmation from the hotel. You will need a passport and, if you are planning to stay in Italy for more than three months, a visa—call the Italian Consulate for information and instructions on how to apply for one.

The best time to visit Rome is in late spring and autumn. Winters are moderate but wet, which means you will primarily see the interiors of the city and miss one of the most important attractions—the street life. July and August are hot, and most Romans flee to the beaches leaving the city half-deserted and many of its restaurants and shops closed. In late September and October the city is in full gear, the weather is dry and warm, and you can still enjoy the many outdoor restaurants and cafés. If you are trying to avoid crowds in the museums, take your chances on February, which can be almost springlike and not as wet as other winter months or early spring.

When choosing your wardrobe don't underestimate

the possibility of extremes. During the summer there are few air conditioners and during the winter it can feel very cold, especially behind Rome's thick damp walls. In the spring and fall temperatures change suddenly, so be prepared to dress in layers. The most basic item in your suitcase should be a comfortable pair of walking shoes; most of the streets in Rome's historic center are cobblestoned and are hard on the feet, and you can't explore the city without a lot of walking. Italians are very style conscious, and, while not formal, they maintain a more conservative approach to dress than we do. Men and women, for instance, do not wear shorts in the city, and these, along with short skirts and bare arms, are not allowed in many of the churches you will want to visit. Remember, too, that Italian electricity is 220 volts with outlets requiring two rounded plugs, so you will need both an adapter and a transformer to use your hair dryer or electric razor. Most medium-priced hotels and up provide hair dryers in the bathrooms.

No other city has been contemplated, discussed, and described as much as Rome, and your impressions of the city will be that much more meaningful for the number of perspectives you bring to it—from the documentations of the ancients, to the insights of Gibbon and Gregorovius, to the awe of Goethe, to the incisive observations of Stendhal, to the romance of Hawthorne, to the enthusiasm of James. You can also look at Rome through the eyes of Piranesi, Lorrain, Franz, and many other artists. Below is a list of books that will help you plan your itinerary and feed your imagination.

General Books on Rome

L. Berarelli, *Roma e Dintorni* (Guide of the Italian Touring Club)

E. Bowen, *A Time in Rome*

E. Clark, *Rome and a Villa*

Information and Advice

A. Hare, *Walks in Rome*

N. Hawthorne, *Notebooks in France and Italy*

P. Hofmann, *Rome: The Sweet Tempestuous Life*

H. James, *Italian Hours*

E. Lucas, *Wandering in Rome*

G. Masson, *A Companion Guide to Rome*

H. V. Morton, *A Traveller in Rome*

W. Murray, *Italy, the Fatal Gift*

R. Rodd, *Rome of the Renaissance and Today*

Stendhal, *Promenades dans Rome*

W. Story, *Roba di Roma*

Roman History

J. Burckhardt, *The Civilization of the Renaissance in Italy*

E. Gibbon, *The History of the Decline and Fall of the Roman Empire*

F. Gregorovius, *History of the City of Rome in the Middle Ages*

E. Hamilton, *The Roman Way*

C. Hibbert, *Rome, the Biography of a City*

J. Klaczko, *Rome and the Renaissance*

R. Krauthimer, *Rome, Profile of a City 312–1308*

R. Lanciani, *The Golden Days of the Renaissance in Rome*

R. Lanciani, *Pagan and Christian Rome*

Livy, *The Early History of Rome*

L. von Pastor, *The History of Popes from the Close of the Middle Ages*

W. Pater, *The Renaissance*

Suetonius, *Lives of the Caesars*

J. A. Symonds, *The Renaissance in Italy*

Roman Art and Architecture

J. Ackerman, *The Architecture of Michelangelo*

M. Armellini, *Le Chiese di Roma dal Secolo IV al XIX*

B. Berenson, *Italian Painters of the Renaissance*

A. Blunt, *Guide to Baroque Rome*

M. Briggs, *Baroque Architecture*

A. Fabber, *Roman Baroque Art*

J. Lees-Milne, *Roman Mornings*

P. MacKendrick, *The Mute Stone Speaks*

W. Mâle and D. Buxton, *The Early Churches of Rome*

C. Marucchi, *The Roman Forum and Palatine*

G. Masson, *Italian Villas and Palaces*

P. and L. Murray, *The Art of the Renaissance*

A. Rinaldi, *L'Arte in Roma dal Seicento al Novecento*

M. Scherer, *Marvels of Ancient Rome*

G. Scott, *The Architecture of Humanism*

A. Strong, *Art in Ancient Rome*

P. Toesca, *Pietro Cavallini*

C. de Tolnay, *Michelangelo*

J. Toynbee and J. Ward Perkins, *The Shrine of St. Peter's*

G. Vasari, *Lives of the Artists*

A. Venturi, *Short History of Italian Art*

R. Wittkower, *Art and Architecture in Italy 1600–1750*

Literature Set in Rome

R. Browning, "The Bishop Orders His Tomb at St. Praxed's Church"

Byron, "Childe Harold's Pilgrimage"

R. Graves, *I, Claudius*

N. Hawthorne, *The Marble Faun*

H. James, *Roderick Hudson*

M. de Staël, *Corinne*

T. Williams, *The Roman Spring of Mrs. Stone*

M. Yourcenar, *Memoirs of Hadrian*

GENERAL INFORMATION

Following the initial flurry of excitement sparked by the sight of Roman pines, the cupolas on the horizon, the jumble of terra-cotta buildings, and the Colosseum, your feelings of Rome may shift to not-so-pleasant frustrations. Rome is a city that has outgrown its narrow streets; the congestion of people, cars, and buses combined with the noise is infamous. At the beginning of the second century Juvenal complained that the noise "could break the sleep of a deaf man," so not all these annoyances are modern. They are a part of the city's culture. It is, however, possible to keep from getting completely overwhelmed by arriving with certain expectations and by learning to cope with the unavoidable. St. Ambrose's advice to St. Augustine still holds, "When you are in Rome, live in the Roman style." Above all, this means coming to Rome with patience, time, and perseverance.

There are two things you can do when planning your trip. First, if possible, make a reservation in a hotel in the center of the city but away from the train station and major streets. The historic center of Rome is easily crossed by foot and you will enjoy your visit much more if you can walk to most of the places you intend to visit. Second, a point that I cannot overemphasize, give yourself plenty of time for everything. It takes almost twice as long to do anything in Italy as it does in America, and you will be the lucky traveler if you don't run into a major strike of some sort. Even if you have come to live in Rome for a while you won't see everything there is to see, so certainly don't try to do so in a week or two. Leave plenty of time just to wander around and make alternative plans in case the museum or church you want to see is closed for lunch and siesta, or for restoration (*"Chiuso per restauro"* is a very familiar sign all over Italy).

When you arrive in Rome, slow down. Rome's enchantment is physical and comes from touch, smell, taste, and sight, so you must allow for all these sensations. The

11

best way to explore Rome is by taking a walk, as confusing as the streets may seem. Without those plunges in the wrong direction Rome will never be yours. Don't hesitate to ask directions even with a ten-word Italian vocabulary; in any case, there will always be a bar at the next corner where you can pull out your map over a cup of coffee or a glass of mineral water or Campari. Sitting in these cafés, especially on a piazza during the summer, is as important to your experience of Rome as the next church or fountain on your list.

The Roman day begins early, ends late, and includes a three-hour siesta that can be unnerving to nine-to-fivers. Most museums and churches are open only in the morning, so you should get an early start and plan your shopping expeditions for the late afternoon. By the time siesta rolls around you will want to sit back at a café or return to your hotel room. This can also be a good time to wander the streets, which are then thinned of crowds, but if you do, you will miss the show—iron gates are pulled down to cover the shop windows, courtyards are closed, and street life is almost nonexistent. When four or five o'clock rolls around it is like the start of a new day. After nine o'clock you should again do as the Romans and spend your time eating. This is one of the city's most delightful forms of entertainment, and even at the cheapest *trattoria* you can linger over several courses. As the Romans wisely say, you don't get old at the table, so relax and enjoy.

As far as perseverance goes, you will have a better sense of the need for it once you have been in Rome for a few days. I learned to be aggressive in Rome, not in New York City. If you want something, don't be shy; ask, point, and politely insist. If you are standing in what appears to be a line be forewarned, lines are not respected in Rome. In terms of sightseeing, unless a sign is posted that clearly states you can't get in, keep asking and looking for the guard; he may just be out for his cup of coffee.

ENTERTAINMENT

Being in a foreign country doesn't mean you have to lose touch with the news or your favorite forms of entertainment. *The International Daily News* is an English-language daily, with local and international news, that is published in Rome. *The International Herald Tribune*, published in Paris, is the major English-language newspaper in Europe. The *Metropolitan*, a biweekly review, is available free at English-language bookstores (see page 282) and most large newsstands. It will have a listing of events in Rome, including galleries, concerts, movies, and nightlife. The Italian papers include *Il Messaggero* for Roman news, *Il Paese Sera* for business news, and *La Repubblica* for the best cultural coverage. The most comprehensive guide to events in Rome is the *Trovaroma* listing distributed with Thursday's edition of *La Repubblica*. "The CBS Evening News with Dan Rather" is also available on TV Montecarlo, channel 21, at 7:30 A.M. and again at 8:00 A.M.

The official opera and ballet season runs from November to June at the Teatro dell'Opera (1 Piazza Beniamino Giglio, tel. 488-1755, for information in English call 675-957-25) and in July and August performances are given at the Baths of Caracalla. *Aida* in the midst of these huge Roman ruins is an impressive spectacle well worth including in your plans if you are visiting in summer. Tickets for the summer programs are available only on the day of the performance and may be purchased either at the Teatro dell'Opera during the day between 9:30 A.M. and 1:00 P.M., and 5:00 P.M. and 7:00 P.M., or the Baths of Caracalla from 8:00 P.M.–9:00 P.M. Advanced bookings for the winter season may be made by mail, otherwise tickets are available two days before the performance. Rather than waste your time at the box office, I recommend asking the concierge at your hotel to get tickets or calling an agency. Il Botteghino, tel. 678-3750, Pronto Spettacolo, tel. 684-7297, and Tre G, tel. 462-428 handle all theater and concert tickets.

Most movies in Italy are dubbed into Italian, but there is one theater in town that always shows undubbed English-language movies, Pasquino (19 Vicolo del Piede, tel. 580-36-22). The Aleagar (14 Via Merry del Val, tel. 588-0089) shows first-run movies in English on Mondays.

Rome's best entertainment offerings are concerts and chamber music. The official season is from October to June with the Accademia di S. Cecilia sponsoring the most important events. Orchestral concerts are held at the Auditorio di Via della Conciliazione (4 Via della Con-ciliazione, tel. 654-1044), and chamber recitals at the Sala Accademia di Via dei Greci (18 Via dei Greci, tel. 679-3617). Recitals are also frequently held during the winter in various churches and palazzi, offering the opportunity to see the interiors of these marvelous buildings flooded in light. Often these concerts are free. During the summer, concerts are held on Michelangelo's piazza (the Campi-doglio) at the top of the Capitoline Hill, Bramante's clois-ter of S. Maria della Pace, Villa Borghese Park and Villa Ada Park, and on the Tiber Island.

Rome has many fairs and festivals throughout the year, but the most important are: the Christmas fair in the Piazza Navona from mid-December to January 6; the International Horse Show at the Piazza di Siena in the Villa Borghese Park in late April; the feast of St. John the Baptist on June 24, celebrated as a street fair in the area around the Church of St. John the Lateran; the Noan-tri Festival in Trastevere from July 16 to the end of the month; and the Summer Festival, with events of all kinds scattered about the city.

On hot summer days, if you are not staying in one of the hotels on the outskirts of the city that has a swim-ming pool, you may want to go to the beach. Ostia is but a forty-five-minute ride and can be reached by train from the Stazione Termini. For the cleaner beaches stay on the train until the last stop. You then pay to use the facilities of a bathing concession where you may rent an umbrella and a beach chair. By far the nicest beach near Rome is Fregene, which can be reached only by car. Several hotels also open their swimming pools to nonguests: the Hilton Hotel (101 Via Cadlolo in Monte Mario) and the Hotel Aldrovandi (15 Via Ulisse Aldrovandi in Parioli). The Piscina Rose, a large olympic pool in EUR (Viale America), is open from June to September.

For tours of the city and its environs, there are several possibilities. American Express (38 Piazza di Spagna, tel. 676-441) is one of the best. There are also the Appian Line (84 Via Vittorio Veneto, tel. 474-1641) and CIT (68 Piazza della Repubblica, tel. 479-4372). Your hotel will probably have more information and can help make the arrangements you want.

If you want to attend a papal audience you must have a ticket. During the winter general audiences are held at 11:00 A.M. every Wednesday in the Audience Hall. During the summer they are held at 5:00 P.M. in the piazza designed by Bernini in front of St. Peter's. Tickets are obtained in person at the Prefettura della Cassa Pontificia at the Vatican, open from 9:00 A.M.–1:00 P.M. on weekdays. You can also write ahead to the Bishop's Office for United States Visitors to the Vatican, 30 Via dell'Umiltà, 00187 Rome, tel. 678-9184.

MUSEUMS AND SITES

Rome has more than fifty museums, some ranked with the most important in the world. Many of the collections are housed in palaces or Renaissance villas that would be a pleasure to visit even if they were empty. Below is a list of some of the most important. Remember that opening hours often change without notice. Also note that entrance fees for Italian museums are no longer cheap and can cost as much as 10,000 lire.

Roman Forum, Via dei Fori Imperiali. Open April through September, Monday and Wednesday through

Saturday, 9:00 A.M.–6:00 P.M.; Tuesday, Sunday, and holidays, 9:00 A.M.–1:00 P.M.; October through March, open Monday and Wednesday through Saturday, 9:00 A.M.–3:00 P.M., and Tuesday, Sunday, and holidays 9:00 A.M.–1:00 P.M.; tel. 679-0333. These are the archeological ruins of what was once the heart of republican Rome and, in a lovely parklike setting, the ruins of palaces on the Palatine Hill.

The Vatican Museums, Viale Vaticano. Open October to June, Monday to Saturday, 9:00 A.M.–2:00 P.M.; July to September 30 and Easter week, Monday to Friday, 9:00 A.M.–5:00 P.M., Saturday, 9:00 A.M.–2:00 P.M. Closed on Sunday except the last Sunday of the month when the hours are from 9:00 A.M.–2:00 P.M. (9:00 A.M.–5:00 P.M. during the summer); tel. 698-3333. These museums hold one of the most important collections of antiquities and Renaissance art in the world. Your trip to Rome should include at least one visit.

The Capitoline Museums, Piazza del Campidoglio. Closed on Monday; open Tuesday to Sunday, 9:00 A.M.–3:00 P.M., and on Tuesday and Saturday from 5:00 P.M.–8:00 P.M. From April 1 to September 30 the museums are open Saturday evenings until 11:00 P.M.; tel. 678-2862. These include the Palazzo dei Conservatori, the Museo Nuovo in the Palazzo Caffarelli, and the Capitoline Picture Gallery. This complex of museums has an impressive collection of art, especially an outstanding collection of antique Roman sculpture.

Museo Nazionale Romano, Piazza dei Cinquecento. Closed Monday; open Tuesday to Saturday, 9:00 A.M.–2:00 P.M., Sunday and holidays, 9:00 A.M.–1:00 P.M.; tel. 460-530. Here is a fine collection of antiquities, many of which were discovered in Rome. Some of the galleries may be closed for restoration.

Galleria Borghese, Via Pinciana. Open Tuesday to Saturday, 9:00 A.M.–3:00 P.M., Monday and Sunday, 9:00 A.M.–1:00 P.M.; tel. 858-577. This is located in the casino of the Villa Borghese, which was built in the seventeenth century by Cardinal Scipio Borghese, who started the collection with some of the best works of his time, including several masterpieces by Bernini. Only the ground floor may be open. The paintings from the second floor are being exhibited during this period of restoration at the Ospizio di S. Michele on Via di S. Michele in Trastevere.

National Museum of the Villa Giulia, 9 Piazzale di Villa Giulia. Closed on Monday; open Tuesday to Saturday, 9:00 A.M.–7:00 P.M., Sunday and holidays, 9:00 A.M.–1:00 P.M.; tel. 360-1951. The villa was built by Vignola in 1550 for Pope Julius III. It contains a splendid collection of Etruscan antiquities found in the necropolis of Veii, Praeneste, Cerveteri, and other Etruscan towns.

National Gallery of Ancient Art, Palazzo Barberini, 13 Via delle Quattro Fontane. Open Monday to Saturday, 9:00 A.M.–2:00 P.M., Sunday and holidays, 9:00 A.M.–1:00 P.M.; tel. 481-4591. This collection of Italian and European paintings from the early Renaissance to the seventeenth century is housed in an imposing baroque building begun in 1625 by Carlo Maderno and completed by Bernini.

The Doria Pamphili Gallery, Piazza del Collegio Romano. Open Tuesday, Friday, Saturday, and Sunday, 10:00 A.M.–1:00 P.M.; tel. 679-4365. The Palazzo Doria was begun in 1435 and completed only in 1660, so it spans two centuries of architectural styles. The gallery contains the Doria family collection of paintings and objets d'art, including paintings by Titian, Raphael, Caravaggio, and many others. It is the finest patrician collection in Rome.

The Museum of Rome (Museo di Roma), Palazzo Braschi, Piazza di S. Pantaleo. Closed on Monday; open Tuesday to Sunday, 9:00 A.M.–2:00 P.M.; tel. 687-5880. The museum documents the various aspects of Roman life from the Middle Ages onward, including a collection of watercolors by Roesler Franz. This may be closed for restoration.

The Galleria Spada, Palazzo Spada, 13 Piazza Capo di Ferro. Open Monday to Saturday, 9:00 A.M.–1:00 P.M., Wednesday through Saturday from 3:00 P.M.–7:00 P.M., and Sunday and holidays, 9:00 A.M.–1:00 P.M.; tel. 656-1158.

This is an important museum of baroque paintings shown in four of the sumptuous rooms of this marvelous palazzo (discussed in Walk 1).

National Gallery of Modern Art, 131 Viale delle Belle Arti. Closed on Monday; open Tuesday to Saturday, 9:00 A.M.–2:00 P.M., Sunday and holidays, 9:00 A.M.–1:00 P.M.; tel. 802-751. This is a large collection that presents the evolution of nineteenth- and twentieth-century Italian art.

Palazzo Venezia Museum, Via del Plebiscito. Closed on Monday; open Tuesday to Saturday, 9:00 A.M. –2:00 P.M., Thursday until 7:00 P.M., Sunday and holidays, 9:00 A.M.–1:00 P.M.; tel. 679-8865. A visit to the museum is the best way to see the interior of Cardinal Barbo's palace, which was begun in 1455. The collection has paintings, bronzes, wood and ivory sculptures, ceramics, and tapestries. The visit includes the Sala del Mappamondo, Mussolini's office.

Churches

So much of Italy's art is found in churches that I have a general rule to never walk by an open church without checking it out. Churches are free of charge but as places of worship rules of silence and modest dress should be respected. Also wait until services are finished to walk past the altars and chapels. Most churches are open in the morning until 1:00 P.M.; some reopen from 5:00 P.M.–7:00 P.M.

ACCOMMODATIONS

Rome's long tradition of tourism gives this city an especially wide variety of places to stay. These range from some of the most luxurious hotels in Europe to the simple *pensione*, "boardinghouse." In between are a great number of possibilities based on price, style, amenities, and location. Standards at all hotels are listed in the *Annuario Alberghi d'Italia* published by the Italian State

Tourist Organization; this book can be consulted at their offices or through your travel agent. Do make these arrangements as soon as possible, since Rome is always crowded, and the choice hotels are booked well in advance. Also remember that mail to Italy often seems to take the slow boat via China.

Most frequent travelers to Rome have a favorite hotel, which says something about the gracious hospitality this city offers. It also reflects the many distinctive personalities these establishments embody, be they luxurious or not. Be forewarned, however, that hotels in Italy are among the most expensive in the world these days. A luxury hotel begins at $400 a night and an inexpensive hotel means $100 a night for a very simple room. There are cheaper options and beginning on page 276 you will find a list of hotels and accommodations that include some for under $100. Because traffic in Rome is so bad and you will primarily be exploring Rome's historic center, I strongly urge you to find a place to stay in the center.

TRANSPORTATION

There are two airports in Rome. The main international and national airport is Leonardo da Vinci in Fiumicino, twenty-six kilometers southwest of Rome near the sea. A modern *autostrada* connects Fiumicino with Rome, and both taxi and public transportation are available. You should count on spending about sixty dollars to get into town by taxi. For slightly more there is a limousine service with comfortable Mercedes cars that hold more luggage than most of the yellow cabs; there are also minivans. As you leave the customs area, go to the right to the CON. CO. RA. counter or just ask someone about a car with a driver.

The cheapest and sometimes fastest way to get into the city is to take the train, which leaves the terminal at Fiumicino Airport every twenty minutes from 5:00 A.M.

to midnight and goes to the train station in Trastevere and the Ostiense Air Terminal. I don't recommend doing this if you have a lot of luggage, as there is quite a bit of walking involved. To get to the train from the international terminal you must go up a flight of stairs and walk out of the building to the sidewalk. Near the large overhead tunnel are both a ramp and an elevator. Go through the tunnel, which connects the airport to the train station. There you will find automatic machines that issue tickets for the train, but you can also buy them more easily at the newsstand on the right. Get off the train at the Trastevere station only if you are staying in Trastevere. There are not many taxis at this station but there are a number of buses down Viale Trastevere. At the Ostiense station you are still a couple of miles from the center of Rome and most hotels. You must find a taxi, which I recommend, or walk the considerable distance to the Piramide Metro Station where you can take the B line Metro to the center. The B line stops running after 1:30 A.M., then bus no. 176 shuttles between the Air Terminal and the main railroad station, the Stazione Termini.

The other airport, Ciampino, is thirteen kilometers southeast of the city and is used exclusively by private aircraft and charter flights. This is also the city's military airport. Bus service connects this airport every hour from 6:30 A.M.–10:00 P.M. to the Anagnina station of the A line Metro, which then takes you to the Stazione Termini.

The central train station, the Stazione Termini, is a large modern structure built between 1938 and 1950 on the Piazza dei Cinquecento. This is the main train station for all the state railways, including those with international connections. In addition to the services one usually finds in a train station—newsstands for a map of the city, coffee shops, shoeshine boys—this one also has a tourist information center in case you have arrived without a hotel reservation, and an *albergo diurno*, "day hotel," where you can take a shower and even have your hair done. In front of the train station is one of the main stops for the city's bus transportation system (your map of the city should also give the bus routes), as well as a large taxi stand.

This station serves the Lazio Line for trains to nearby towns in the region such as Palestrina, Frascati, and Fiuggi. You go downstairs to the Metro station for services to Ostia and EUR. The station where Rome's two subway lines cross is reached from the railroad terminal's front arcade. Look for red signs with a large white "M" for the Metropolitana.

Chances are you will not be traveling by bus when you arrive or leave Rome because the train system is so good. Bus service is, however, efficient for some of the small towns near Rome, or you may be interested in the tourist coach services. There is no central bus station in Rome. On the northeast corner of Piazza dei Cinquecento on Via Gaeta are the buses of the Azienda Tramvie Autobus Comunali (A.T.A.C.) to Tivoli. On the southwest side of the Piazza, in front of the train station, are the buses of the S.T.E.F.E.R. company to Colonna, San Cesareo, Palestrina, and Fiuggi, as well as the S.I.T.A. buses to Terracina, Sperlonga, Gaeta, Naples, and beyond. The Piazza della Repubblica is the terminus for the luxury auto-pullmans of the Compagnia Italiana Autoservizi Turistici (C.I.A.T.) with transportation to Naples, Assisi, Perugia, Florence, Pisa, Rapallo, Genoa, and Siena.

Taxis are plentiful but expensive in Rome. They are clearly identified by a sign and their bright yellow color. Though it is possible to flag one on the street, the usual procedure is to go to a taxi stand, marked by a large blue sign. The base fare is 6,400 lire and is good for three kilometers. A 3,000 lire *notturno* surcharge is added from 10:00 P.M.–7:00 A.M.; 1,000 lire is added on Sundays and holidays; and there is a 500 lire charge for each piece of baggage. If you call a cab (tel. 3570 or 4994), the meter starts as soon as the call comes in, so be prepared to pay for the convenience. There are gypsy cabs with no taxi sign or meter; you should avoid these unless you are desperate—and then bargain before you get in the car.

The entire city is serviced by a very good bus system that, while often crowded, uncomfortable, and known for its pickpockets, is often the best way to get about town other than walking. You must first buy an A.T.A.C. ticket at a green booth near major stops or at a bar or newsstand. Remember that there are four rush hours in Rome—mornings from 8:00–9:30, twice during the lunch break from 1:00–2:00 and from 4:00–5:00, and evenings from 7:00–8:00, and you do not want to be fighting your way on and off a bus during these times.

Bus stops are marked *"Fermata"* and give the numbers for the buses that use them along with a listing of the main stops made by that line. The final destination point will be listed last. There is a prescribed etiquette for bus riders in Rome: you enter from the rear of the bus, unless you have a monthly pass, and exit from the center of the bus. Stick the ticket into the card punch machine in the direction of the arrow; keep the stub until you have left the bus or you may be charged a forty dollar fine. Pay attention to your route because you will have to maneuver your way to the exit with a polite *"permesso"* before the bus arrives, otherwise you may miss the stop entirely. Don't be surprised if your return trip is different from the trip going; this is often the case because of all the one-way streets in the city.

With much difficulty, caused by the numerous archeological sites, two subway lines have been built in the past thirty years. The first line of the Metropolitana, completed in 1952, line B, connects the northeastern outskirts with the southern sections of the city including EUR and Ostia. Among line B's stops are the Church of St. Paul Outside the Walls, the Ostiense Air Terminal, the Circus Maximus, and the Colosseum. Line A, opened in 1981, crosses line B at the Stazione Termini and runs from the eastern part of the city, stopping at St. John the Lateran on its way to the Stazione Termini, and from there to Piazza Barberini, the Spanish Steps, the Piazza del Popolo and on to Ottaviano, near the Vatican and its museum. This is certainly the fastest way to get across Rome if you are located near its route, but the coverage is limited. The Metro opens at 5:30 A.M. and the last train leaves each terminal at 1:30 A.M.

Another form of transportation popular with tourists is the horse-drawn carriage available at Piazza di Spagna, Piazza S. Pietro, and the Trevi Fountain. They are not cheap, and you should establish the price before you get in for a ride. During the day also be aware that you may just be stuck in traffic.

FOOD AND DRINK

Above all, Romans like to eat, and eating is an all-day ritual. So much respect is given to their produce and cuisine that you will be tempted at every turn: in the shops the windows are filled with decorative displays of hams, salamis, cheeses, breads, and pasta; the restaurants entice you with succulent samples of cold platters and fresh fish; the open markets are a dramatic collage of some of the most beautiful produce you will ever see; the street vendors offer tempting slices of coconut, melon, and, in the winter, roasted chestnuts; and even the bars have their counters piled high with an assortment of *tramezzini*, crustless sandwiches. You can snack all day, but dinner is sacred, and you must leave room for at least three courses. At mealtimes you are doing more than just nourishing your body; you are attending one of Rome's best shows. For lunch this begins at 1:00; for dinner not before 9:00. Always, it is a theater of colors, flavors, odors, sounds, and gestures, but from April through October, when the tables move outdoors, the people-watching is at its best. Then, too, you will be amused by countless street musicians and entertainers. There is no need to rush to a movie; the spectacle is right there, coupled with a delicious plate of pasta.

As eating begins in the morning, let's start there. A

cappuccino, rich Brazilian coffee with steamed milk, and a *cornetto*, a sweet crescent-shaped roll, are the standard Roman breakfast, which is usually taken standing at a counter. First you pay the cashier, then you take your *scontrino*, "receipt," to the bar and give your order (and a 200 lire tip) to the man behind the espresso machine. While cappuccino is the typical morning coffee, drunk only until noon, you can have your coffee in a variety of other ways. Espresso is the highly concentrated black brew that can be made *lungo*, watered down, or *macchiato*, with just a dab of milk. If you don't like steamed milk there is *caffè e latte*, coffee with plain cold milk, or, if the coffee is too strong for you, try a *latte macchiato*, which is a glass of steamed milk with a drop of espresso. Those who want a little kick in their coffee can have a *caffè corretto*, with a bit of brandy, and there's always *caffè hag*, decaffeinated coffee, which is available the world over. During the summer you can have iced coffee, black or with milk, *caffè freddo* or *cappuccino freddo*. Coffee is a good way to begin the day, but it is also a good excuse for a break anytime, and, of course, it's the only way to end a meal.

Almost every bar has a plate of *tramezzini*, sandwiches, for a quick snack, but larger bars provide additional selections, including pastries and ice cream. The largest have a *tavola calda* and *tavola fredda*, hot and cold prepared dishes usually eaten right at the counter, and are a good option for a cheap meal. Though tables and chairs are provided in these establishments, be prepared to pay double for the pleasure of sitting. These bars also offer the only possibility of a clean restroom.

Roman ice cream has a justly deserved high reputation, and the *gelaterias*, or ice cream parlors, are another favorite place to grab a snack. This ice cream is made only with eggs, cream, sugar, fresh fruit, and natural flavorings. Try Giolitti's, Rome's most popular parlor, on 40 Via Uffici del Vacario, or any of the other ice cream parlors listed in the "Restaurants, Hotels, and Shops" guide, on page 275. In any case, wherever they make homemade ice cream it is bound to be delicious.

Italy is a country of regional cuisines that vary greatly from north to south. In Rome you eat primarily *cucina romana*, though there are some restaurants that specialize in dishes from other regions. As a rule Roman cuisine is not refined, which is not to say that it isn't tasty; it is just a hardy, peasant form of cooking that uses a variety of pastas. Among the best are: *penne arabiata*, a spicy tomato sauce on macaroni; *spaghetti alle vongole*, with sweet small clams cooked in their shells with garlic; and *bucatini alla Matriciana*, large macaroni with a tomato, cheese, and bacon sauce. Standard main courses include tripe, salt cod, sweetbreads, brains, oxtail, and salt pork, but there are also more luxurious foods, such as fish (especially in Trastevere), baby lamb, suckling pig, and veal.

Roman bread is among the best in Italy, but if you want *burro*, "butter," you have to ask for it. Vegetables and salads are served as separate courses. Unless vegetables are fried these are served cold and dressed in lemon juice and oil. Some of the best Roman dishes fall into this category: *carciofi alla giudia*, fried artichokes; *fiore di zucca fritti*, fried zucchini flowers stuffed with mozzarella cheese; and *funghi porcini*, a huge brown-and-white fleshy mushroom available in the fall that is usually grilled with garlic. Dessert is customarily fresh fruit.

Your meal is not complete without a bottle of wine and *acqua minerale*, "mineral water." Italians seem to have an unquenchable thirst for *acqua minerale*, which has nothing to do with the tap water's being untasty or polluted, because it is neither. It is a habit, but it is also consumed for health reasons. The impressive labels always contain a testimonial by an eminent professor of medicine and a chemical analysis of the bottle's contents. The professor explains in technical terms that the water will relieve digestive miseries, kidney ailments, or whatever. The analysis is as complicated and comprehensive as any blood test. This is all taken very seriously and some waters are better for some things than others: Sangenini for children's digestion, Fiuggi and Uliveto for people with kidney problems, Chianciano for liver problems, and Crodo for dyspepsia and colitis. Neri, Claudia, and San Paolo are alkaline waters and good for hangovers. Both mineral water and wine are inexpensive, and most restaurants have a wide selection of wines from all over Italy. Wine is usually arrayed on shelves around the dining room and not on a wine list unless you are in a restaurant known for its wine cellar. In most restaurants one asks the waiter for a wine from a particular region, such as a Chianti or a Barolo. The house wine is the cheapest way to order wine and it will give you a familiarity with some of the wines from the region around Rome, which includes Frascati.

If you are willing to take the time, one of the nicest and cheapest lunches is a picnic in Villa Borghese Park. This also gives you an opportunity to shop for bread, wine, cheese, and salami along the Via della Croce. You can buy vegetables and fruit at a small outdoor market on one of the side streets. Remember, when going to the market, that you are not supposed to touch the produce, tempting as it may be. Tell the person behind the stand how much you want; he or she will be very good about picking the best for you. The outdoor markets are open only in the morning, and all food stores are closed on Thursday afternoons, except during the summer when they close with everything else on Saturday afternoons.

Another cheap way to eat lunch is to do as many Romans have started doing since restaurants became expensive. Buy a *tramezzino* or *panino*, both sandwiches, one made with soft bread and the other with a hard roll, and take it to your favorite piazza. A cheap dinner can be had by eating at a pizzeria. On page 273 I list a few places where you can get a pizza or a sandwich but they are easily available all over Rome.

The perfect way to end your day is to pass the evening sitting at one of the big piazzas—Piazza Navona, Piazza del Popolo, or Piazza S. Maria in Trastevere—over a glass of Sambuca, licorice liqueur; *vin santo*, sweet wine;

or brandy. There you can continue people-watching until the wee hours of the morning.

TIPPING

A 15 percent service charge is added to hotel and restaurant bills, but you should leave a small tip in addition. At the hotel tip the porters and service personnel as you would anywhere: 2,000 lire a bag to the bellboy and 10,000 to 20,000 lire to the concierge depending on how helpful he or she has been. In restaurants leave 5 to 10 percent of your total bill for the waiter. When buying a cup of coffee or a drink at a bar leave a 200-lire coin on the counter or, if you sit at a table, 5 to 10 percent of the bill. While cab drivers do not expect a tip it is customary to round up the change.

You should be generous to custodians who do special favors for you, such as opening doors to churches, cloisters, and sections of museums not generally open to the public. In such cases it is appropriate to give them the equivalent of a dollar. Theater ushers expect 500 lire per person when they seat you.

TELEPHONE, TELEGRAPH, POST OFFICE

Public telephones are available throughout the city, particularly in bars. They take either a 200-lire coin, two 100-lire coins, or a token known as a *gettone*. *Gettoni* may be purchased at a bar or newsstand; they are worth 200 lire and can also be used as money. Each 200-lire deposit allows you a three-minute conversation; when you begin to hear a clicking sound just add more money. In many locations you will also find *scheda* phones that take cards instead of coins. You buy the card from the tobacconist for 3,000, 6,000, or 10,000 lire. To use the card, insert it into the slot on the telephone and the value of the card will appear. After the call, hang up and the card will be returned with the telephone automatically deducting the toll from the credit recorded on the card. This is a good way to make long distance calls within Italy. International calls can be made from your hotel room, but you may be charged as much as twice the normal rate. An easy way to make your calls is at the S.I.P., the main telephone office, located on the Piazza S. Silvestro. It's open from 8:00 A.M.–9:00 P.M. weekdays and from 8:00 A.M.–noon on Saturday. There are also S.I.P. offices at the Stazione Termini and at Leonardo da Vinci airport. Calls from Italy to the U.S.A. are always far more expensive than calls made in the United States. If possible, arrange to have calls made to you at a certain time and place or use an American telephone credit card; dial 172-1011 for AT&T, 172-1022 for MCI, or 172-1877 for Sprint.

You can buy stamps at any tobacconist, usually located in bars and identified by a "T" sign outside. The mailboxes along the street are red, but it is wiser to go directly to the post office to mail your letters. Neighborhood post offices are open from 8:00 A.M.–2:00 P.M., but the main office, Palazzo delle Poste, also at Piazza S. Silvestro, is open Monday through Friday from 8:00 A.M.– 9:00 P.M. and on Saturday from 8:00 A.M.–noon. The Vatican, as a separate principality, has its own mail system; the post office there is on the piazza in front of St. Peter's. It is open Monday through Saturday from 9:00 A.M.–5:00 P.M. All mail should be marked "air," and if you are especially concerned about the delivery of a particular letter send it *espresso*, special delivery.

Packages sent out of the country must be tied with a string, not sealed with tape, for customs purposes. If packages weigh more than 1 kilo (2.2 pounds), the end of the string must be attached to a *piombi*, a small lead clasp that can be purchased at a stationery store or *cartoleria*.

MONEY AND BANKING

Banks are open from 8:30 A.M.–1:20 P.M., Monday through Friday. Most banks cash traveler's checks, but be prepared to stand in several lines and spend more than a few minutes. This is especially true on Monday mornings when all the shopkeepers do their banking. You must have a passport to make this transaction. The Banco di Santo Spirito, with branches around town, usually has the best exchange rate for the dollar. The American Express Office (38 Piazza di Spagna, tel. 67–64) is open from 9:00 A.M.–5:00 P.M. You won't have any language problems there, but you will face huge crowds during the summer tourist season. In a pinch you can usually cash a traveler's check at a hotel, but the convenience will cost you. If you are having money transferred to you in Italy, use American Express and not an Italian bank where it can take as long as a week.

If you are interested in knowing the lira/dollar exchange rate before you leave for Rome, check the business section of your local paper or call the bank. The Sunday *New York Times* travel section also gives you the exchange rate averaged over the week. While credit cards may be used for shopping and in some hotels and restaurants, Italy is still run on cash, so check before counting on using credit.

A Value Added Tax (I.V.A.) is included in the price of all luxury items. In Italy, as opposed to other European countries, you cannot be reimbursed for this tax. The only exception is very large purchases that are shipped out of the country by the dealer.

SHOPPING

Italian design has a terrific reputation the world over, and it is almost superfluous to say that Rome is a shopper's paradise. Even knowing this, you will be surprised by the opulent window displays along the main shopping streets at the foot of the Spanish Steps. This area centers on the Via Condotti, south along the Via del Corso to Via Frattina and north to Via della Croce. Here you will find all those familiar names: Gianni Versace, Fendi, Missoni, Carlo Palazzi, Valentino, Gucci, Bulgari, Ginori, Mila Schön, Buccellati, Ferragamo, Pratesi, and Roberta di Camerino. Needless to say, this is not a place for bargain hunting, although there are good sales in July and February. This is where you buy quality—the very best money can buy. A word of warning about shopping in these stores: you will be treated as well as you are dressed.

Rome is full of shopping areas. Less expensive ready-to-wear shops are found on the Via del Corso, Via Tritone, and Via Nazionale. The best bargains in nonname leather goods and shoes are found on the Via Cola di Rienzo in a neighborhood near the Vatican. On our walks you will find small neighborhood craft and specialty shops. Although there is a major department store, La Rinascente, this is not the Roman way of shopping.

For the lover of antiques there are many exciting possibilities. Some of the bargains left for the dedicated hunter are in prints, etchings, and music scores. They are sold under the sign *"Libreria-Antiquaria."* The Piazza Borghese is famous for its stands of old books and prints. You get more of a feel for Roman history in an hour of browsing among these prints than in days of reading. Rare, old, first- or second-edition prints command high prices, but there are numerous eighteenth-century prints of piazzas, churches, and monuments that are quite reasonable. The illuminated parchment music sheets, some dating as far back as 1630, are also in abundance. At much higher prices are fine Italian drawings, antiques, and reproductions.

Do remember the shopping hours. They are normally from 9:00 A.M.–1:00 P.M. and from 3:30 P.M.–7:30 P.M. In the summer shops reopen at 4:00 P.M. and close at 8:00 P.M. All shops are closed on Sunday; and from September through April shops are closed Monday mornings. From May through September they are closed on Saturday afternoons.

On Sunday mornings you can shop as the Romans do at the Porta Portese flea market. While not the best flea market in the world, it is quite a spectacle. This is the only place in Rome where bargaining is still expected and you can find anything—coffeepots, car parts, cheap clothing, books, ballet shoes, and drafting sets sold by the Russian immigrants, antique furniture, and seventeenth-century ceramics. For something very special you will have to look hard and arrive as early as 7:00 A.M.

See the list of selected shops on page 279.

EMERGENCIES

The most important number to know in case of an emergency is that of the American Embassy (tel. 46-741), located at 119A Via Vittorio Veneto. They have a list of all American-trained physicians and dentists and can explain the procedure for reporting thefts or accidents. Rome also has several English-speaking hospitals and clinics: the Salvator Mundi International Hospital, Viale delle Mura Gianicolense, tel. 58-6041, and the American Hospital, 69 Via Emilio Longoni, tel. 256-71. For English-speaking doctors, call the Medical Diagnostic Center, 125 Via del Tritone, tel. 481-8429. If you lose your passport you will not be able to go very far— it is needed to exchange money and to register at a hotel. The American Consulate at the Embassy can provide you with a new one in a matter of hours. While chances are slim that you will ever recover stolen property, it is worth filing a report with the Italian police for insurance claims and tax deductions.

Pharmacies have late-night and holiday rotations that

31

are posted at the nearest pharmacy. If none are nearby dial 1921 for information. If you are taking medication you should bring a supply with you; many American products are not readily available in Italy.

A WORD OF WARNING

You are not likely to be in any physical danger as you walk around the city, but there are some conditions of which you should be aware. Among the many reputations Rome holds is one for its cunning motorcycle thieves who grab for purses, jewelry, and anything else of value. You can also get hurt as they swiftly breeze by you taking their plunder. The best thing, of course, is to not carry a purse or wear jewelry, but this isn't always possible, especially when you are traveling. If you do wear jewelry be discreet; those thin gold chains are a favorite. As for your purse, you will notice that most Roman women wear their shoulder bags across their chest, not just dangling from the shoulder. Follow their example and walk with your bag toward the buildings and not the street. Buses are another danger zone. Keep your wallet and purse close to you. One other thing: beware of the gypsy children—they have been skillfully trained to steal from you as you give them money. It is best not to be taken in by their pitiful acts, but to ignore and avoid them. They are very persistent, and you may have to be quite stern.

The traffic is as crazy as it seems, so make sure the cars have come to a complete stop before crossing the street; where there are no lights, cross at the white zebra markings, and use underpasses when they are available. As you follow the walks in this book, you will notice that there are usually no sidewalks; cars and motorscooters especially will come whizzing by at terrifying speeds. Stay close to the buildings and look around the corner before crossing an intersection.

One thing women may find disarming but needn't worry about is the overtures made by men. These are harmless displays of one of Italian men's favorite pastimes, women-watching. Just remember that any acknowledgment is a form of encouragement. Keep walking. If flirting becomes a major annoyance during your trip it may be because you are calling attention to yourself. It is wise to respect the city's dress code, which is generally elegant and a bit conservative.

GLOSSARY OF ARCHITECTURAL TERMS

architrave: the molded band or group of moldings that rests immediately above the columns.

atrium: originally the principal room in an ancient Roman house; later it became used to define the porch enclosed on three sides and attached to the front of a basilica.

basilica: an early Christian church with a broad nave ending in a semicircular apse and flanked by colonnaded aisles; the basilica type of church in its simplest form has a wooden roof, brick walls, and an interior decorated with mosaics and frescoes.

belvedere: a structure or tower on the top of a building commanding a fine view; from *bel,* "beautiful," and *vedere,* "to see."

campanile: a bell tower next to a church.

capital: the uppermost part of a column or pilaster crowning the shaft.

cella: the part of an ancient Roman temple within the walls, as distinct from the open porticoes; it contained the image of the deity.

corbel: a projection from the wall or structure to support a weight lying or resting on top of it.

Corinthian: the most elaborate of the three Greek orders

of architecture, characterized by its bell-shaped capital enveloped with acanthus leaves.

cornice: the horizontal molded projection that crowns the façade.

cross-mullions: the crossed bars dividing the windows into panes.

Doric: the oldest and simplest of the Greek orders of architecture, distinguished by low proportions and saucershaped capitals.

entablature: the wall resting upon the capital of columns and supporting the pediment or roof plate; it is divided into an architrave, the part immediately above the columns; a frieze, the central space; and a cornice, the upper projecting molding.

frieze: that part of an entablature between the architrave and the cornice; usually a sculpted or richly ornamented band.

herm: a statue consisting of a head supported on a quadrangular pillar.

Ionic: one of the three Greek orders of architecture, distinguished by the spiral volutes of its capital.

lintel: the horizontal piece spanning an opening or carrying a superstructure.

loggia: a roofed, open gallery that is part of the main structure.

parapet: a low wall or railing.

pediment: the triangular space forming the gable of a two-pitched roof, used as a decoration over porticoes, doors, and windows.

pergola: a colonnade of beams and poles supporting an open roof, usually treated as an arbor or a trellis.

peristyle: the inner court of an ancient Roman dwelling.

pilaster: a rectangular architectural device that is used as a pier but treated as a column with capital, shaft, and base.

portico: a colonnade or covered walkway.

spandrels: the space between the curved arch and the frame.

stelae: a slab or pillar of stone used as a gravestone.

Tuscan order: a crude version of the Doric order of architecture with unfluted columns and a general lack of ornamentation.

tympanum: the recessed space of a pediment within the frame of the upper and lower cornice.

A BRIEF HISTORY OF ROME

The story of Rome's founding is steeped in mythology and goes back to the end of the Trojan War, circa 1200 B.C., when Aeneas, escaping with his father Anchises on his back, landed on the coast of what was called Latium. Three hundred years later, Rea Silvia, a vestal virgin descended from those Trojans, gave birth to twins, Romulus and Remus, whose father was the god Mars. According to the law of the time, Rea Silvia was punished for her infidelity by being buried alive. The twins were left to drift on the Tiber, which carried them to the foot of the Palatine Hill, where they were found and kept alive by a she-wolf and raised as shepherds. On this spot they later decided to build a city. On April 21, 753 B.C., Romulus began to build a wall around the Palatine Hill; the city that rose here was called Roma Quadrata because of the hill's square shape. Modern excavations have uncovered portions of this wall and the necropolis that belonged to this earliest settlement.

Favored by its central position on the Italian peninsula, by the proximity of the sea, and by the bold character of its inhabitants, Rome grew rapidly in importance. Under its seven legendary kings—Romulus, Numa Pompilius, Yullius Hostilius, Ancus Marcius, Tarquinius Priscus, Servius Tullius, and Tarquinius Superbus—it successfully waged war against the Latins and the Etruscans. Toward the close of this "period of the kings," a new civic community was organized; its constitution was memorialized by the erection of the Servian Wall.

Also built at this time were the Temple of Jupiter Capitolinus, the Circus Maximus, the Carcere Mamertinus, and the Cloaca Maxima, which drained the swampy site of the Forum. The energetic development of the city under the kings of the Tarquinian family came to an end in 510 B.C. when the city became a republic ruled by two consuls.

Despite a protracted period of internecine struggle between the plebeian and patrician classes, Rome became strong enough finally to conquer the Etruscans of Tarquinii and Veii, who had continually threatened the city. Shortly after this victory, Rome was almost completely destroyed by the Gauls in 390 B.C. She recovered to conquer the Latins, the Samnites, and the Tarentines, and finally Pyrrhus, becoming in 275 B.C. the mistress of Italy.

Rome flourished. She built fleets, conquered Magna Graecia and Sicily, and challenged the naval prowess of Carthage. Hannibal transferred the Second Punic War to Italy and inflicted severe defeats in the north; but the Romans marched on to conquer Spain and moved the Punic wars back to Africa. In 146 B.C., at the end of the Third Punic War, Carthage was defeated and Rome began a period of aggressive conquest. New countries were disarmed, taxed, and treated as provinces under the control of a Roman magistrate, a proconsul who had wide parameters of power and the opportunity to acquire great fame and wealth. All of Asia Minor, Syria, and Palestine were brought under Roman rule, and Julius Caesar bore the Roman eagles to Gallia Transalpina and Britain. Soon, Rome ruled the Mediterranean. Cato the Censor asked himself, "What will become of Rome when she no longer has any State to fear?" This was the republic's major problem during its last years.

In 49 B.C. Caesar crossed the Rubicon at the head of his troops and marched into Rome; thus began another era in the city's history—the Roman Empire. Caesar became dictator, and his administration included reforms of the calendar, the census, money, and weights and measures. His greatest work, however, was the unification of the Roman world under one leader and under one system of law.

Following Julius Caesar's murder, Cicero remarked that the tyrant was dead but the tyranny survived. The civil war that followed made it plain to all that good government was no longer possible, except under a beneficent tyrant, and no man was better fitted to play that part than Caesar had been. Though most of Caesar's successors were also murdered, the Roman Empire lasted another five hundred years.

Until the time of Augustus Caesar, Rome was anything but a handsome city. Her steadily increasing power over the then-known world, however, demanded that she display the pride of a capital city, and the funds were available to do so in an impressive manner. Augustus's reign also provided an unusual forty-five years of peace. The result was magnificent; of all the ancient Roman monuments, those built during the reign of Augustus are among the best. Augustus's boast that he "found a city of wood and bricks and have left a city of marble," was not unfounded! In the Campus Martius rose the original Pantheon, the Portico d'Ottavia, the Theater of Marcellus, the Mausoleum of Augustus, and the Ara Pacis. Also credited to his reign are the Basilica Julia, the Domus Augustiana on the Palatine, and the Forum of Augustus with the Temple of Mars. No fewer then eighty-two temples were restored by Augustus, and the brick in Roman architecture that we admire today came into use at that time, supplemented by travertine from Tivoli or marble from Carrara, Paros, and other Greek islands.

Augustus's successors followed his example in the building of public monuments, each man striving to surpass his predecessors. In this respect Nero (A.D. 54–68) displayed the most unbridled ambitions. In A.D. 64 he reduced large parts of the city to ashes in order to rebuild it in a more modern style. Most of Nero's work, however, was destroyed by his successors, including his "Golden House," a palace with gardens that extended from the Palatine Hill across the valley of the Colosseum and up the Esquiline Hill.

The Flavian dynasty continued the tradition, building the Colosseum, to this day considered a symbol of Rome's power, and the Triumphal Arch of Titus, which commemorated the destruction of Jerusalem. Under Trajan, Roman architecture received a new impetus and may have reached its zenith. The Forum of Trajan, with its column named after him and its reliefs now found on Constantine's Arch, are eloquent testimonies to this period's achievements. Under the next emperor, Hadrian, the majestic dome of the Pantheon was raised to dominate the city's skyline, and the Temple of Venus and Roma and his Mausoleum (now Castel S. Angelo) were also added to the city's inventory of great architecture.

Under Marcus Aurelius, the Stoic, there was a period of such peace and prosperity that to this day the Romans believe that "the good old times" will return when the equestrian statue of Aurelius, once gracing the Campidoglio, is again returned. But this peace was short-lived; during the century following the reign of Marcus Aurelius the empire was beset with civil wars, barbarian invasions, famine, and the plague. The decline of Rome as the capital of the ancient world began under Diocletian in 284. Despite all this adversity, contributions to the city's landscape were made during this epoch: the column of Marcus Aurelius, the Arch of Septimius Severus, the Baths of Caracalla, the huge Thermae of Diocletian, and the Aurelian Walls—all of which stand today much as they did then.

Diocletian divided the empire into east and west, but it wasn't until Constantine moved the seat of government to Byzantium in 330 that this division became a reality. It marked a turning point in the history of the city and the empire. The last important ruins of antiquity, the Basilica Thermae and the Triumphal Arch, bear Constantine's name. Statistics about Rome at this point indicate that the city had 19 aqueducts, 8 bridges, 425 streets, 1,790 palaces, 46,602 homes, 11 thermae, 856 baths, 1,352 street fountains, 36 triumphal arches, and 10 basilicas. After Constantine's reign no new works were begun, and the city fell into a long period of decay.

The Roman religion was based on the belief that the gods intervened in human affairs with rewards and punishments for good and bad actions. Propitiated by sacrifices and offerings, the gods' favor was always sought on any projected enterprise. The chief religious officials were the Pontifex Maximus; the minor pontifice; the flamens; the augurs, who interpreted the mood of the gods; and the vestal virgins, who kept alive the sacred fire of Vesta that had been brought from Alba Longa. It wasn't a sophisticated religion, rather one steeped in tradition, and tradition formed the basis of Roman law and order. Though generally tolerant of various religious beliefs, Roman religion and rule was contradicted by Christianity at almost every level—the belief in only one divinity, the condemnation of idolatry, the assertion of human equality, and the belief in future punishment for evildoers. Despite three centuries of persecution the Christians gained increasing strength and organized themselves into independent, self-governed republics. By the time Constantine issued his celebrated decree in 313, which granted Christianity equality with other religions, the bishop of Rome was in a position to be recognized as an official of the state. This office, which became known as "pope" after the Romans' Pontifex Maximus, quickly filled the vacuum of power left by the decaying empire. When Alaric the Barbarian appeared before the walls of Rome in 408 it was Pope Innocent I who acted as the city's representative. In 451, Pope Leo I saved Rome from Attila the Hun; and in 455 his intercession softened the blows of Genseric the Vandal. After these events the Romans regarded the pope as their leader and defender, a position that was further strengthened by the fall of the Western Empire in 476.

The great struggles and victories of Christianity helped preserve Rome from total destruction. The city's transformation from pagan to Christian was accompanied by the gradual development of the papacy as the supreme ecclesiastical power in the West. Pope Leo the Great (440–461) and Pope Gregory the Great (590–604) are credited with this scheme of aggrandizement. Their objective was the independence of Rome from Byzantium, the subjection of the Eastern Church to the Court of Rome, and the conversion of the Germans. In 727 the Longobard king gave the ancient Etruscan town of Sutri to the pope, and this was the first step in the formation of the Papal States. This act was reinforced in 755 when Pepin, at the pope's request, defeated the Lombards and gave a portion of their territory to the papacy. On Christmas Day in 800, Charlemagne, son of Pepin, was crowned augustus and emperor by Pope Leo III in St. Peter's. The Holy Roman Empire endured until the abdication of Francis II of Austria in 1806.

Characteristic of this period are the once-numerous towers of red brick that stand in such strong contrast to the monuments of ancient Rome. This style of architecture was developed during the Carolingian epoch, though most of the towers we now see were not erected before the twelfth century. During this time the great monuments of antiquity were doomed to desecration and destruction. Gregorovius gives us a colorful description of their fate:

> Charlemagne had already set the example of carrying off ancient columns and sculpture to adorn his cathedral at Aix-la-Chapelle; the nobles and even the abbots took possession of magnificent ancient edifices which they disfigured by the addition of modern towers; and the citizens established their work-shops, rope-walks, and smithies in the towers and circuses of imperial Rome. The fisherman selling his fish near the bridges over the Tiber, the butcher displaying his meat at the theater of Marcellus, and the baker exposing his bread for sale, deposited their wares on the magnificent slabs of marble which had once been used as seats by the senators in the theater or circus and perhaps by Caesar,

Mark Antony, Augustus, and other masters of the world. The elaborately sculptured sarcophagi of Roman heroes were scattered in every direction and converted into cisterns, washing-vats, and troughs for swine; and the table of the tailor and the shoemaker was perhaps formed by the cippus of some illustrious Roman matron for the display of her jewellery. For several centuries Rome may be said to have resembled a vast lime-kiln, into which the costliest marbles were recklessly cast for the purpose of burning lime; and thus did the Romans incessantly pillage, burn, dismantle, and utterly destroy their glorious old city.

Upon Charlemagne's death a turbulent period ensued for the papacy. The Crusades against the Turks in Jerusalem began and lasted two hundred years. The city was repeatedly besieged and captured by German armies, and within the city itself various families fought for control. These increasing civic and national crises led Pope Clement V (1305–1316) in 1309 to transfer the papacy to Avignon, where it remained until 1377. During these years Rome was successively governed by Guelphs and Ghibellines, Neapolitans and Germans, Orsinis, Colonnas, and Caetanis; and, for a brief period in 1347, by Cola di Rienzo, who succeeded in restoring the ancient republican form of government. This was an unhappy time in Rome's history. Poverty, war, and disease reduced its population to less than 20,000 inhabitants.

A change was inaugurated with the return of Gregory XI (1370–1378) to Rome in 1377. The schism between the Eastern and Western churches engaged the attention of the popes immediately upon their return, and it was not until 1420 that Pope Martin V began to restore the city, which had deteriorated both physically and socially during the so-called Babylonian Captivity. Under Pope Julius II and Pope Leo X, Rome, aided by vast sums of money that flowed into the papal coffers, attracted the greatest artists of the Italian Renaissance. Slowly the city regained its pride and again transformed itself into a capital, this time of the Christian world.

Yet even at this point in time Rome was not safe from barbarian invasion. In 1527 the city was sacked by German troops of the Imperial General Charles of Bourbon. Restoration after this attack, as well as further embellishments, occupied succeeding popes. The population increased; palaces were built by members of the Papal Court; popes and cardinals restored old churches and vied with each other to build new ones. Their efforts, combined with what has been left of ancient Rome, are what distinguishes Rome from other Italian and European cities.

In the 1700s Italy was divided into a number of small states. Genoa and Venice were republics; the king of Sardinia held Savoy, Nice, and Piedmont; Lombardy was under the last emperor of the Holy Roman Empire, Francis II; Tuscany, Modena, and Parma were under dukes; the pope ruled the states of the Church; and a Bourbon was king of Naples and Sicily. In 1798 the French, under the leadership of Napoleon, entered Rome and declared a republic. Pope Pius VI was taken prisoner and died in France in 1799. This occupation was but one step in Napoleon's plan to conquer all of Italy and the Holy Roman Empire. In 1810 the French senate proclaimed Rome their second capital, and in 1811 Napoleon conferred the title of king of Rome on his newborn son. In 1815, when Napoleon finally fell, the Congress of Vienna divided Italy among the conquerors: the north (except Genoa, which fell to Victor Emmanuel, king of Sardinia) went to Austrian princes; the Bourbon family obtained Naples and Sicily; and Rome was restored to the pope along with the Papal States.

A general revolutionary movement spread throughout Italy in 1848. It was headed by Mazzini, whose aim was to create a United Italian Republic. Insurrection broke out in Rome; after the pope fled south to Gaeta a triumvirate of Mazzini, Saffi, and Armellini proclaimed Rome a republic and entrusted its defense to Garibaldi. This, however, did not last long because the French came to the defense of the pope and his territory. While Victor Emmanuel was proclaimed king of Italy in 1861, it wasn't until 1870, when the French troops left to fight the Prussian War, that the Italians were finally able to capture Rome and, in 1871, make it their capital. This ended the papacy's temporal power and its rule over Rome.

After World War I a Fascist movement was organized by Benito Mussolini. It grew rapidly. In October 1922 the Fascists marched into Rome; King Vittorio Emanuele III invited Mussolini to form a government, which he did and which prevailed until the middle of World War II, when it was overthrown on July 25, 1943. During the Fascist reign, in 1929, the Lateran Treaty was signed declaring the Vatican an independent sovereign state. From September 1943 until its liberation by Allied troops in 1944, Rome was occupied by Germans.

In 1946 Vittorio Emanuele III abdicated. In December 1947 the Constituent Assembly approved a new republican constitution. Since then there have been numerous governmental crises, but the Italian people have maintained a strongly democratic and united republic.

When Rome resumed her place as capital of Italy much was done to improve the amenities of the city, often at the cost of the picturesque. Old quarters, such as those of the Campitelli and Suburra, were leveled and new quarters were built outside the walls to accommodate a rapidly increasing population. The climax of replanning was reached in the 1930s. Broad thoroughfares were built and many of the historic monuments were isolated from the surroundings. The construction plans facilitated the excavation of important areas, especially around the Forum. The most significant development, however, was the establishment of the Esposizione Universale, EUR, which is now an important business center and suburb on the edge of town—Mussolini's equivalent of the late-nineteenth-century monument to Vittorio Emanuele that dominates the city skyline.

Walk · 1

Streets of the Papacy

THE NEIGHBORHOOD OF
THE CAMPO DEI FIORI

The courtyard of the Palazzo Spada

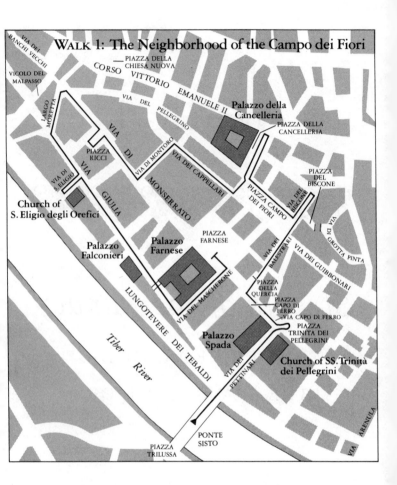

WALK 1: The Neighborhood of the Campo dei Fiori

VIA DEI BANCHI VECCHI

VICOLO DEL MALPASSO

PIAZZA DELLA CHIESA NUOVA

CORSO VITTORIO EMANUELE II

VIA DEL PELLEGRINO

Palazzo della Cancelleria

PIAZZA DELLA CANCELLERIA

LARGO MORETTA

VIA DI

PIAZZA RICCI

VIA DI MONTORO

VIA DEI CAPPELLARI

PIAZZA DEL BISCONE

VIA DI S. ELIGIO

VIA

PIAZZA CAMPO DEI FIORI

VIA DEL BISCONE

VIA DI GROTTA PINTA

Church of S. Eligio degli Orefici

GIULIA

MONSERRATO

PIAZZA FARNESE

VIA DEI GIUBBONARI

Palazzo Falconieri

Palazzo Farnese

VIA DEI BALESTRARI

PIAZZA DELLA QUERCIA

LUNGOTEVERE DEI TEBALDI

VIA DEL MASCHERONE

PIAZZA CAPO DI FERRO

VIA CAPO DI FERRO

PIAZZA TRINITA DEI PELLEGRINI

Tiber River

Palazzo Spada

VIA DEI PETTINARI

Church of SS. Trinità dei Pellegrini

PONTE SISTO

PIAZZA TRILUSSA

VIA ARENULA

Starting Point: Ponte Sisto between Piazza Trilussa and Lungotevere dei Tebaldi
Buses: 26, 44, 56, 60, 65, 75, 96, 170, 710 (From Via Arenula, four blocks upriver along Lungotevere Vallati)
Length of Walk: three hours

In the middle of the eighth century, Pepin, king of the Franks, formally granted Rome to the Papal Court. This decision saved the city from extinction and also marked a turning point in its social history. Built on the ruins of a pagan city and nurtured by the heritage of a pagan empire, Rome became for centuries the capital of Christianity.

With no productive life of its own and surrounded by malarial swamps and sparsely inhabited plains, Rome needed the sponsorship of the Papal Court. During the great papal schism, for example, the city failed to develop the flourishing civic and economic life of other central and northern Italian cities and the population of Rome dropped from 35,000 in 1200 to 17,000 in 1400. Petrarch, one of the pilgrims of 1350, says that Rome gave the impression of having just been stormed and pillaged by barbaric hosts. Things remained as such until 1417, when Martin V reestablished the papal seat in Rome. Platina, Martin V's biographer, says that when the pope returned to Rome he found the city "in such a state of devastation that it could hardly be considered a city fit for human habitation: whole rows of houses abandoned by their tenants; many churches fallen to the ground; streets deserted and buried under heaps of refuse; traces of plague and famine everywhere." Rome's improvement was neither sudden nor immediately noticeable, but the simple fact that the head of the Church returned to Rome gave the city a new lease on life. The Papal Court brought wealth and distinction to this struggling community, and a new tradition of grandeur rose amidst the ancient ruins. Hundreds of thousands of pilgrims from all parts of the world brought not only money, but the vitality of a cosmopolitan life.

Rome began to flourish again between 1450 and 1650 as each pope proposed a building program and hired architects and builders to carry it out. Grandiose plans were drawn up by Renaissance artists who were anxious to apply their theories of geometry, proportion, and perspective to a single, magnificent vision of a capital that combined the great Roman and Christian traditions. Most of these plans were never carried out; instead, the new Renaissance and baroque city evolved slowly based on incremental plans seldom committed to paper. Yet, despite the lack of a master plan, the twenty popes and the hundreds of architects, craftsmen, and administrators who rebuilt Rome achieved a remarkable unity of style and effect.

Our walk through the neighborhood of the Campo dei Fiori presents us with many of the physical changes that were created by the Catholic Church's decision to make Rome the embodiment of its wealth and power. Situated across the Tiber from the Vatican, the area lies between the Vatican and the Capitoline Hill, making it a natural site for much of the Church's reconstruction efforts. Despite these efforts, the desired example of Renaissance city planning was never produced. The city's medieval framework is still clearly visible, if not directly before one, then around the corner. The charm of this neighborhood does not rest solely in historical lore or architectural vistas but is magnified by sharp contrasts both visual and social. Here Renaissance and baroque Rome are at their secular best, circumscribed by the less-refined requirements of modern urban life and the tastes and structures of other periods.

At first glance, it is difficult to envision the much older character of this area—when it was the western end of the Roman Empire's Campus Martius. Little remains intact, but there are enough hints to tickle the imagination with impressions of the influence and richness of ancient Roman culture. The best description of the early period was written in the seventh century B.C. by a Greek geographer, Strabo, who was one of the first of numberless foreigners who, taken in by Rome's personality and beauty, have felt compelled to share it with others.

> Superior to all is the Campus Martius. The greatness of the plain itself is wonderful, all open for horses and chariot racing and for the great multitudes who take exercise in ball games; in the circus and in gymnastics. The ground is covered with grass, green all year round, surrounded by buildings and hills that reach to the river's edge; it presents a scenic effect from which it is difficult to tear oneself away.

Vitigis the Goth unwittingly initiated the decline of the Campus Martius as it was described by Strabo when he cut off Rome's water supply by destroying the aqueducts in 537. This act not only killed the verdant fields but forced the dwindling population of Rome to move from the hills to the edge of the Tiber, a part of the city that had never before been residential. Slowly the Campus Martius's few ceremonial buildings fell to ruin, and any portable fragments of columns or stone were recycled as decorative or structural objects in nearby homes. The lack of water marked the beginning of a long struggle that helped shape the history of medieval Rome and changed the face of the city. The glory of ancient Rome became a sentimental memory as the city turned into the huddle of huts, tenements, and battlements that Pope Martin V described to his biographer.

In 1429 Poggio Bracciolini, one of Pope Martin's secretaries, found a lost manuscript in the library of the monastery of Monte Cassino. The manuscript, called *De Acquis* and written by Fontinius, was a handbook to the aqueducts, mountains, and waters of imperial Rome. This handbook became an important tool for Rome's revival— a revival that will appear more dramatic as we walk through the streets of this neighborhood.

We begin our walk in the middle of the **Ponte Sisto**, the bridge that spans the Tiber from the Lungotevere dei Tebaldi to the Piazza Trilussa. Stand in the middle of the bridge and enjoy the view. Upstream we see the curve of the river and the dome of St. Peter's. On the left bank the dense and colorful quarter of Trastevere edges up the Gianicolo Hill covered with large, elegant villas and green parks, and on the right bank loom the palazzi of Renaissance Rome. Downstream is the Tiber Island and a lovely silhouette of the ruins on the Palatine Hill.

Before he was elected pope, Sixtus IV lived near the Campo dei Fiori and must have been greatly inconvenienced on his trips to the Vatican, because he vowed that if elected pope he would rebuild the Pons Janiculensi, also known as the Pons Agripae, the bridge that had been destroyed by a flood in 792. This desire was reinforced when during the Jubilee of 1450, congestion on the Ponte S. Angelo caused the death of more than two hundred pilgrims. At the time, the Ponte S. Angelo was the only bridge to the Vatican. When Pope Sixtus IV laid the foundation stone for this bridge in April 1473 its completion was given the highest priority in preparation for the Jubilee of 1475. The pope was also interested in providing a convenient link to Trastevere, which was then an especially poor section of town. In time the bridge did, in fact, attract new settlements to that community and helped tie it to the growing business center across the river.

The area bordering the river has changed completely in the last 125 years. Embankments were built, as were the wide streets along both sides of the river, which provide a direct route between the northern and southern ends of the city. Before this construction humble dwellings stood all the way down to the river's edge, and there were huge fortified walls that protected the gardens and homes of the rich. The contrast between what we see today and what existed a century ago is best seen in etchings and paintings at the Museum of Rome on the Piazza S. Pantaleo.

The Tiber itself has taken on a very different role in the life of the city. In the late nineteenth century terrible floods plagued Rome year after year—floods so bad that one etching depicts people visiting the Pantheon in a boat. The Tiber was used as a means of transportation and for power to churn wheat mills located on barges in the middle of the river. Now there are but a few houseboats, and transportation is possible only on short stretches. The Tiber today functions primarily as a point of reference—one is more likely to be aware of the bridges than the river flowing beneath them.

The fountain at the end of the bridge in Trastevere is also a relatively new addition to the landscape, though it dates to the early seventeenth century. In 1611 Pope Paul V repaired an ancient aqueduct that had been built by Trajan to carry water to Rome from a group of springs thirty miles northwest of the city. To display this new source of water, which became known as the Acqua Paola, he commissioned Giovanni Fontana to design an elegant fountain to be incorporated into the wall of a hospice for beggars between Via Giulia and the Ponte Sisto. These fountains were not mere decorations, for many centuries they were the primary source of potable water and were also used for bathing. When plans for the Tiber embankment called for the demolition of both the fountain and the hospice, great protests arose, for the fountain had become one of the most popular in Rome. Despite the agitation it was pulled down in August 1879, but it was saved from oblivion some years later when, stone by stone, the fountain was rebuilt on the **Piazza Trilussa**, at the Trastevere end of Ponte Sisto.

Keeping the fate of the old bridge in mind, architects were careful to ensure that the Ponte Sisto could withstand the strong currents of a flooding river. This single-lane bridge is composed of four supporting arches and a large round eye in the center that allows water to pass through when the river swells. In 1878, at the same time that the embankments were constructed, the two footpaths supported by corbels were added. Also that year sections of an arch from the ancient bridge were found at the bottom of the river; the remains bore an inscription to Valentinian, emperor of Rome in 365, and undoubtedly the builder of the original Pons Janiculensi. Other treasures, including a bronze statue and some pedestals, were also excavated; they now rest in the Capitoline Museum. The only remnants of an earlier structure are a few large stones seen near the Trastevere embankment when the river is low.

The earliest Romans, along with many other primitive peoples, believed that building a bridge offended the gods of the river because it robbed them of a certain number of victims who would otherwise have drowned. With this in mind, the most important duty of the bridge-builder was to pacify the river god with expiatory sacrifices in the form of living human beings and dummies made of rushes. For much the same reason it was unlawful to use nails or other metals in any part of the bridge's woodwork. It was also unlawful to use stone since a more temporary structure was considered less offensive than a solid piece of masonry. This sacrificial tradition seems to have been a burden to the early Christian Church: St. Calipius, St. Saba, and St. Symphorosa were all thrown into the Tiber from the Pons Janiculensi. Between the fourth and fifteenth centuries Rome became solidly Christian and a gentler place if the inscription at the beginning of the bridge near the Lungotevere dei Tebaldi is any indication: "You who pass, invoke the divine bounty so that Sixtus IV, excellent Pontifex Maximus, may be healthy and for long be preserved. You then, to whom this request is made, whoever you are, be healthy, too."

Walk across the Lungotevere dei Tebaldi and toward the shop called Handles on the corner of Via Giulia and Via dei Pettinari. On the corner to your right is one of the few arcaded buildings in Rome, styled after so many in northern Italian cities. The fountain at Piazza Trilussa would have been located in the same spot as the children's clothing store, Il Paloncino Rosso (The Red Balloon).

Continue straight on the **Via dei Pettinari**, named for the combmakers or wool-combers who once lived and worked on this street. Nothing remains of these artisans; now jewelers and watchmakers occupy the small shops on the ground floor. This change probably took place in the eighteenth century when the state office for stamping gold and silver was established just a few blocks away. The right-hand side of the street is dotted with the kind of signs that are such a trademark of Rome's center-city streets—signs of ownership, law enforcement, and religious fervor. Here, such signs are more noticeable because they are not upstaged by dramatic architecture or obscured by hanging laundry.

At 39–40 Via dei Pettinari is an *edicola*, an image, of the Virgin Mary. This is a rather simple example of the popular displays of religious fervor, which are often associated with particular events—a tragedy, a feast day, a miracle. Such images are seen all over the city with the Virgin and Child a favorite theme. Their manifestations range from simple photographic images protected by a glass box to great pieces of art almost always accompanied by a candleholder and some flowers. As with most *edicole* the emotions behind it are not revealed and are now long forgotten.

Embedded in the wall of **no. 36A**, a few yards to your right, is a very common street sign engraved in marble that often causes confusion among tourists. It reads:

> Per ordine espresso di monsig. ill.mo. rev.do. presidente delle strade si proibisce espressamente a qualqunque persona di gettare immondizie e fare mondezzaro in questa strada sotto pene di scudi diece ed altre pene ad arbitrio di sua sig.ria. ill.ma. in conformita dell edito emanato il p.o. marzo MDCCXXXXI.

This merely states that it is illegal to throw trash in the street and that a fine is imposed.

Ten feet farther is a sign that marks the dedication in 1944 of the building to the Madonna of Divine Love for saving Rome from the destruction that befell other Italian cities during World War II. Just around the corner once stood one of the few buildings destroyed by Allied bombing.

On the left-hand side of the street are two buildings of architectural interest. The first, **no. 79–80**, is a small fifteenth-century house with a loggia on the top story. This house's exterior was once completely covered with paintings in the decorative style so popular during the century in which it was built. The other building is the palazzo on the corner of Via dei Pettinari and Via Capo di Ferro, **no. 81–87**. This is the **Palazzo Salmoni Albertischi**, which belonged to a family known in Rome since the twelfth century. This building, in the style of Renaissance Roman palazzi, has two large portals bearing inscriptions that identify the Salmoni Albertischi family. The portals and the cornice are decorated with motifs from the family's insignia—lions' heads and the knot of Solomon.

The **Piazza della Trinità dei Pellegrini** is a landmark that dates from the golden age of the Catholic Church, when hundreds of thousands of pilgrims came from all parts of the world to celebrate the Jubilee year. This celebration originated in the ancient Jewish Jubilee and gradually became one of the most popular events in the Catholic Church's calendar. Proclaimed by Pope Boniface VIII in 1300 this tradition of celebrating every twenty-five years has continued to the present day, except for the nineteenth century when because of political tensions in Europe there was only one. The idea of a pilgrimage to Rome seems to have existed even before the first Jubilee. The Jesuit scholar Thurston tells of Pope Boniface questioning a 107-year-old man being carried into St. Peter's Basilica in January 1300. "I remembered," the old man said, "that at the beginning of the last century my father, who was a laborer, came to Rome and dwelt here as long as his means lasted in order to gain the indulgence. He bade me not to forget to come at the beginning of the next century, if I should live so long, which he did not think I should do."

Though pilgrims are still very much a part of the Roman scene today, patterns, style, and even the ways of manifesting religious devotion have changed. Earning a plenary indulgence, which is the difference between purgatory and heaven for the pious Catholic, is certainly not what it used to be. Buses and cabs make the journey to the five basilicas a rather simple task, and this is not to mention the availability of water, hotels, and paved streets. Pilgrims arrive with their sneakers and practical dress like all other tourists; only during the weeks before and after Easter, when the main streets to the Vatican suddenly become obstacle courses, is one particularly aware of any pilgrims. This sudden influx of foreigners is always a surprise, yet it is more predictable than the weather. Soon they become part of the huge tourist crowd though they come to Rome as Petrarch did "in a spirit of fervor because I wished to put an end to the sinfulness of my life, which overwhelmed me with shame" and whose visit held a higher importance than a mere "poet's curiosity."

When pilgrims were Rome's only tourists the Piazza della Trinità dei Pellegrini, where we now stand, was as important as the Via Condotti is today. Here a church with an attached hospice was built for the Jubilee of 1550 by S. Filippo Neri, perhaps the most appealing figure among the saints of the Counter-Reformation and dear to this day as the patron saint of Rome. The hospice was for centuries one of the city's more important centers of hospitality, receiving and feeding for a period of three to seven days pilgrims of "pious intent" who had traveled more than sixty miles. An example of the traffic on this piazza is a statistic from 1675: that year the hospice accommodated 582,760 pilgrims. During Holy Week princes and cardinals came here to wash the feet of the pilgrims. Augustus Hare, who witnessed this custom that endured into the nineteenth century, was shocked by the fact that "here the washing is a reality, the feet not having been prepared beforehand."

The inscription on the façade to the left of the church is in memory of the poet Goffredo Mameli, who was brought to the hospice to die after he was mortally wounded in the defense of Rome in 1849. (The hospice had been turned into a hospital for the Garibaldi forces.) All this came to an end during World War II when, in 1940, one of the few bombs to drop on Rome fell here and destroyed the building as well as a small oratory that stood in the middle of the piazza. In its place rose an apartment complex and garage, one of the few examples of postwar architecture you will see during this walk.

The **Church of SS. Trinità dei Pellegrini** was built between 1587 and 1597 from a design by Martino Longhi the Elder. The façade, however, was not executed until 1723. Designed by Francesco de Sanctis, it is a skillful variation of Carlo Fontana's façade for the Church of S. Marcello on Via del Corso. The curved façade first introduced by Borromini and Cortona in 1630 is here reinterpreted as a single, steady curve instead of the double **S** curve or the play of convex against straight or concave. During the seventeenth and eighteenth centuries this principle of baroque architecture, with its many variations, was probably more frequently imitated than any other in Rome. The expressive, oversized statues of the four evangelists by Bernardino Ludovisi are also worthy of attention.

The bar in any Roman neighborhood is an institution. Bars do a thriving business on practically every corner and each has its attraction—it makes the best coffee or ice cream, it is a gathering place for friends, or it has the right atmosphere. The one on this piazza is a good example of the true neighborhood bar that has nothing going for it but the fact that it is where the people who live and work on this street congregate to pass the time. Certainly it is the best place to get any information about apartments, people, directions, and local history.

At this point we turn onto the **Via Capo di Ferro**, which borders the Palazzo Salmoni Alberteschi and intersects with Via dei Pettinari. At the very beginning of the street to your right is another example of the inexhaustible treasures of Rome. For months I walked this path daily without noticing the four Ionic columns embedded in the wall of this house. How these Roman columns found a place in the walls of a thirteenth-century house is not known for certain. They may have been a small section of the miles of porticoes built during the empire, or they may be an example of the widespread vandalism of the Middle Ages. In any case, the columns were undoubtedly bricked in after 1475 when Pope Sixtus IV, acting on a warning by King Ferrante of Naples that it was impossible to keep order in a city that provided dark hiding places for rebels and thieves, decreed an end to all open porticoes in Rome. The few that exist today are on a small number of free-standing medieval houses or were built during the nineteenth and twentieth centuries. This house lost its medieval character when it was completely remodeled in the eighteenth century.

Via Capo di Ferro is named for an old Roman family distinguished as early as the 1100s. Throughout the late Middle Ages and well into the sixteenth century they controlled this part of the city and in the name of their successors, the Spada family, they have left two very different examples of Renaissance architecture. Capo di Ferro literally means "chief of the sword"; in time their name changed to Spada, the more common word for sword. To your left, at **no. 7**, the **Palazzetto Spada**, is a stately and classical example of early sixteenth-century architecture. This *palazzetto*, "small palace," is attributed to both Peruzzi and Vignola, two of the greatest architects in Rome at the time. Debate over attribution aside, one look at the elegant façade leaves little doubt that its conception was the vision of a master. In addition to the harmony of its arched shop doors on the ground floor and the classical lines of the *piano nobile* with windows separated by Ionic pilasters, the charm lies in its scale—more human and livable than the grand palazzi that often dazzle by sheer volume.

Before reaching the second and most famous palazzo of the Spada family there are a few interesting digressions. To your right, the **Vicolo della Madonnella** is a narrow street that ends in one of the undistinguished but nevertheless alluring courtyards that are so characteristic of Rome's medieval vestiges. In its short passage we step away from the carefully conceived spaces of the sixteenth century.

Back on the Via Capo di Ferro, **no. 10**, to the left, is a relatively new addition on the block. Until the beginning of the seventeenth century this was the site of a street named Arcaccio after an arch built as part of its promenade. The street connected the end of Via Giulia

An ancient sarcophagus-turned-fountain in the Piazza Capo di Ferro

to the Via Capo di Ferro. While a small segment of that street still exists off the Via Giulia, both the arch and this entrance to the street disappeared when a building was erected in the 1600s to connect the two Spada palaces. **No. 12** is a house built in the fifteenth century adorned at the time with a picturesque monochrome design. To make room for that decorative flourish, the proportion of window to wall varies from the norm.

Just another ten steps brings us to a by-now-familiar opening in the road called a piazza. Here we have the Piazza Capo di Ferro, dominated by the fanciful **Palazzo Spada**. This building's architecture is full of unrestrained and captivating touches meant to stimulate our historic sensibility.

The piazza was designed around 1635 by Francesco Borromini, a good friend of Cardinal Bernardino Spada's brother. His intention was to destroy or hide some of the hovels that could be seen from the palace windows and to ensure the cardinal's privacy. After clearing the area for the piazza, the architect built a wall with battlements and blind windows to keep the neighbors from seeing who was entering and leaving the palazzo. (Only recently have a few of these windows been opened.) These details turned the piazza into a private courtyard, virtually an extension of the palazzo. Borromini built a niche beneath the sundial and belvedere to hold a fountain of Venus standing on a shell with water flowing from her breasts. That statue has long since been replaced by the less suggestive, but still beautiful configuration of a lion's head spurting water into a sarcophagus, also decorated with lions' heads.

The façade of the palazzo rises above a stonework base. On the *piano nobile* the windows alternate with statues representing figures from Roman history: Trajan, Pompey, Fabius Maximus, Romulus, Nema, Marcellus, Caesar, and Augustus. Above that, the windows are surrounded by stucco tondi and garlands. The boxed inscriptions refer to the figures in the niches below. This stucco decoration, so popular in the later days of the Renaissance, is seen here at its very best. All, or nearly all, of this work is by Giulio Mazzoni, who was commissioned by the Papal Apostolic Camera in 1550 during the reign of Pope Julius III.

A document dating from the first half of the sixteenth century suggests that the palace may originally have been intended as the French Embassy. In 1555 the building became the property of Cardinal Girolamo Capo di Ferro. When he died in 1559 the palace was inherited by the Mignanelli family who in turn sold it to Cardinal Bernardino Spada in 1632. As soon as he purchased the palace Cardinal Spada had it adapted to his own needs. He employed Borromini, whose design is seen not only in the piazza but in the wing that houses the Galleria Spada, the great staircase, and the garden that extends to the Via Giulia.

Walk through the grand portal, and don't be intimidated by the guards with machine guns. Since 1927 the palace has been the headquarters of the Council of State. If approached, explain (or gesture) that you are here to look at the building and its courtyards.

The main courtyard surrounds us with the world of Greek mythology, which had such a strong influence on the Romans, depicted on the façade. This courtyard was also decorated by Giulio Mazzoni. There are still a few traces of faded frescoes in the panels between the top-story windows, but the walls covered with exquisite stucco decoration are the highlight here. Amidst the acanthus and struggling fauns are images of the sea demigod Triton, the son of Poseidon; Amphitrite, with his conch-shell trumpet; and centaurs, the half-man half-horse descendants of Ixion, who dwelt in the mountains of Thessaly. The niches are filled with the most important Olympian deities: Hercules, Mars, Venus, Juno, Jupiter, Pluto, Persephone, Minerva, Mercury, Amphitrite, and Neptune.

On the wall opposite the entrance, between the second-floor windows, nude male figures hold shields bearing the coats of arms of Pope Julius III and the king of France. This either reinforces the theory that the palazzo, begun under Pope Julius's reign, was intended as the French Embassy, or it refers to Cardinal Capo di Ferro himself, who was the pope's treasurer and served as the Apostolic Delegate to France.

Facing the coats of arms turn to your left, where a large window on the ground floor opens onto the library with its beautiful painted globe. Beyond that and the orange trees is Borromini's most famous contribution to the palazzo: an arcaded gallery at the end of which is a statue on a pedestal. Although the gallery was originally meant to be seen from this courtyard, it is best to find the custodian and actually walk through it. (He sits in the entrance to the museum, through the courtyard and to your left.) Approach, or watch someone else approach, the statue. You will soon realize that there is an optical illusion created by progressively diminishing columns and arches. Even the floor changes dimensions. In reality the gallery is but ten meters long while the seemingly life-size statue is but a foot in height. Built in 1663, Borromini's conceit replaced a false perspective painted on the wall in 1644. Such *trompe l'oeil* were popular throughout Italy at the time, another example being the Scala Santa at the Vatican. This one, however, also served a very specific function, that of extending the axis of the side court, which was restricted by the surrounding buildings.

The museum in this palazzo is known as the **Galleria Spada**. The collection fills four rooms on the second floor. Go through the arch to the garden, turn to your left, and wind your way up a narrow circular stairwell. Of the many small family collections in Rome this is the only one to have survived in its original setting consisting primarily of baroque paintings acquired by Cardinal Bernardino Spada while papal legate to Bologna in the mid–seventeenth century. Among the paintings are Breughel's *Landscape with Windmills*, Titian's *Musician*, and Andrea del Sarto's *Visitation*. The state rooms hold further marvels but written permission to visit must be obtained from the Ufficio Intendenza, Palazzo Spada, 13 Piazza Capo di Ferro, 00186 Roma.

There in the great throne room presides the **statue of Pompey** that Byron describes in "Childe Harold's Pilgrimage":

> And thou, dread statue! Yet existent in
> The austerest form of naked majesty,
> Thou who beheldest 'mid the assassins din,
> At thy bathed base the bloody Caesar lie,
> Folding his robe in dying dignity
> And offering to thine altar from the queen
> of Gods and men, great Nemesis! did he die
> and thou, too, perish, Pompey? have ye been
> Victors of countless kings, or puppets of a scene?

It was at the foot of this statue, which stands eleven feet high and is among the first representations of the male nude, that Caesar is thought to have died. There is no real proof to support this generally accepted notion except that the statue was found near the Theater of Pompey, not far from the Roman Curia. Of greater interest is the story of its discovery.

The Pompey statue was found in the cellar of a private home on Via dei Leutari. The statue was positioned with the wall of the neighboring house passing over its neck, and the owner of that house claimed the entire statue on the grounds that the head was more important than the body. When the matter went to court the judges, remembering the verdict of Solomon, decided that the head should be detached from the torso and each party given the portion found on his property. This decision so offended Cardinal Capo di Ferro that, with the help of Pope Julius III, he was able to obtain a stay of execution. Pope Julius promptly ended the debate by paying each of the rivaling parties a fee for the sculpture. He then presented it as a gift to the cardinal who ensured its preservation and safety here in this palazzo. More recently, after the proclamation of the republic by the French in 1810, the statue's integrity was again threatened. At that time it was transported to the Colosseum to lend a heightened sense of reality to a performance of Voltaire's *Brutus*. Later, when the statue wouldn't fit into the carriage, the right arm was severed.

As you leave the Palazzo Spada, turn to your left through the piazza and make an immediate right. Within a few feet is the unusual sight of a solitary oak tree rising from the cobbled street. It marks the adjoining **Piazza della Quercia**, "of the oak," and memorializes the cult of the Madonna of the Oak Tree. Tucked into the corner is the **Church of S. Maria della Quercia** built by the Confraternity of Butchers, a profession in Rome dominated by men from Viterbo who, with their families, brought this cult to Rome.

In 1523 the Confraternity of Butchers bought this site, which housed the medieval church of S. Nicolò. The foundation stones for the existing church were laid in 1727 by Pope Benedict XIII, and it was consecrated in 1738. The façade was designed by Filippo Raguzzini, an architect whose design for the Piazza di S. Ignazio is one of the most ingenious and lively examples of baroque architecture in Rome. The Church of S. Maria della Quercia also has elements of this design, but on a smaller scale. To fully appreciate them one has to look at the façade from different perspectives. First, stand back as far as possible so you can see the flowing convex curves. As you move forward to the first step of the church's entrance the soft curves disappear and are replaced by the strong vertical lines usually associated with the linear architecture of the Gothic period. Though a minor work, this church certainly depicts the complexity of form and a sense of the dramatic that is essential to the precepts of baroque architecture. The church is generally closed, with the exception of one Sunday service and the celebration of the annual feast of the Confraternity.

Across from the Church of S. Maria della Quercia is the **Palazzo Ossoli**, on **Via dei Balestrari, no. 1**. Built in 1527 it is attributed to Rome's "ghost" architect. "Ghost" because there are three buildings of this period whose authorship is unknown—Peruzzi? Vignola? Sangallo the Younger? Another? In a city whose architectural history is so well documented it is amusing to think what might have caused this lack of attribution or that there might have indeed been another architect less needy of acclaim.

Proceed *sempre diritto*, straight ahead. This is a typical Roman phrase that you will hear whenever you ask directions. Even if what you are asking about is on the other end of town you will be told to go *sempre diritto*.

Via dei Balestrari is named for the makers of crossbows who were replaced when the crossbow was superseded by the harquebus, a portable firearm that had a matchlock operated by a trigger and was supported for firing by a hook. This is where you came during the Renaissance if you needed a crossbow or harquebus. Walking down the street today we won't see anything so exotic. Instead, there is a wonderful mixture of the new and the old—an Erboristeria, which sells herbal potions and cosmetics; wine shop; and some craftmen's studios, including a frame shop and a pizzeria.

This street is of little interest, but a few of the buildings can be singled out. To your left, at the beginning of the street, is a large building of the 1700s with medallion windows belonging to the Confraternity of Butchers. Only in the last century has this organization been located anywhere near a major market (the Campo dei Fiori is but a couple of blocks away). When they first came to this neighborhood the meat market was at the foot of the Capitoline Hill; later it moved to the neighborhood of Testaccio, a few miles downriver from here.

Across the way, at no. 15, is a house used by a religious order associated with the nearby church of S. Lorenzo in Damaso. That church's coat of arms hangs on the corner of this building at the intersection of Via dei Balestrari and Vicolo del Giglio. **No. 8** is a building of the 1600s with stone encasements around the windows and door. The house at **no. 42–43** with its shrine to the Virgin also belongs to the Church of S. Lorenzo in Damaso and is used by the Archconfraternity of the Immaculate Conception.

At the end of the street, where it intersects with the Campo dei Fiori, is a large marble plaque (to your right above the street sign) that commemorates one of the many efforts by the Vatican to clean up and pave the streets of Rome:

> Earth of Marcius which until a short time ago was ugly and drowned in squalid mud, and full of diseases, now under the reign of Sixtus IV, you have been liberated of this undignified aspect and everything appears admirable in the same spot. These dignified changes are due to Sixtus, giver of health. Oh how Rome is indebted to his reign!

The inscription continues with the names of the builders of the street, Battista Arcioni and Ludovico Margani, and the date, 1483.

The plaque's message hints at the philosophy that motivated the popes' urban plans during the Renaissance. They wanted to make Rome the first city in Europe, the *caput orbis*, a city owing its existence and splendor exclusively to the papacy. In this regard Sixtus probably achieved more than any of his predecessors. The street was paved and widened for aesthetic reasons, but this effort was also a crucial ingredient in Pope Sixtus's attempt to fuse the many settled areas of Rome into a single city whose arteries centered on the Vatican. Moreover, Sixtus was concerned with the problems of hygiene and went so far as to arrange for the regular sweeping of this newly paved street, which was known at the time as the Via Flora.

Walk across this end of the Campo dei Fiori past the local movie theater and fresh pasta shop and turn right. You will find yourself in the **Piazza del Biscione**. Though the name of this piazza no doubt refers to the snake that figured on the coat of arms of the Orsini family (they were responsible for initiating the settlement of this section of town in the twelfth century), its history goes back to the Roman republic. On this piazza stood the temple that, at the height of his success, Pompey dedicated to Venus Victrix. It stood within the first permanent theater built in Rome. This combined temple and theater complex was created for very pragmatic reasons. During the republican period there was a great prejudice against constructing a stone theater because it was associated with the luxurious habits of the decadent Greeks. In 55 B.C., in order to bypass the senate's anxieties, Pompey built this first stone theater with a temple to Venus Victrix in the top of the auditorium. It was constructed in such a way that the stone steps and seats formed the access to the temple and were made to appear an essential part of the temple and not the theater. In any case it was an impressive structure—150 meters in diameter with a stage 95 meters long and a seating capacity of up to thirteen thousand people. Although it is said to have been in-

*A vegetable stand at the Campo
dei Fiori*

spired by a Greek theater on the island of Mitylene,
it was not an exact replica; its semicircular form differed
from the Greek archetype that was either a complete
circle or, in later times, always more than a half-
circle.

Pliny, the great chronicler of the Roman republic, tells
us that Nero had the theater completely gilded, both inside and out, in a single day. One of Nero's many fits of
extravagance, in this case it was part of his preparations
for the arrival of King Tiridates of Armenia. Pliny also

describes the great slaughter of beasts that celebrated the theater's opening. This kind of extravagance and bloodshed continued for most of the theater's tenure. During the reign of Augustus, spectacles and fights between wild beasts and gladiators took place in which no fewer than five hundred lions and twenty elephants were killed.

Aside from the temple and the theater, there was another magnificent architectural display: the Hectostylon, or Hall of One Hundred Columns. Standing at the back of the stage, this building was supported by several lines of numerous columns forming a great portico; the center was planted with avenues of sycamore trees and decorated with fountains and rows of marble and gilded bronze statues. It was here that the Roman Curia assembled. It was also here that Brutus administered his form of justice to Caesar on the fatal Ides of March.

Little is known of the vicissitudes of the Teatro di Pompeo after its restoration by Theodoric in 510 and before the twelfth century. In 1150 the Orsini family built a large towered fortress known as the Arpacata within the ruins of the theater. Centuries later this tower became famous for its clock, which initiated a fad for clocks all over Rome. Under Pope Eugene IV, who began the reconstruction of medieval Rome in the fifteenth century, the Venetian Cardinal Condulmer built a palazzo overlooking the Campo dei Fiori on the ruins of the theater and the fortress. In 1677, when the palazzo became the property of the Pio di Carpi family, it was again remodeled and took on the appearance of the building we now see to the right as we stand facing the enclosed end of the piazza.

This building must have enjoyed a wide reputation for elegance in the fifteenth and sixteenth centuries because a number of important dignitaries were hosted here: Caterina Sforza in 1477; the ambassador to the king of France in 1485; a retinue of distinguished visitors from Spain in 1486; and, in 1492, Giovanni de' Medici, who later became Pope Leo X. During the sack of Rome in 1527 the man who was in effect governor of the city chose to make this his home. Today the building, known as the Palazzo Pio, seems not to have kept up its reputation, but its heritage is certainly greater than its façade admits.

In 1864, during a renovation of the palazzo's court-yard (which is not noteworthy), a large bronze statue of Hercules was excavated. This find, along with that of the statue of Pompey, has led to speculation that there is a precious treasure buried in this area. The construction of Rome's subway certainly proved that this is the case for most of the city, and given Pliny's description of Pompey's theater and the condition of the two sculptures al-ready found, one can easily imagine that there is a great deal of truth to that speculation.

Ruins of the theater can be seen in the basement of several houses in the area. The best way to visit the vaults and arches of the theater is over lunch or dinner at two restaurants: Da Pancrazio, here at 92 Piazza del Biscione, or Costanza, at 65 Piazza del Paradiso. Both restaurants occupy the cellars of this 2,000-year-old structure, but at Da Pan-crazio you must ask for a table downstairs in the *buca*.

In the far corner of the Piazza del Biscione is a small archway with a gate that leads to the semicircular **Via di Grotta Pinta**, whose outline follows that of the audito-rium of the ancient Theater of Pompey. In the 1930s and 1940s an elderly man sat near this passage at a table under a tattered awning with pens, ink, and a few sheets of notepaper. He was the local letter-writer who com-posed paragraphs of complaint, lyrical love poems, or any other missives needed by the illiterate. At night he stored the equipment of his trade in the archway.

Also on the piazza is one of the rare Roman houses that still bears traces of its painted façade. In recent years different shopkeepers have occupied this site, but the in-signia tells us that it was once either the local horse stable or a shop that sold horsemeat.

If you turn onto **Via del Biscione** you will see the once-famous **Albergo del Sole**, said to be the oldest hotel in Rome. Burckhart, Pope Alexander VI's secretary, noted that the French ambassador had stayed there in 1489. Before its restoration in 1869 the entrance was built like a fortress and the courtyard was decorated with a fountain and a sarcophagus.

The junk shops and peddlers that set out their wares during the weekdays are probably much like those that cluttered this street in the fifteenth century. One big difference is the lack of elegant courtesans strolling, shopping, and flirting on their way to the Campo dei Fiori. At the end of the fifteenth century a powerful and beautiful courtesan, La Grechetta (the Little Greek), lived somewhere on this street. She is primarily remembered for a jealous duel over her favors that turned into a major riot. During the fight a Frenchman killed a member of the prestigious Sanguigni family—who, in revenge, set fire to La Grechetta's home. The fighting grew to such proportions that it involved nearly 2,000 people and moved to the Campo dei Fiori.

Retrace your steps to the **Campo dei Fiori**. Whether you are here in the morning, afternoon, or evening this long rectangular space will always be filled with activity and local color. Every morning except Sunday, it becomes the largest outdoor produce market in the historic center. In the afternoon it is often a favorite forum for local demonstrations, and in the evening it becomes a casual hangout, the neighborhood's living room. Beside all this activity are the warm stucco façades of multilevel buildings whose roofs cut a busy network of textures against the sky.

The market day begins at about six o'clock in the morning when the men roll in their carts laden with boards, sawhorses, poles, and awnings. (These are hidden away for the evening in warehouses occupying the ground floor of buildings in the surrounding area.) As soon as the stalls are set up the women arrive with crates

Cartons stacked at the market in the Campo dei Fiori

of the previous day's fruits and vegetables. It is never a one-person operation, but almost always a family endeavor. While the installation takes place another member of the family is at the wholesale market buying the day's produce and delivering it before the market starts hopping at 9:00 or 9:30. Fresh seasonal produce is an absolute requirement. (Only "rich man's row," the aisle on the right with your back to the movie theater, which caters to the many foreigners in the neighborhood and the new expensive boutique restaurants, supplies artichokes in the summer and asparagus during the winter.)

Between the stalls and the shops on the piazza, one's entire shopping list can be filled. In front of the movie theater are the fishmongers, who have an especially abundant selection on Tuesdays and Thursdays. To the left of the movie theater is the fresh pasta shop, which makes a delicious tortellini with spinach and ricotta. The left aisle has a number of butchers' stalls displaying the various innards that are a staple of the Roman cuisine. Ruggeri sells canned goods, cheeses, and salamis in the shop on the corner of Via dei Balestrari and the "Campo," as it is colloquially known.

While the temporary stalls in the middle of the piazza disband around 1:30, the shops in the buildings reopen in the afternoon. So if you are not here in the morning you can still appreciate some of the flavor of the market, though not its full vitality. Past Ruggeri's and down the length of the Campo is the *confetti*, or candy, shop. The most popular item in this store is the candy-coated almonds (*confetti*) that are an integral part of family celebrations. Blue and pink *confetti* are given as party favors at a baptism; at weddings the individually wrapped and decorated pouches of white almonds take precedence over the cake. A few doors down is the wine shop where you can sip at the bar and investigate the selection of wines.

As you round the corner of the piazza you will see a bread store with a picture window where you can get a peek at the ovens inside. The man who sells delicious olives in the morning in front of the bread store measures the state of the economy by the amount of bread people are buying. Recession or not, this shop is one of the market's biggest attractions, especially for the *pizza bianca*. This flat bread covered with olive oil and salt is a Roman specialty that you should definitely sample while you're here. You buy it by the weight and one *etto*, one hundred grams, is more than enough per person.

Campo dei Fiori means "field of flowers" and elicits an image of a huge flower market. While there are only three stalls selling flowers, the sumptuousness of their selection mitigates their small number. The name of the place, however, is much older than the market, which has been here only since 1869. Before the twelfth century this was indeed a huge field extending down to the river banks. "Flowers," however, probably derives not from the real thing but from Flora, Pompey's lover at the time he built the Theater and the Temple of Venus Victrix.

Past the clothing and sundries shops, along the other length of the piazza, is the pork shop, the *Norceria Viola*, where every part of the pig is sold in all its many forms and reincarnations. Carefully displayed on beds of laurel are varieties of sausages made in many combinations of grind and spice, salamis from all over Italy, prosciutto, and much more. This shopkeeper's eye for display is always catching, especially at Christmas when the portal is draped with laurel branches and outlined with pigs' heads.

Not much is known about what went on here between the sixth century, when the theater fell into ruin, and the twelfth century, when the Orsini family built their fortress. During the fifteenth century other construction began; by mid-century the area assumed such a degree of importance and desirability that the most powerful Roman families vied with one another to buy up the barren land. Toward the end of the fifteenth century, with the help of the papacy—which paved roads into the

Campo, built bridges, and ensured a constant supply of water and pilgrims—the piazza became not only the most popular spot in the area, but, after Pope Sixtus IV's constructions, the very center of the city. At that time economic activity shifted from the foot of the Capitoline Hill to the Campo, and the area boomed with artisans' workshops, business establishments, and hotels. This upswing was reinforced by the transfer of the horse and grain market, which came to be held here every Saturday and Monday until the beginning of the nineteenth century.

At the turn of the sixteenth century the Campo was selected as the site of public executions, which may have only added to its diverse spectacles. The most important of these executions occurred in 1600, and the statue erected in 1889 in the middle of the piazza stands as a memorial to that event and a testament to free speech.

Born in 1550, Giordano Bruno committed the heresy of being an ardent advocate of the Copernican view of the universe (Copernicus died seven years before Bruno's birth). This belief, of course, was that the sun, not the earth, was the center of the universe and that the planets revolved in their orbits about the sun. To Bruno's contemporaries the Copernican theory aroused serious objections. Some thought it naïve and irresponsible; others deemed it an outmoded Pythagorean notion, an absurd form of sun worship. The Vatican considered it heresy. Bruno also strongly opposed the philosophy of Aristotle and offended many Catholic scholars by setting forth views of his own that strongly tended toward pantheism, the doctrine holding that the natural universe, taken or conceived as a whole, is God. Bruno visited France, England, and Germany, and in each of these countries the uncompromising expression of his opinions excited only hostility. It was in Venice that he first fell into the hands of his ecclesiastical enemies. After six years' imprisonment he was brought to Rome to be burned to death on

The statue of Giordano Bruno above the market

the corner of this piazza where Via dei Giubbonari and Via dei Balestrari meet. Surprisingly, Giordano Bruno's solemn stance in the middle of the Campo is one of the few reminders in this city of the Inquisition, a period of several centuries in the Church's history when there was a very thin line between rational thought and heresy. Today, a magazine of political satire, *Il Male*, places the occasional wreath at the foot of Giordano Bruno to call attention to contemporary examples of blows to the expression of free speech.

The Campo was also the meeting place of the cultural bourgeoisie, ambassadors, cardinals, noblemen, businessmen, artisans, and foreigners. All Papal Bulls, court sentences, marriage banns, and citizen complaints were posted here. By the mid-1500s almost every house on the piazza had a public bar or dining facility, and there were numerous hotels. These were run primarily by Germans who did such a good job that Pope Pius II is quoted as saying "it's best not to find others" to manage hotels. On the corner near the entrance to Via del Pellegrino, Antonio Blado opened the first printing press in Rome during the first part of the sixteenth century. Bufalini's map, the first perspective view of Rome, was printed here, as were numerous volumes in Greek. Blado's bread-and-butter work, however, consisted of pamphlets for great feasts, such as the tournament of 1565 held in the Belvedere Courtyard; public notices; statements of miracles; and information on natural phenomena.

We leave the Piazza Campo dei Fiori by the intersection of Via del Pellegrino, at the far end opposite from where we entered. As you face the bread store turn right and walk into the connecting **Piazza della Cancelleria**. Dominating the piazza is one of the most important palazzi in Rome, the **Palazzo della Cancelleria**. This building's reputation is based not only on the simple beauty of its structure, but also the design, which marked a clean break from fifteenth-century Roman architectural traditions. Here, for the first time, are the basic elements that have come to be associated with the design of Roman palazzi. The body, an immense quadrangle of travertine, reintroduced the luxurious scale and materials of the ancient Romans. The base is of incised stonework, and above that, the façade is offset by a series of classical pilasters that create a pattern of symmetry and a rhythm of wide and narrow bays. The windows, arched and set in rectangular frames, became a popular architectural detail after the construction of this palace, as did the arcaded courtyard in the center of the building. While most architectural historians consider this the best example of early Renaissance architecture in Rome, not all are in agreement with the attribution sometimes made to Bramante, who arrived in Rome after the inscription date of 1495 engraved on the façade marking the completion of the palazzo.

The Cancelleria is also a monument to papal nepotism. It was built by Cardinal Riario, nephew of Pope Sixtus IV, with money he won in one evening of gambling with another papal nephew, Franceschetto Cibo, whose uncle later became Pope Innocent VIII. Following a plot by the Riario family to assassinate him, Pope Leo X (1513–1521) confiscated the property and installed the Papal Chancellery in the palazzo, hence the name Cancelleria. This is the Vatican office that deals with the correspondence of the papal hierarchy. While it still functions in that capacity, and is today under the jurisdiction of the Vatican, not Italy, this palazzo has been an important site of events in Italy's civil history. In 1798–1799 it was the seat of the Tribune of the Roman republic; in 1810, of the imperial court; and in 1848, of the republican parliament, which was summoned here by Pope Pius IX. In July of that year an angry mob of citizens burst into the council chambers and demanded an instant declaration of war against Austria, making Rome one of the centers of the nationalist movement. The papacy's neutrality on this issue led to the beginning of a serious rift between the Church and the state. Tensions grew in Rome—which since the fifth century had been ruled by the papacy—until they erupted with the assassination of Pellegrino Rossi, the pope's minister, at the foot of the palazzo's grand staircase. One of the manifestations of the tension was the establishment of two Roman aristocracies: the "white" civil aristocracy and the "black," allied to the Vatican. The Church's position following the establishment of the republic of Italy was not resolved until the 1920s when, with the signing of the Lateran Treaty, the Vatican's realm of jurisdiction was clearly circumscribed. Today the palazzo no longer tugs on the emotional cords of the anticlerics and few people have qualms about listening to the chamber concerts played in the Hall of One Hundred Days, so named because it was painted by Vasari in little more than three months.

Walk into the courtyard; it is one of the most beautiful works of the Renaissance in Rome—a city whose landscape is dominated by the baroque architecture produced a hundred years later. The courtyard is a model of perfection and simplicity and stands free of decorative details except for the elegant architectural lines and Cardinal Riario's rose motifs, which are visible in the spandrels of the arches, on the corner pillars, and as the central theme of the pavement. The forty-four Doric columns of granite supporting the portico are said to have been plundered from the ruins of Pompey's Hecatostylon. They may also, however, have come from the barracks of the Green Squadron, whose site is hinted at in the original name of the church attached to this palazzo, S. Lorenzo in Prasino (in leek green). Of the four squadrons of charioteers that used the Campus Martius during the days of the empire—Red, White, Blue, and Green—the Green were favored by the Romans and their barracks were undoubtedly sumptuous, befitting the quarters of popular heroes who, similar to modern sports heroes, amassed fortunes in gifts and prizes from their admirers.

As you leave the courtyard, turn left to see the church

now named **S. Lorenzo in Damaso**. (It is part of the palazzo with its entrance just ten yards from the main gate of the Cancelleria.) Founded by Pope Damascus I, it was conceded to a chapter of the canons, which are said to be one of the most ancient establishments of the sort in Rome. Later it became the titular church of Cardinal Riario and was thus positioned within a courtyard of this palazzo. Because of its placement the space inside the church is nearly square with a double elliptical groined vault. It is also decorated with some interesting works of art and tombs, among them that of the poet Annibale Caro. For more details about the interior of the church listen to the tape-recorded description provided inside, just through the doors designed by Vignola.

Returning to the Campo dei Fiori we pass the **Via del Pellegrino**, to the right at the juncture of the two piazzas. Named after a route used by the pilgrims in the fifteenth century to get from their hotels near the Campo to the Vatican, the Via del Pellegrino is one of the few medieval streets to retain its original name. Later, at the end of the seventeenth century, the city required all jewelers to live and work there. Though no longer the "gold ghetto," it preserves part of that heritage in the few jewelry shops along its path. Continue walking past this street straight to the bread store on the Campo.

If you stand on the corner of the Piazza Campo dei Fiori and the Via dei Cappellari you will be next to a building whose reputation as an inn at the beginning of the sixteenth century was no doubt enhanced by that of its owner, Vanozza Cattanei, the mistress of Pope Alexander VI and mother of his children, Lucrezia and Cesare Borgia. Her crest, which includes the emblem of the infamous Borgia pope, can be seen if you take a few steps down the **Vicolo del Gallo** to **no. 13**. Vanozza's relationship with the pope was no secret at the time, as he adopted her children and even made Cesare a cardinal. Nevertheless, adding his family emblem to her shield would have been considered audacious. Vanozza waited ten years after the pope's death before she hung this crest on the front of her hotel.

Turn right onto **Via dei Cappellari**, "Street of the Hatmakers." The hatmakers are long gone, but little else has changed on this street, which is perhaps one of the most characteristic to have survived from the 1500s. The narrow street lined with aging façades often festooned with laundry, is still trafficked by wooden carts used to transport produce from the ground-floor storage areas to the market. Here, for a block, we again step into an area that recalls medieval Rome, and the contrast between this street and the High Renaissance elegance of the nearby Via di Monserrato, Piazza Farnese, and Via Giulia is striking.

As you begin down the street notice the stucco *edicola* from the eighteenth century on the corner to your left. The image is always flanked by plastic or fresh flowers that ten years ago were always left by old ladies dressed in black. A sign of the changing times is that the task is fulfilled by women in suits on their way to work, no doubt the daughters or grandaughters of the women I observed not so long ago. **No. 127–130** is a house owned by the Vatican. Until 1937, when Gnoli, a Roman historian, wrote about it, frescoes could still be seen on its façade. The building at **no. 61–62** was also once decorated with geometric designs. This sixteenth-century fashion for decorating houses with architectonic motifs or scenes from mythology and the Old Testament began in Venice, became fashionable in Florence, and finally took hold in Rome, where as many as two hundred façades were painted. It became such a fad that it was often cited as one of the elements that differentiated Rome from other Italian cities during the Renaissance. Polidoro da Caravaggio and Maturino da Firenze, two of the most important artists of this style, distinguished themselves by painting houses with such energy and fecundity that Vasari wrote, "Rome, laughing, became drunk with their efforts."

The arch over the street, named the **Arco dei Cappellari**, was built in the seventeenth century. Under it, at **no. 29–30**, a marble plaque states that here Pietro Trapessi, the boy who recited his verses in the Piazza S. Andrea della Valle and became the famous poet Metastasio (a Hellenized form of his family name), was born in 1698.

Just to the right of the arch a passageway terminates with a picture from the fifteenth century known as the *Crucifixion of the Hatmakers*. The picture depicts Christ on the cross with the Virgin Mary, Mary Magdalene, and other worshipers on their knees; it is an object of veneration on September 14, the occasion of the feast of the Exaltation of the Cross. Directly across the street is a courtyard whose walls and small-grated windows are said to be relics of the Corte Savello, one of Rome's grim medieval prisons. The prison was placed under the jurisdiction of the Savelli family, who, in the thirteenth century, were given the title of Hereditary Marshals of the Conclave. With a guard of five hundred men and some sort of criminal court the Savelli Marshal's function was to control, among other things, the courtesans from whom he exacted a tax (in addition to license fees) adding a nice sum to the papal coffers. The prison, which extended to Via di Monserrato, was closed by Pope Innocent X for its unsanitary conditions and was replaced by a new one on Via Giulia.

In about ten yards there will be an intersection. On the right, the **Vicolo del Bollo** is named for the office that stamped hallmarks on gold and silver. This office was established here in the eighteenth century for the convenience of the jewelers on the neighboring Via del Pellegrino. Straight ahead, rows of rustic antique furniture shops line the remainder of Via dei Cappellari where a bargain can be found if you are interested, but it takes some patience and a good eye.

Turn left onto **Via di Montoro**, whose name was taken from the palazzo immediately to your right. This street

Antique shops for rustic furniture

functions as a bridge between the older medieval quarter of this neighborhood and the more elegant creations of the Renaissance and the baroque periods. The **Palazzo Montoro**, a building that extends the length of nineteen windows, was built in the mid–eighteenth century by a noble family from Umbria who came to Rome as part of the Savelli Court. The family did well for themselves in the city. One of their daughters married into the famous Sienese banking family, the Chigis, and added that family's name and insignia to their own. You can see the Chigi insignia, an oak and a star, decorating the building. Later a son married the last member of one of Rome's oldest families, Maria Verginia Patrizi, and assumed her family name. Since the longevity of a family name is very important in an aristocratic society, this young Chigi Montoro rescued the Patrizis from oblivion.

When we reach the intersection of Via di Montoro

and **Via di Monserrato** we enter a section of the neighborhood and the city distinguished for its refined beauty.
Via di Monserrato is lined with palazzi built between the
late sixteenth century and the eighteenth. From the corner take note of the house at **no. 105**, the **Palazzo Giangiacomo**, with its beautiful portal and broken pediments
supported by female heads. **No. 111–112**, the house belonging to the Confraternity of S. Caterina da Siena, is a
replica of the saint's birthplace in Siena.

From the sixteenth century until recent times this
section of Rome was known as the *quartiere degli stranieri,*
"quarter of the foreigners," because so many people of
foreign nationality or from other regions of what is now
Italy lived here. On one end of the street is the Venerable
English College, established in 1362 and said to be the
oldest English institution abroad. To our right and across
the street is the **Church of S. Maria in Monserrato**, the
national church of Spain. This church is dedicated to the
celebrated Black Virgin, whose miraculous appearance in
the mountains outside Barcelona made her one of the
most loved of Spanish idols. The two Borgia popes, Calixtus III and Alexander VI, are buried here.

Pope Calixtus III suffered from the reputation of his
nephew, Pope Alexander, who was considered capable
of any crime. Just as some people would like to attribute
every monumental work in Rome to Michelangelo, so,
too, crime during the fifteenth century was popularly associated with the Borgia name. Both popes were originally buried in the vaults of St. Peter, but when Julius II,
a great enemy of the Borgias, was elected, their bodies
were promptly exhumed and turned over to the Spanish
Church here on Via di Monserrato. The gesture was tan-
tamount to transferring their remains to Spain, and it was
more than three centuries before the passage of time could
allow the acknowledgment of their positions as leaders
of the Church. A proper monument was finally built for
them in 1881.

S. Maria in Monserrato was built on the site of a house

bought by Pope Innocent VI (1352–1362) as a hospice for Catalan pilgrims. Work on the present structure was begun in 1518 by Antonio Sangallo the Younger but was not finished because of political problems between Rome and Spain, which lasted more than a century.

Turn right onto Via di Monserrato. Pass the church and to your left you will see a small street called the **Via della Barchetta**, named after a boat service that operated between here and Trastevere in the days when only two or three bridges spanned the river. Across from the beginning of this street, at **no. 34**, is the **Palazzo Capponi**. Walk into the courtyard. There, a large amorphous space is divided by a fountain portal into a small paved area and a large garden beyond. The sound of water and the gentle swaying of palm trees are a pleasant contrast to the city streets.

Return to the street. **No. 17**, to the left, is a house whose renovation in 1870 caused enough of an uproar that its owner had the following motto inscribed over the door: *"Trahit sua quemque voluptas,"* meaning that everyone has his own taste and that in finding his, the owner had done what pleased him. What "pleased him" was removing the frescoes, antique travertine windows, cornices, and the ancient family crest of the previous owners.

The **Palazzo Pallavicini**, at **no. 25**, was built by a family who came to Rome from Cremona. The family included two cardinals and a city magistrate, and all are buried in a family chapel at S. Maria in Monserrato. Carlo Maderno designed the main entrance, the windows of the façade, and the main staircase of this residence. The balcony above the entrance was added in the eighteenth century. At that time the palazzo became home to the Carmelite Order, and they built a church to S. Teresa just to the right of the entrance. A watercolor by Achilli Pinelli shows the façade of this palazzo with a church, but when the Carmelites moved to S. Maria della Vittoria

A garden courtyard on Via di Monserrato

(one of the "must" churches in Rome, if only to see Bernini's sculpture of St. Teresa) all traces of the church were also removed.

Across the street from the Palazzo Pallavicini, on the corner of **Piazza Ricci**, is the charming, ancient **Church of S. Giovanni in Ayno**, which has been converted into a private residence. The church dates back to 1186. In the fourteenth century it was described as a basilica with an entrance porch similar to other early Christian churches such as S. Cecilia and S. Maria in Cosmedin. In the fifteenth century, however, it was given this delicate face-lift. Some signs of its medieval origins remain in the corbeled cornice and the sawtoothed decorative design.

On the far end of the square is the palazzo that gives the piazza its name. Built in the 1500s by Nanni di Baccio Bigio, **Palazzo Ricci** boasts probably the best example of the frescoed façades that were so much a part of the city's character at that time. It was once entirely covered by the monochromatic paintings of Polidoro da Caravaggio and Maturino da Firenze, but time has taken its toll, especially in the last forty years. Photographs taken by Alinari show that these frescoes were still prominent during the 1940s; their recent destruction is blamed entirely on auto pollution. At the end of the nineteenth century Luigi Fontana restored the paintings and added the family crest on the third floor and the scenes on the fourth. With a sharp eye and some imagination you can decipher these historical and mythical studies: the Tiber, the she-wolf with Romulus and Remus, Faustolo with his wife, Romulus with a plough marking the position for the walls of Rome while men around him dig the foundations for the new city, and the rape of the Sabines.

Polidoro and Maturino were quite a pair during the early days of the sixteenth century. Vasari in the *Lives of the Artists* says of them:

> They began to study the antiquities of Rome, and copied the ancient marbles until they both alike ac-

quired the antique style, and the one was so like the other that, as their minds were moved by the same will, so their hands expressed the same knowledge. Of what great use they have been to the art of painting may be seen by the number of foreign artists who continually study their works; for all artists in Rome copy the pictures of Polidoro and Maturino more than all the other modern paintings. . . . But if I were to name all their works, I should have to make a whole book of the doings of these two men, for there is no house or palace or vineyard where there are not works by Polidoro and Maturino.

A member of the Ricci family still keeps an apartment in this palazzo, which otherwise has been divided into numerous dwellings. Not too long ago, when he decided to have the main salon painted, workmen found under the wallpaper a beautifully preserved painted frieze with figures of seated women. The painter is unknown but the style is mannerist, of the period between 1570 and 1590. This kind of story, while infrequent, is not unusual in Rome.

The restaurant on this piazza is especially popular among a crowd of young professionals. While the specialties change with the season there is always a chocolate cake for dessert, and it's one of the few in Rome spared a dousing of liquor. Most months of the year you can sit under a large umbrella and admire the decoration of the Palazzo Ricci or the façades of the Palazzo Pallavicini and the former Church of S. Giovanni in Ayno.

Return to Via di Monserrato and turn left. About twenty feet on the right is the **Palazzo Corsetti**, at **no. 20**. Peer through the gate at the miniature courtyard rich with classical fragments. The arches, the outside staircase, the columns, the stone, and stucco create a most delightful atmosphere for this space between the street and the house. The marble fragments and plaques recall the glory of classical Rome, while beyond is a small garden with orange trees. The courtyard and the Palazzo Corsetti were built by Monsignor Podocatori, the doctor to Pope Clement VII and rector of the University of Padova, one of the oldest universities in Europe. Across the street are two other palazzi built during the sixteenth century by families connected to the Vatican.

Via di Monserrato ends in a rather desolate piazza where several important streets—Via dei Banchi Vecchi, Via del Pellegrino, and Via di Monserrato—converge. The restaurant to the left on **Largo Moretta** may be located in the same place as another that in the seventeenth century gave the piazza its name. The customers of that long-ago restaurant were taken with the owners' daughter, an exotic mulatto child. Nicknamed "La Moretta," she soon gave her name to the street and the piazza. At that time a pharmacy famous for its antique vases and a bronze mortar made by Cellini also took the name.

The Largo Moretta is located at an important juncture in the street map of old Rome called the Chiavica de Santa Lucia. At this point the Cloaca di Ponte, one of the ancient Roman sewers, flowed into the Tiber. These *cloacas*, "sewers," were incredible feats of engineering. The drains flushed not only the sewage of the city but all the water from a large number of fresh-water springs and all of the water that constantly poured into Rome from the aqueducts. As a result of this draining system, places like the Forum and the Campus Martius, originally soggy marshes, became dry, habitable land. What's more, this was not just a system of narrow pipes; Pliny describes Agrippa, when minister of public works in 33 B.C., as inspecting the *cloaca* by boat.

Cellini's autobiography mentions this spot on several occasions. The famous mortar was given to the pharmacist as a gift in gratitude for the protection given Cellini during one of his violent adventures, which may well have been this one described in his autobiography:

In the meantime my enemies had proceeded slowly towards Chiavica, as the place was called, and had arrived at the crossing of several roads, going in different directions, but the street in which Pompeo's house stood was the one which leads straight to the Campo dei Fiori. Some business or other made him enter the apothecary's shop which stood at the corner of Chiavica, and there he stayed a while transacting it. I had just been told that he had boasted of an insult which he fancied he had put upon me, but be that as it may, it was to his misfortune; for precisely when I came up to the corner, he was leaving the shop, and his *bravi* had opened their ranks and received him in their midst. I drew a little dagger with a sharpened edge, and breaking the line of his defenders, laid my hands upon his breast so quickly and coolly, that none of them were able to prevent me. Then I aimed to strike him in the face, but fright made him turn his head round; and I stabbed him beneath the ear. I only gave him two blows, for he fell stone cold at the second. I had not meant to kill him, but as the saying goes, knocks are not dealt by measure. With my left hand I plucked back the dagger, and with my right hand drew my sword to defend my life. However, all those *bravi* ran up to the corpse and took no action against me, so I went back alone through Strada Giulia considering how best to put myself in safety.

During the sixteenth century Rome witnessed a huge upsurge of construction as popes, cardinals, and other nobles tried to outdo each other, building homes along grandiose classical lines. The house to your right, between Via di Monserrato and Via del Pellegrino, is one of the vestiges of an earlier Rome—not a palazzo but an elegant human-scale townhouse. For centuries it was known as the "house of the treasurer" after its owner, Pietro Paolo Francesci, the first person to be appointed to supervise the coinage of money. The capitals on the top-floor loggia, facing the piazza, are similar to others on buildings of the late fifteenth century, and, in keeping with the fad of the time, there are still traces of frescoes on the façade (depicting Cloelia crossing the Tiber). An equally dramatic fresco could have been painted about an event that took place within its walls. In 1462 the Austrian emperor Fredrick III came to Rome to ask for the hand of Elenora di Portogallo, a guest of the Francesci family. Until 1870, when it was moved to the German Hospice of S. Maria dell'Anima, the crest of the Austrian emperor with its overreaching motto—*Austriae est impe-rare orbi universo*—hung on this house and overlooked the group of streets that facilitated the rebirth of Rome as the center of the Christian world.

Across the way, at the beginning of **Via del Pelle-grino, no. 145**, is another emblem that adds poignancy to the fates of great nations. Here, embedded in the wall of the local grocery store, is a carved boundary stone from the reign of Claudius in A.D. 49. This stone was one of the many that marked the boundary between the city and the country, which by Roman law was redefined according to the size of the empire. This particular stone indicates the enlargement of the city at the time of the conquest of Britain.

Walk through the Largo Moretta toward the dilapi-dated church and the Tiber. Despite the images conjured by Cellini, by the ancient Roman *cloaca*, or by the bor-dering Vicolo del Malpasso (Street of the Wrong Step—a warning against all the courtesans who once lived here), this is one of the least picturesque spots in the center of the city. Essays advocating its restoration periodically ap-pear in Rome's papers and many architects have designed, their solution to this sixty-year-old problem created when the war aborted Mussolini's plan to build a wide avenue through here to connect the Mazzini Bridge to the Corso Vittorio Emanuele II. Even the church dedicated to Rome's patron saint, S. Filippo Neri (or the Pipo Buono as he is endearingly referred to), stands in semiwrecked

The boundary stone on Via del Pellegrino

abandon; its architectural credentials, built in 1728 by Raguzzini on the orders of Pope Benedict XIII, have not been enough to rescue it from ruin.

The Largo Moretta opens onto **Via Giulia**. At this point we find ourselves about halfway down the famous one-kilometer stretch of road created by Pope Julius II. This street was to be another monumental entrance to the Vatican (from the Ponte Sisto), and Bramante was hired to design a magnificent gate and to construct a new, huge court of justice on the end closest to the Vatican. Both these projects were abandoned for lack of funds, but the foundation stones for the court of justice can still be seen along the walls of the Hotel Cardinale (a few blocks to your right); they have been nicknamed the pillows of Via Giulia. What Pope Julius did accomplish was the alignment and pavement of the street. All protruding porches and stairways obstructing the thoroughfare were removed, and to this day the road's course is one of the few straight lines on the map of the center-city.

As you stand at the intersection with Via Giulia look to your right. A block away is a large building with guards at the entrance; this is what replaced the Corte Savello jails on the Via dei Cappellari. This forbidding structure, built in 1655 by Antonio del Grande and known as the **Carcere Nuovo**, "new prison," was considered for centuries a model of prison design. Now the building is used as offices by the police.

Directly across the street is a public high school, the **Liceo Galileo**, and its parking lot. Though this building is new, the site has been associated with education since 1670. At that time one of the earliest educational institutions in Rome, the Collegio Ghislieri, built its boarding school here. Primarily it served the sons of noble families in the Papal Court; the descendants of the founder, Ghislieri; and the descendants of Ghelmino Crotti who contributed to its founding—but every year one boy was selected for admission from the general Roman population. This school played an important role in the life of the city until 1928 when it was closed for financial reasons.

Turn left onto **Via Giulia** and enjoy a full view of this street, which is framed by the arched bridge at the far end. This is undoubtedly one of the most attractive streets in the city and certainly, since the sixteenth century, one of the most fashionable. It could be a set design for an Italian Renaissance play and often seems so during the spring and summer when circus and music festivals add their spectacles. These festivals are a revival of the street entertainments popular in the seventeenth and eighteenth centuries that kept the torches of Via Giulia burning late into the night. Attracted to both its beauty and street life, artists also came to live and work here. Sangallo built himself a huge palazzo (now the Palazzo Sachetti), and Cellini, Pier Luigi da Palestrina, Raphael, and many others helped create a tradition of art now long associated with this street's name. Today that tradition lives on in the structures that continue to excite the eye and in the antique trade that for the last forty years has occupied the ground-floor shops. Another enticement along this street is that Via Giulia is closed to traffic during the day. This does not mean that you won't see any cars but you will be able to stroll down the middle of the street and examine the architecture of the façades without risking life and limb.

Our walk down the Via Giulia leads us toward the bridge and past enough palazzi, churches, and shops to give the full flavor of this street's ambiance. To your left, past the simple house of the 1600s at no. 146–47, is another entrance to the Palazzo Ricci, whose painted façade we admired from Via di Monserrato.

On the other side of the street, next to the school, is the Neapolitan **Church of S. Spirito**. While this church is hardly representative of the grandeur of the kingdom of Naples in the mid–seventeenth century, it is the "pantheon" for the last sovereigns of that kingdom, who died in exile waiting to be restored to their throne. The design itself doesn't even hint at the grand tradition of church building fostered in Naples.

A dozen yards to your right, before the intersection, look above the wall and you will see the small but beautifully proportioned cupola of the **Church of S. Eligio degli Orefici**. Turn right onto **Via di S. Eligio** for a closer look at this church. St. Eligio, a goldsmith, became the patron saint of jewelers, who were a wealthy and important group in Rome at the turn of the sixteenth century. They commissioned Raphael to design their church in the form of a Greek cross surmounted by a cupola, reproducing, on a small scale, the lines of St. Peter's. The work was completed by Baldassare Peruzzi.

S. Eligio is a good example of the type of design that has come to be referred to as the "golden period" of the Renaissance when Bramante, Michelangelo, and Raphael were all working in Rome. The church established Raphael, a man who considered himself above all a painter, as one of the best architects of his time. Climb the stairs at the end of the street, which lead to the sidewalk along the Lungotevere, for a better view of the cupola.

Return to Via Giulia. At **no. 151**, on the left side of the street, is the only nineteenth-century palazzo on this street which, despite its recent vintage, blends in well with the rest of the buildings. The inscription on this building, known as the **Palazzo degli Stabilimento Spagnoli**, tells us that it was built by Queen Elizabeth II of Spain for the poor, the pilgrims, and the sick. Attached to the Spanish Church of S. Maria di Monserrato, this building encloses a courtyard containing the tombs of famous Spanish clergy. Among them is one designed by Bernini for Monsignor Pietro Foix de Montoya. Also note the intricate iron work of the gate.

To the right, **no. 16** is the **Palazzo Varese**, built by Carlo Maderno in 1617 for a Milanese monsignor. The cornice, richly decorated with flying eagles and towered castles, is a fine example of this architectural detail. Inside the courtyard is a four-story loggia with two stories of arcaded openings and two with flat entablatures, all of the Tuscan order.

The **Church of S. Caterina da Siena** is often referred to as the last baroque work in Rome. Originally built under Leo X for the Sienese colony, which had a defense tower near here along the banks of the Tiber, it was rebuilt in 1766–1770 by Paolo Posi. The firmly curved concave design of the façade, which makes such a strong impression while one walks down this street, was built at a time when the baroque was superseded by flatter, more classical lines. Note the coat of arms of the city of Siena over the door and above that the two medallions of the she-wolf and twins, symbols of the city of Rome.

Next to the church, at **no. 163**, is the **Palazzo Cisterna**, built in the sixteenth century by the sculptor Guglielmo della Porta as his home and studio. At the beginning of this century, it was the home of the painter Eugenio Cisterna. **No. 167** is another sixteenth-century palazzo; it was restored in 1928 by Lord Rennel Rodd, British ambassador to Rome and author of *Rome of the Renaissance and Today*.

We have already passed several antique shops, but there are many more along this street, among them some of the best in Rome. For the last two centuries Via dei Coronari and Via del Babuino have been known as the centers of the antique trade. Only after 1950, when dealers looking for cheap, desirable space bought out the mechanics and garage-owners who occupied the ground-floor shops of the palazzi, did the Via Giulia also acquire this reputation. Originally, these ground-floor spaces were used as stables. When horses were replaced by cars in this century, the noble families sought new ways to earn income to maintain their palazzi, and the spaces were rented out or sold to people involved in the automobile business. Now, only a motorcycle repair shop farther down the street hangs on as a reminder of this short period in Via Giulia's history. Today it is hard to imagine that rents on Via Giulia were ever cheap since it has become one of the most desirable addresses in Rome.

As we approach the arch over Via Giulia, another great palazzo rises to the right, at **no. 1**, with large falcon heads suspended from the corner pilasters. This is the **Palazzo Falconieri**, now the seat of the Hungarian Academy of Art. In the early nineteenth century it was the home of Cardinal Fesch, Napoleon's uncle and one of the greatest collectors of Italian art. When Orazio Falconieri bought this palace from Pietro Farnese in 1638 it had a frontage of seven windows. In 1645 Falconieri bought the adjacent palace and commissioned Borromini to remodel the whole complex. In this instance the great architect's work on the façade is not characterized by his usual overwhelming individuality—lots of movement and perspective, as in the Palazzo Spada or my favorite work, the Church of S. Ivo. His most interesting contribution here is the belvedere on top of the south wing, which can be seen from the river's edge or the Gianicolo (the best point in town from which to admire the entire cityscape). This belvedere, with its concave corners and herms of the two-headed Janus, isolates the palazzo on the skyline and stands in clear contrast to the nearby loggia on the Palazzo Farnese, which was designed by yet another of Rome's great architects, Giacomo della Porta.

Just beyond the palace is the rather macabre **Church of S. Maria dell'Orazione e Morte**, whose façade is adorned by skulls and a sculpture of a winged skeleton pointing to a scroll on which is written "me today, thee tomorrow." This image became the famous "wizened hag of Strada Giulia" in one of Belli's poems. The church itself is considered the finest example of the architecture of Ferdinando Fuga, one of the masters of the late baroque who incorporated into his designs elements from the three founding fathers—Bernini, Borromini, and Cortona. The church was built between 1732 and 1737 and is a rare example of a single, cohesive style. The macabre symbols, such as the winged heads on the tops of the pediments, are in reference to the confraternity established here whose job it was to provide a Christian burial for all abandoned bodies and all those unable to afford a proper burial. This group was similar to the Confraternity of Sacconi Rossi on the Tiber Island, which occupied itself with the burial of bodies drowned in the Tiber.

At one time there were underground burial chambers connected to this church extending to the Tiber. All but one of these were destroyed in 1886 during the construction of the river embankment. The vaults and walls of these chambers were covered with bones and skulls displayed with such fantasy that they became mere decorative elements. In the only remaining chamber, for example, there is a candelabra created out of vertebrae and other small bones; in a niche a skeleton hangs much like a Halloween display representing not our present image of horror, but the popular decorative tastes of the seventeenth century. In fact, this church, along with the Capuchin Church of S. Maria della Concezione on the Via Veneto (which today is a more extensive representation of this macabre baroque style—and easier to get into), was for centuries one of the important tourist sites in Rome. This fact is illustrated by the numerous engravings and lithographs of the burial chambers that were sold to make money for the confraternity. Gregorovius's conclusion to this fascination is that it transformed fears of death into playful familiarity.

At this point in our walk down the Via Giulia we stroll under the bridge that spans the street. This bridge is Via Giulia's mark of distinction, now almost a souvenir of Rome because of Roesler Franz's paintings of the last century. This arch is the only structural trace of Michelangelo's grand scheme to connect the main Farnese house with yet another of their possessions, the Farnesina, across the river in Trastevere.

Just beyond the bridge, to the left, is the back gate to the Palazzo Farnese. I will discuss the story of this palace when we reach the main entrance at the end of our walk. For now, enjoy the sight of the green garden (a luxury in this crowded neighborhood) and the elegant three-bay loggia facing the river that was built by Giacomo della Porta.

You have probably already heard the sound of trickling water that flows from the combined wall-fountain and horse-trough a dozen yards away to the right. This is the **Mascherone fountain**, named for the colossal marble face of Roman origin spewing a steady stream of water. It is not a favorite among Romans except for three days at the end of the nineteenth century when it sent out a stream of wine rather than water to help with the celebrations of a particular feast. Its importance on the Roman street scene is that of being one of three puzzling ancient faces; the other two are the Bocca della Verità (the Mouth of Truth) at S. Maria Cosmedin (covered in Walk 2) and the large face with a moustache in the little square near S. Sabina on the Aventine Hill.

The Mascherone fountain was built in 1570 by the Farnese family, who crowned the piece with their emblem of a lily. Completed before there was any water flowing to this section of Rome, it was hoped that the aqueduct known as Acqua Virgine would reach this far. However, the Acqua Virgine made it only to the Campo dei Fiori, and this fountain, as well as the two on the Piazza Farnese, stood empty until Pope Paul V, in 1613, piped the Acqua Paola across Ponte Sisto to the left banks. Before the river embankment was built, this fountain stood on the landing for the *traghetto*, "ferry," to Porta Settimiana.

Turn left onto **Via del Mascherone**, directly across from the fountain. To the right, at **no. 63**, is a house with two plaques mounted in the wall. One was posted in 1926 by the city government to inform us that the celebrated intellectual Francesco Cancellieri (1751–1826)

The doors of a Renaissance building

lived here. The other, mounted in 1930, is a memorial to the German poet William Frederick Waiblinger, who died here in 1830. The entrance hall of this house has a touching inscription: "I belong to Francesco Cancellieri, may I, a small and not illustrious house, be always frequented by faithful friends."

Next door is the **Church of SS. Giovanni e Petronio dei Bolognesi**. On this site was a medieval church dating back to at least 1186 that was given to the Bolognese community by Pope Gregory XIII in 1581. The present church was built in the last years of the sixteenth century to the design of the Bolognese architect Ottaviano Mascarino.

Having passed the Spanish, the Neapolitan, the Sienese, and now the Bolognese churches, you can understand better why this neighborhood was considered for centuries "of the foreigner." One must remember that only at the end of the nineteenth century was Italy united. The neighborhood's foreign community currently includes large numbers of Americans, British, French, and reflecting more recent changes to the city's faces, Asians and Eastern Europeans.

As you walk up the Via del Mascherone you can't

help but be aware of the mass and height of the structure to your left, the **Palazzo Farnese**. It is the largest palazzo in Rome, and its construction involved many of the greatest architects and artists of the sixteenth and seventeenth centuries. The result is a sumptuous monument to the power and wealth achieved by the Farnese family, primarily through the pontificate. It was the elite of the Church, and not the merchants and politicians as in Florence who were responsible for the domestic architecture of Renaissance and baroque Rome.

As this palazzo should be appreciated from the piazza in front, walk there and rest on the bench conveniently built across from the façade or near one of the two huge vases of gray Egyptian granite that have been turned into fountains. Known as the Farnese bathtubs, these were brought here by Alessandro Farnese from the Baths of Caracalla by way of the Piazza S. Marco. Here, listening to the soothing sound of water and looking at one of the most impressive piazzas in Rome, you can read the story of the Palazzo Farnese, a story that tells a lot about the Renaissance in this city.

A whole chapter could easily be devoted to the history—architectural, artistic, and social—of this palace that was so grandly conceived by Alessandro Farnese. The Farnese name derives from a castle near Lake Bolena and appears rarely in the chronicles of Roman history until Alessandro's time. One of the first stories set a tone for spunk and drama: Alessandro was imprisoned for forging a paper as a student in the Collegium de Parco Majori during the reign of Innocent VIII. Cellini refers to Alessandro's escape from the prison at Castel S. Angelo with a basket and a rope. As with other memorable stories, the real force behind Alessandro's rise to power was the face of a beautiful woman, his sister Giulia. The wife of Ursino Orsini and known as Giulia Bella, Alessandro's sister so captivated the Borgia Pope Alexander VI that she replaced Vanozza in his affections. Alessandro Farnese's appointment as cardinal was a direct result of this liaison. Once a prince of the Church, he seems to have rapidly assumed leadership in the hierarchy and, as was the case at that time, concomitantly amassed a huge fortune.

Following the example of his papal patron and namesake, Alessandro Farnese never disguised his affection for his children, Pierluigi and Constanza. His son became duke of Parma, Piacenza, and Nepi, while his daughter carried on her aunt's reputation for beauty and fortune. Even his grandchildren were able to benefit from his position; one was made a cardinal at the age of fourteen and the other was married to Margaret of Austria, the widow of Alessandro de' Medici.

Both as cardinal and later as Pope Paul III, his taste for magnificence (passed on to his grandson, Alessandro) left Italy a far more beautiful and interesting place. The inheritance includes not only this example in front of us, but also the Villa Caprarola designed by Vignola and the famous collection of antique sculpture that is now the treasure of the National Museum of Naples, to say nothing of Pope Paul III's artistic influence on the Vatican.

Though Alessandro remained a cardinal for forty years, it wasn't until he was made the titular cardinal of S. Eustachio that he called upon Antonio Sangallo to design his new palazzo on land acquired from the monks of S. Maria del Popolo. The construction spread over many years; seventeen years into the project, when Alessandro finally assumed the papal tiara, Vasari says "he felt he should no longer build a cardinal's but a pontiff's palace." Immediately, Alessandro had Sangallo enlarge the building from three to five bays in the court and from eleven to thirteen on the façades. The row of shops on the street was eliminated, and the entrance was enlarged by the addition of a monumental colonnaded vestibule. Ironically, this papal palace was inhabited not by Alessandro Farnese, who moved to the Vatican, but by his ancestors.

Upon the death of Sangallo, Michelangelo was called in to finish the work. He is generally credited with the top story, the famous cornice, and the central loggia window above the Piazza Farnese entrance. James Ackerman says of this collaboration:

> Michelangelo, though noted for his inability to collaborate with colleagues, showed remarkable skill in harmonizing his own dynamic style with the portions already built by Sangallo. No two architects of the mid-sixteenth century were less congenial than these; it is symptomatic of their relationship that at St. Peter's Michelangelo erased almost every trace of Sangallo's Basilica. Perhaps he would have done the same at the Farnese palace if it had not been so far advanced when he started, but economy must have forced him to keep what was there and even to make use of members that had been carved but not put in place, such as the uppermost façade windows. Consequently the palace has a Sangallesque personality throughout. Michelangelo enhanced and gave vigor to his personality and at essential points rescues it from dull propriety; in doing so he created Sangallo's masterpiece.

Michelangelo did have one scheme that, completed, would have left his distinctive mark: the single arch, which we saw over Via Giulia, is all that remains of his plan to connect the garden of this palace with that of the Farnesina. His intention was to create a vista and access that spanned the courtyard, the garden of the Farnese Palace, the Via Giulia, the river, all the way to the other garden. When Michelangelo died, Giacomo della Porta completed the palazzo with a loggia on the riverfront and left the bridge unfinished. An inscription assigns the final year of work to 1589.

Besides its rich architecture, the Farnese palace became the recipient even before its completion of the rarest and best collections of art ever formed by a private individual. The collection may have begun in the early days of construction when Sangallo discovered the walls of the barracks and stables of the Red Squadron of Charioteers, which dated back to the heyday of the Campus Martius. The collection comprised works of statuary, pictures, books, manuscripts, *objets de vertu*, and curiosities. Many of the statues came from Cardinal Alessandro's excavations throughout Rome but especially from those in the Baths of Caracalla, which brought him a great reputation as a savior of antiquity. Notwithstanding his will, which declares "that none of my heirs and successors shall dare to sell or give away, or transfer to other places, or pawn any of the objects of art and curiosity which exist at the moment in my collection," Pope Pius VI did manage to ship the entire collection to Naples to assuage the Bourbon dynasty. It is this collection that now distinguishes the National Museum of Naples.

The collection and the love of art from which it stems dictated the design and decor of many of the rooms, which unfortunately are now closed to the public. If possible, catch a fleeting glimpse of the **vestibule** leading to the courtyard while the gate opens to what is now the French Embassy. It is one of the most beautiful features of the palace—a quadruple row of columns and semicolumns holding a stuccoed ceiling.

The windows to the left of the center balcony, including both the *piano nobile* and the row of windows above, look onto one room—the **Salon d'Hercule**, named after the gigantic statue of Hercules standing in that room. The original statue, now in Naples, was found in 1540 at the Baths of Caracalla and is signed by Glycon of Athens. It was the pride of the Farnese collection, and the room that was designed around it more than matched its size. (The beautifully coffered ceiling in this room is sometimes visible from the piazza in the evenings when the lights are on in that room.)

The other room worthy of mention is the **Carracci Gallery**, which is used on state occasions as the French Embassy's dining room. There the themes of the loves of gods and goddesses from Ovid's *Metamorphosis* are spread across the walls in a colorful praise of pagan voluptuousness. This work, done between 1597 and 1604, had a tremendous influence on subsequent decorative painting in Rome. It is also believed to have led to Carracci's death; disappointed at the fee he received he took to drink and died at the age of forty-nine.

During the pontificate of Clement VII, Cardinal Farnese's (Alessandro's grandson) records show that he had 306 people living in the palace, including family and servants. Both the palace's reputation and its magnificence attracted famous dignitaries. In 1635 Cardinal Richelieu stayed here, lured by the library, which at the time was considered the best in Italy; and in 1655 Queen Christina of Sweden made this her home. But the opulence of the Farnese family was never again matched. During the late seventeenth century this served as a residence for the French ambassador to the Holy See. Through marriage it was inherited by the Bourbon kings of Naples, who lived here in utmost seclusion after their exile in 1861. The French classic historian Jerome Carcopino tells a story about flocks of chickens kept on the attic terraces during this time of decline for the Bourbon dynasty. Since the union of Italy in 1871 the palace has been the home of the French Embassy under a remarkable arrangement that must have been negotiated during the French occupation of Rome. The palace was exchanged for the Hotel Galiffet in Paris for a rent of one lira payable every ninety-nine years. Thus, the French now have an exclusive right to one of the most magnificent palazzi in all of Italy.

Today this monumental palace still induces the awe and thrill that it was intended to—maybe more awe than ever. Pope Martin V, who started the ball rolling with his dismay and concern over the sight of Rome in the early fifteenth century, would probably be both surprised and thrilled at the efforts of his successors. Here in the neighborhood around the Campo dei Fiori, the Vatican certainly accomplished what it set out to do—to make Rome the queen of cities.

Walk·2

The Empire and the Church

AT THE FOOT OF THE
CAPITOLINE HILL

Ruins of the Temple of Apollo

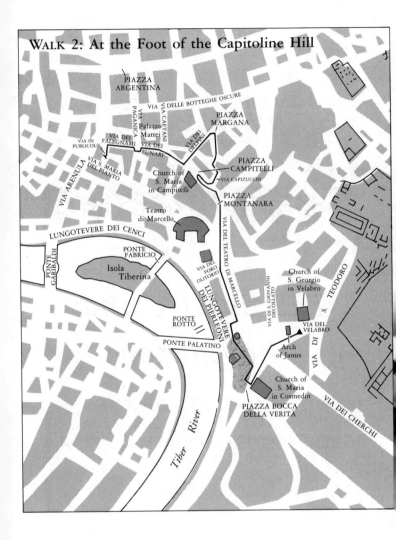

WALK 2: At the Foot of the Capitoline Hill

PIAZZA ARGENTINA

VIA DELLE BOTTEGHE OSCURE

VIA CAETANI

VIA PAGANICA

PIAZZA MARGANA

Palazzo Mattei

VIA DEI FUNARI

VIA DEI DELFINI

VIA IN PUBLICOLIS

VIA DEI FALEGNAMI

PIAZZA CAMPITELLI

VIA S. MARIA DEL PIANTO

VIA CAPIZUCCHI

VIA ARENULA

Church of S. Maria in Campitelli

PIAZZA MONTANARA

Teatro di Marcello

LUNGOTEVERE DEI CENCI

VIA DEL TEATRO DI MARCELLO

PONTE FABRICIO

S. TEODORO

Isola Tiberina

VIA DEL FORO OLITORIO

Church of S. Georgio in Velabro

PONTE GARIBALDI

LUNGOTEVERE DEI PIERLEONI

VIA DI S. GIOVANNI DECOLLATO

PONTE ROTTO

VIA DEL VELABRO

PONTE PALATINO

Arch of Janus

VIA DI

Church of S. Maria in Cosmedin

PIAZZA BOCCA DELLA VERITÀ

VIA DEI CHERCHI

Tiber River

Starting Point: Via del Velabro between the Arch of Janus and the Church of S. Giorgio in Velabro (Due to a terrorist bomb in July 1993 some of the immediate area around the Church of S. Giorgio will be closed to the public. Renovations are in progress.)
Buses: 57, 89, 90, 92, 94, 95, 716
Length of Walk: three hours

This walk leads us through an area of Rome at the foot of the Capitoline Hill toward the Tiber. Here twenty-seven centuries of the city's history are evoked and a visitor can get a fairly clear sense of how carefully planned Rome's development has been despite modern appearances to the contrary. Originally this area was a swamp that the ancient Romans drained and filled with markets, later with temples; and during the time of Augustus it became the site of some of the Empire's greatest splendors. Elaborate triumphal receptions were celebrated in the Theater of Marcellus. The Forum Olitorium, the oil and vegetable market, and the Forum Boarium, the meat market, established a center of commercial activity that remained strong, in one form or another, until the eighteenth century. It was in this zone that local Romans had their initial contact with foreign traders and later pilgrims.

Here the early Christian Church established the first shelter for visitors. Even during the city's bleaker periods, when many sections of Rome were abandoned, this quarter retained its inhabitants and commerce. In the sixteenth and seventeenth centuries, baroque splendors replaced those of the Empire and, in our century, Mussolini ensured that the city's architectural heritage was clearly visible.

Today, this quarter is not as densely populated and commercial as it was, which only facilitates our ability to enjoy its many vistas on the history of Rome. Here the grandeur of the Roman Empire, the simplicity of the Middle Ages, the elegance of the late Renaissance, the embellishments of the baroque, and the functionalism of the twentieth century are viewed in the intimacy of a residential quarter.

Our walk begins on the tranquil **Via del Velabro** between the massive Roman arch and the Romanesque church. This bowl-shaped area between the Tiber River, the Capitoline Hill, and the Palatine Hill has been known since ancient times as the Velabrum. In the legend of the founding of Rome, this is where Faustulus discovered the infants Romulus and Remus and, until King Tarquinius Priscus (616–579 B.C.) built the Cloaca Maxima to drain the area, it remained a marshy swamp. This drainage system, completed in 33 B.C., is essentially a large, vaulted underground canal that captures all the water streaming down the Quirinal, Viminal, and Esquiline hills and carries it into the Tiber River. The Cloaca Maxima drained not only the Velabrum, but also the area of the Roman Forum and is in use to this day. Pliny, writing at the end of the first century, was astonished that the Cloaca Maxima had already withstood the earthquakes, inundations, and accidents of seven hundred years.

Soon after the Velabrum was drained, during the time of the Roman Republic, this became the Forum Boarium, an open-air cattle market, extending from here south and toward the river. During the Roman Empire it continued as a cattle market but also became a busy commercial

Relief sculpture from the Arco dei Argentari

center crossed by the main road leading from a bridge over the Tiber to the Roman Forum. Not far away, between the Ponte Rotto and the Ponte Fabricio stood the Forum Olitorium.

In the middle of the ancient Forum Boarium stood a large bronze bull brought back from Aegina, Greece, to commemorate the legend of the cattle of Geryon that Hercules left to pasture on this site and which were stolen by Cacus. The Forum Boarium, until the Colosseum was built, was also the arena of the gladiators, who began fighting here in 64 B.C. when Marcus and Decimus Brutus mourned the death of their father by engaging three pairs of gladiators to fight to their deaths. Ninety years later when his father died, Titus Flaminius engaged seventy-four pairs of gladiators to fight over a thirty-day period. These fights became so popular that almost any excuse was used to hold them and by the height of the Empire, Julius Caesar (110–44 B.C.) entertained the Roman populace with as many as three hundred pairs of gladiators. These men were mostly prisoners of war, slaves, or criminals with a death sentence hanging over their heads. If they won the fight, they were rewarded with instant glory, wealth, and freedom.

The oldest remaining structure here on the Via del Velabro is the miniature classical arch attached to the left side of the Church of S. Giorgio in Velabro. This was erected in 204 by the silversmiths with shops in the Forum Boarium in honor of Emperor Septimius Severus and is known both as the **Arco dei Argentari** (silversmiths) and the Arco de Septimius Severus, not to be confused with another one in the Roman Forum. The delicately carved figures portray this emperor's wife and sons, Caracalla and Geta, offering a sacrifice to the gods. Following Caracalla's murder of his brother, he ordered Geta's effigy removed from this bas-relief as well as the larger triumphal arch.

The massive squared arch that dominates this site is the **Arch of Janus Quadrifons** built during the reign of Constantine (313–337). The word Janus in this case probably refers to a covered passage and not the Roman god of beginnings represented with two faces. Such arches were built at the crossroads of important commercial centers, in this case the roads leading from the Roman Forum to the Forum Boarium, and were also used as shelters for the merchants. The arch has four equal sides covered with marble and its forty-eight niches were undoubtedly designed to hold statues. As was so often done by noble families in Rome during the Middle Ages, this arch became the fortified stronghold and home of the Frangipane family until they moved in the eleventh century and built themselves a tower near the Piazza Navona.

When Constantine became emperor in the early fourth century, Rome was still the showcase of the Empire and the center of the civilized world. Visitors to the city were awestruck as they looked from the Capitoline Hill across the Forum to the Colosseum, entered temples gilded with bronze, and counted the number of basilicas, triumphal arches, statues, obelisks, fountains with water running from aqueducts built to the surrounding hills, libraries, circuses, theaters, and bridges. Nevertheless, Constantine moved the imperial capital to Byzantium on the Bosporus Strait, later known as Constantinople, so that he could defend the northern and eastern frontiers of the Roman Empire. By the end of the fourth century this empire was clearly crumbling. In 378 the Visigoths defeated the Roman army at Adrianople, and in 408 they invaded Italy and started marching south to Rome. When they first appeared at the Aurelian Wall, which had been fortified and raised to almost twice its original height, they were kept at bay with bribes. In 410, however, the gates were opened by traitors within the city and for the first time in eight hundred years Rome was occupied by hostile forces. There followed two hundred years of struggle for the Roman population with various invading forces. As noble families fled to Constantinople, the papacy became Rome's chief defender and Christianity established itself as the form of religious expression, dominating all aspects of life in Rome.

By the end of the sixth century Rome was impoverished, her population diminished from 500,000 to 30,000, and she was merely another town in one of the outer provinces of the Byzantine Empire. Eyewitnesses painted a bleak picture of a city in which buildings, aqueducts, and sewers were crumbling into ruins; monuments and statues were looted; the river's muddy waters carried dead animals and disease; and the entire population lived in dread of starvation and infection. While most of the structures of imperial Rome were in shambles, the skeleton of a city survived, and it was the church that maintained the economic, social, and political fabric of the city.

When Pope Gregory the Great ascended to the papacy in 590, he devoted himself to the relief of the poor by reorganizing the system of food distribution that the papacy had taken over from imperial authorities, and he established relief centers known as *diaconiae*, which were later converted into churches. The lovely Romanesque **Church of S. Giorgio in Velabro**, to the left of the Arch of Janus, is an example of this process of change and renewal that occurred in Rome beginning in the seventh century and set the tone for the Middle Ages in Rome.

Here on the edge of the Forum Boarium, Pope Gregory established a *diaconia* that fed the poor, cared for the sick, and took care of the increasing number of pilgrims. Aside from solving some of the urban problems of Rome, Pope Gregory dedicated himself to the spreading of the faith and sent missionaries to all corners of the then-known world. As a result, Christian pilgrims began coming to Rome to pray in the basilicas, catacombs, and shrines and turned to the *diaconiae* for food and shelter. Among the many visitors, there continued to be those who came to see the monuments of antiquity. When Emperor Constans II came to Rome in 667, a member of his retinue scratched the sovereign's name on the Arch of Janus. This remained a busy commercial center and all visitors to the city would have come here.

The Church of S. Giorgio in Velabro was built on the site of the *diaconia* in the ninth century. The portico and the campanile were added in the twelfth. The long nave is lined with sixteen columns each with different capitals

The campanile of S. Giorgio in Velabro

plundered from nearby temples. The altar, which contains part of St. George's skull, and the canopy were added in the thirteenth century. It is a refreshingly plain interior with the cosmatesque mosaic of the canopy and the fresco on the apse, attributed to the school of Cavallini, providing the only decorative touches. Note the original window with mica instead of glass. In recent times this church has become a popular setting for wedding ceremonies and is almost always open on Sundays for this purpose. According to James Lees-Milne, in his book of essays on Rome, *Roman Mornings*, the square campanile which is so much associated with the Romanesque style, and which we see a good example of here, is a legacy of the Lombards:

> These barbaric people were impressed by the solitary round towers which everywhere they saw punctuating the Italian landscape. A few of these towers now stand at Ravenna detached from the churches which they serve. The Lombards felt impelled by some odd instinct to emulate them. But they did not build their own towers on a round plan. They built them square. At first they made them severely plain; later they adorned them with plaster strips and engaged shafts and provided arched openings which increased in size towards the summit.

In 1347, on the architrave above the portico of S. Giorgio in Velabro and facing a busy intersection, Cola di Rienzo posted his notice: "In a short time the Romans will return to their good ancient government." Once again there was a power vacuum in Rome following the papal move to Avignon. The city was torn by violence as noble families waged war against each other. With retainers and priests joining factions, they paraded through the streets of the city fighting with daggers and swords. Cola di Rienzo tried to restore the Republic with the help of the papacy and managed a six-month hiatus until he himself fell victim to his own grandiose visions. He is referred to as the first Italian liberator.

Before leaving the Via del Velabro, note the gate with an "S.P.Q.R." sign in the corner directly across from the church and to the left of the brick apartment building. This gate closes off a lane leading to an entrance to the **Cloaca Maxima**. Until recently, one could peer into this ancient drainage system much as Henry James did in 1869. In a letter to his mother he wrote:

> A man sallied forth from the neighboring shades with an enormous key and whispered the soul-stirring name of the Cloaca Maxima. I joyfully assented and he led me apart under a series of half buried arches into a deeper hollow, where the great mouth of a tunnel seemed to brood over the scene and thence introduced me into a little covered enclosure, whence we might survey a small section of the ancient sewer. It gave me the deepest and grimmest impression of antiquity I have ever received. He lit a long torch and plunged it down into the blackness. It threw a red glare on a mass of dead black travertine and I was assured that I was gazing upon the masonry of Tarquinius Priscus. If it wasn't I'm sure it ought to have been.

Walk in the direction of the river and across the parking area toward the large Romanesque bell tower on the **Piazza Bocca della Verità**. The space we are crossing, all part of the ancient Forum Boarium, was the site, beginning in the fifteenth century, of a prison and until this century was used as a stage for public executions. The name of the piazza, which means "mouth of truth," refers to a circular stone about five feet in diameter that resembles the dramatic masks used in ancient theater. It now resides inside the portico of the Church of S. Maria in Cosmedin, the church attached to the campanile we are heading toward. This stone is probably a classical drainage cover whose open mouth allowed the water to easily flow into the Cloaca Maxima. In the Middle Ages it was believed that Virgil, a great enchanter, created the mask to single out perjurers. In a sort of trial by ordeal, suspects were required to place their hands in the open mouth and if they had lied, the lips would close, severing the fingers. Augustus Hare relates the story of an incredulous Englishman who was persuaded to put his hand in the mouth and tell a lie. He was promptly bitten by a scorpion. La Bocca della Verità is popular with Romans as well as tourists and seems to have become a real drawing card for the **Church of S. Maria in Cosmedin**, which easily stands on its own as one of the finest early Christian churches in Rome. According to James Lees-Milne it is the best example of medieval church architecture in Rome because "the story of S. Maria in Cosmedin is that of a church begun, rebegun, and continued intermittently throughout the course of the Middle Ages."

Like S. Giorgio in Velabro, S. Maria in Cosmedin began as an early *diaconia*. In fact, the church itself incorporates fragments of the *Stato Annonae*, or the fourth-century grain market attached to the Forum Boarium. It became a *diaconia* in the sixth century, and in the eighth Pope Hadrian I built the church for the ever-increasing Greek Christian population in Rome. These Greeks were fleeing the iconoclastic persecutions of the Byzantine emperors, who did not believe in the worship of images. Since the papacy had persistently condemned the iconoclasts, Rome began attracting a large number of Greeks arriving on Sicilian merchant vessels that traded between Rome and Byzantium. They came to the Forum Boarium seeking food and shelter, and by the eighth century the *diaconia* assumed the name of Santa Maria in Schola Graeca, having become not just a welfare center for the Greek community, but a place of worship and a school for their children.

Go into the church if it is open. As James Lees-Milne says:

The relief it offers after the relentless roar of motor traffic over the cobbles outside is heavenly indeed. On entry you step down quite literally into the refreshing austerity of the twelfth century. The chill air is rinsed in that charnell smell of must and damp which is inseparable from all medieval Catholic Churches on the continent, and which the initiated church-roamer learns to recognize and grows to love. It is the breath of his being, the effluvium of stale incense, bones, decaying parchment, and sacramental oil.

First, Pope Hadrian I removed the crumbling remains of the Temple of Ceres, which was threatening to fall on the *diaconia* hall. He used the existing hall as the basis for the new church, extending it east into a nave and added two aisles, a portico, and a crypt that was hewn out of the foundations of an even older temple, that of Hercules, patron of the cattle market. If you look carefully down the nave of the church you will note the irregularity of its shape.

Another reference to the church's early heritage are the two black granite objects the size and shape of a wheel of cheese on either side of the main door. They are Roman standard weights that were used in the old grain market, and according to stories of early Christianity, they were also used to kill Christians. As a concession to the Greek custom that men and women worship separately, a women's gallery was built above the aisles, though this was later taken down in the twelfth century. One thing to remember is that this church was Greek Catholic and not Greek Orthodox. The decor was carried out by Greek artists and could account for the use of the word *Cosmedin* in the church's name. It means "to adorn" in Greek. It could also be in reference to the Kosmidion in Constantinople. The beautiful cosmatesque pavement, the choir, and the paschal candlestick were commissioned in the twelfth century and are wonderful examples of the marble craftsmanship of the Cosmati

School. This art, particular to medieval Rome, reached its highest perfection between the end of the twelfth and the end of the thirteenth centuries.

These geometrical patterns of marble mosaics have their origins in Roman art and survived until the fourteenth century. It is worth observing the contrast between the pavement under the altar created in the eighth century with the more intricate design on the rest of the floor done three centuries later. Cosmati art was practiced exclusively by certain families who designed objects such as tombs and pavements using mosaics of every color. They had their workshops in the ruins of ancient Rome on the nearby Campus Martius, where they found both the inspiration for their art and their material, the marble that had decorated Augustan Rome.

The canopy is one of the very rare Gothic features to be found in Rome, and this thirteenth-century work is by Cosma Deodatus. *"Deodatus me fecit"* is inscribed on the entablature. Within the altar are the remains of the skull of St. Valentine, patron of lovers, and on February 14 it is brought out and crowned with roses. The portico and the campanile, one of Rome's best, were built in the twelfth century. In the eighteenth century the church was given a baroque façade, but this was removed in 1899, returning the entire structure to its pristine medieval state.

Leave the church and cross the busy street identified as Piazza Bocca della Verità toward the small park and the **fountain with tritons**. This area became a busy market and maintained itself as a commercial hub until this century because of the availability of water. Having the Tiber nearby certainly helped, but its water was neither dependable nor always safe to drink. It was the aqueducts bringing fresh spring water from the Alban Hills that kept this area habitable and commercially active. The first aqueduct to the Forum Boarium was the Acqua Alessandrina built by Emperor Alexander Severus in 208–35. In fact, the sculpture of the ox in the market

A view of the fountain and temple on the Piazza Bocca della Verità

was part of a fountain. In the late eighth century when Pope Hadrian I built S. Maria in Cosmedin, he also rebuilt the aqueduct, ensuring that there was plenty of water for his new church and farther north where we will be walking. In the late sixteenth century, Pope Sixtus V (1585–1590), who left his mark on Rome more indelibly than any other pope of the Counter-Reformation, restored the water supply to this area by mending the Acqua Alessandrina and renaming it Acqua Felice, after his given name, Felix. All the fountains on the Quirinal Hill and the Capitoline Hill are fed by the Acqua Felice. In 1717 Pope Clement XI (1700–1721) commissioned this fountain.

Just beyond the fountain are two lovely Republican temples, one circular and the other rectangular. They were built during the first century B.C. and are among the oldest existing buildings in Rome. The circular temple is known as the **Temple of Vesta**, but it was probably a temple built in honor of Hercules, patron of the Forum Boarium. The rectangular temple was dedicated to **Fortuna Virilis**, a goddess who among other things had the power to conceal personal imperfections from the eyes of men and was therefore very popular among the women

The Temple of Fortuna Virilis and the Casa dei Crescenzi

of ancient Rome. Both of these temples reflect the strong influence of Greek culture on Rome during the last century before Christ. By then Macedonia was a Roman province and designs were being made on the rest of Greece, which was to become the province of Actaea. Soldiers returned to Rome with enormous respect for Greek architecture, philosophy, and art. Soon Greek teachers were being imported and every aspect of Roman life was influenced by Greek models. The Temple of Fortuna Virilis is especially representative of the inception of Greco-Roman architectural traditions. Thanks to Mussolini's dictate that "the millennial monuments of our history must loom gigantic in their necessary solitude," we can enjoy these temples in a parklike setting without the urban clutter that surrounded them until the 1930s.

Cross the **Via di Ponte Rotto** directly in front of the rectangular temple. This road name refers to the one-arched bridge segment standing in the middle of the Tiber right where the Cloaca Maxima expels its water. The bridge was originally built in 179 B.C. by Aemilius Lepidus and was an important passage from the southeast into the city, leading directly across the Forum Boarium.

Across the street on the corner of **Via del Teatro di Marcello** is an interesting medieval house known as the **Casa dei Crescenzi**. Originally a tower built in the 1100s, now only the ground floor and fragments of an upper story with an arcaded loggia remain. While visually exciting, with columns and a collage of architectural fragments purloined from ancient Roman buildings, it is also representative of the important changes taking place in Rome during the early twelfth century. The inscription placed by Nicolò, son of Crescenzio and Theodora, speaks of his pride in his ancestry and his aim to renew Rome's ancient grandeur. It was a period of heightened sensitivity to Rome's glorious past, which was manifested in the culture of that time by an interest in ancient writers and poets; a revival in the appreciation of the antique remains; and politically, in a revolt that took place in 1143. The Roman people demanded the banishment of all nobles from the city, proclaiming the establishment of a republic and the restoration of the Senate. No doubt the popular belief that this is the house where Cola di Rienzo was born springs from the identification of Rienzo's fervor and aspirations with that which preceded him by two hundred years. The house has also been referred to as "Pilate's House," a name that dates back to the medieval passion plays that were enacted in this area, in which it was used as Pilate's palace.

The twelfth-century concept of Rome reborn and interpreted along the lines of contemporary political aspirations and Christian realities manifests itself clearly in one of the earliest guidebooks written between 1140 and 1143, the *Mirabilia*. This guide, in contrast to earlier pilgrim guides that led the faithful to the relics of saints and martyrs, centers attention almost exclusively on ancient Rome. Finally, pagan Rome had been fused into and had become an integral part of Christian Rome.

Continue walking down Via del Teatro di Marcello

Ancient capitals as benches

past modern municipal buildings. Since this is a rather bleak twentieth-century block full of exhaust fumes and noisy traffic, let me quote Juvenal, for whom Rome was no less congested or noisy in the first century.

> Rest is impossible. It costs money to sleep in Rome. There is the root of the sickness. The movement of heavy wagons through narrow streets, the oaths of stalled cattle drivers would break the sleep of a deaf man or a lazy walrus. On a morning call the crowd gives way before the passage of a millionaire carried above their heads in a litter, reading the while he goes, or writing, or sleeping unseen: for a man becomes sleepy with closed windows and comfort. Yet he'll arrive before us. We have to fight our way through a wave in front, and behind we are pressed by a huge mob shoving our hips, an elbow hits us here and a pole there, now we are smashed by a beam, now biffed by a barrel. Our legs are thick with mud, our feet are crushed by large ubiquitous shoes, a soldier's hobnail rests on our toe. . . .

As far as Juvenal was concerned, "most sick men die here from insomnia."

In 1932 Mussolini told the City Council, "In five years, Rome must appear wonderful to the whole world, immense, orderly, and powerful as she was in the days of the first empire of Augustus. The approaches to the Theater of Marcellus, the Campidoglio, and the Pantheon must be cleared of everything that has grown up round them during the centuries of decadence." The Via del Teatro di Marcello is the result of that edict. On the corner of the Via del Teatro di Marcello and the **Via del Foro Olitorio** the foundations of the **Church of S. Nicolà in Carcere** were exposed after all the many residential buildings surrounding it were cleared. The church incorporates part of three temples, which along with the two we just visited on the Piazza Bocca della Verità, are among the few remains of the Republican era.

These temples dedicated to Janus, Juno Sospita, and Hope were built during the third century B.C. during and after the First Punic War. They stood very near one another so that when the church was constructed in the *cella* of the middle temple its side walls enclosed columns of the other two. Along the Via del Foro Olitorio, we can see six columns of the original Doric temple. The façade of the church incorporates three much restored columns from the middle temple; and facing the Theater of Marcellus are seven columns from an Ionic temple. In the basement of the church, which can be visited Thursday mornings from 10:30 to 12 noon, are more remains of the middle temple. Another object associating this church to the earliest days of the city is an extremely rare and ancient urn of green prophyry under the main altar.

The name "St. Nicholas in Prison" gives rise to several explanations. The Greek immigrant population of this area introduced to Rome the cult of St. Nicholas, a saint who spent much of his life in prison, and the ascription could just be a natural association with his name. Another explanation has evoked much more interest over time. This one states that the church was built on the foundations of an ancient prison referred to in Pliny's history of Rome by Emperor Appius Claudius's remark that it was the *"domicilium plebis Romanae"* (home of the Roman people). It is quite possible that the temples would have been used as prisons two hundred years after they were originally dedicated. A legend associated with this prison tells the tale of a young woman's effort to keep her father alive by offering him the milk of her breast. This act of filial loyalty so impressed the Roman Senate that they spared the old man's life and erected a temple to Piety. Lord Byron's "Childe Harold's Pilgrimage" recalls this legend:

> There is a dungeon in whose drear light
> What do I gaze on?—Nothing—Look again!
> Two forms are slowly shadowed on my sight—
> Two insulated phantoms of the brain:
> It is not so/I see them full and plain,
> An old man and a female young and fair,
> Fresh as a nursing mother—but what doth she there,
> With her unmantled neck and bosom white and bare?
> But here youth offers to old age the food,
> The milk of its own gift: it is her sire
> To whom she renders back the debt of blood
> Born with her birth—No he shall not expire
> While in those warm and lovely veins the fire
> Of health and holy feeling can provide
> Great Nature's Nile, whose deep stream rises higher
> Than Egypt's river; from the gentle side
> Drink, drink, and live, old man! Heaven's realm has no such.

The façade of this church was designed in the sixteenth century by Giacomo della Porta but a plaque tells us that the church was first dedicated in 1128. Over the centuries it has gone through several renovations and it is probable that the church is even older than the plaque states. For example, there is mention of S. Nicolà in Carcere with reference to Pope Urban II who ruled from 1088–1099. Inside there is a stone bearing the date 369, but Christian churches did not start occupying the ruins of pagan Rome until after the seventh century.

In the eleventh century S. Nicolà in Carcere was known as the "Church of Petrus Leonis," referring to the converted Jewish family who built their fortress on the ruins of the Theater of Marcellus. In 1286 Pandolfo Savelli, who followed the Pierleoni as occupant of the theater, donated a bell made by Guidotto Pisano. This association to the occupants of the Theater of Marcellus continues to this day, no doubt encouraged by the fact that the palazzo, now built into the ruins of the ancient theater, is the only residential space standing in this spot once crowded with narrow streets, houses, and shops.

Before moving on to the Theater of Marcellus, note the classical ruins and medieval house across the Via del Teatro di Marcello from the church. The ruins, known as the **Portichetto de Via della Consolazione**, are fragments from the first century when the Forum Olitorium, the oil and vegetable market, was lined with a series of porticoes, among them the *porticus dei frumentari*, of the wheat merchants, and the porticus Minucia where indigent Romans received their monthly dole. Seen from this corner are two arches supported by semicolumns of the Tuscan Order; opposite that are three arches and a corniced architrave. These were once incorporated into the structure of a medieval house, and a few walls and columns still remain from that phase of their history. Porticoes became an architectual phenomenon only at the time of the Empire, when a taste for luxury and comfort superseded the previous austerity of Roman life. The columns of such porticoes were often made of the rarest kinds of marble and had gilded Corinthian capitals and floors laid with jasper and porphyry. Each portico contained a museum of sculpture, pictures, and enclosed gardens with thickets of landscaped boxwood, trees, fountains, and even waterfalls. More incredible than their decor is the fact that by the end of the fifth century these porticoes extended from the Roman Forum to the area of St. Peter's, a stretch of almost two miles.

The medieval house to the left of the *portichetto* dates from the twelfth century. It has undergone a great deal of restoration, but its tower and its arched bifurcated and trifurcated windows still convey the charms of another era. This is an especially imposing view at night, when the lights from the Campidoglio outline it against the wooded hillside.

Just ahead is the **Theater of Marcellus** looming over an enclosed and isolated landscape of fallen columns and ancient marble fragments. Our approach today is in sharp contrast to that of Charles Dickens and other visitors in the nineteenth century and before: "I soon struck upon the remains of the theater of Marcellus which are very picturesque and the more so from being closely linked in, indeed identified with the shops, habitations and swarming life of modern Rome." The Piazza Montanara, named for the mountain people who converged here to sell their goods or seek employment, stood at the edge of the theater whose arcades were used as shops by blacksmiths and scrap iron dealers. From the Middle Ages until early in this century the piazza served as a market and was a gathering place for day laborers in search of work.

Goethe was also captivated by the local color on this piazza and he wrote of it during his visit to Rome in 1786–1788. Peasants, many in costume, filled the piazza where they enjoyed a famous puppet theater and used the services of a town scribe. Here Goethe met the people of Rome, far removed from the Rome of the Catholic Church and the palaces of the gentry. Here too he met the famous Faustina of his *Roman Elegies*; she was the daughter of the owner of a local tavern.

The Teatro di Marcello may be one of the oldest inhabited buildings in the Western world. First a Roman theater it was afterward, by turns, a fortress, an elegant

Renaissance palace, and, today, a complex of apartments and offices. Built by Augustus and dedicated to his nephew and intended successor, Marcellus, son of Ottavia, it was inaugurated in A.D. 11 with great pomp, ceremony, and not without incident. During the festivities the ivory stand from which Augustus was viewing the spectacle broke and sent him tumbling into the crowd of senators and dignitaries. Accounts of this event claim Augustus rose with great dignity and commanded that the spectacle resume.

Augustus, referring to himself as "an adventurous man of the world" on the dedication plaque, offered this theater to the Roman people for assemblies and grand spectacles. Not until the reign of Domitian (181–196), however, was this function realized with the greatest flair. Then theater and poetry were introduced as part of the celebrations that were held in March in honor of Minerva, the goddess of wisdom. This feast was called the *quinquatrie* because it lasted five days; *quinquatrie* is a name still used for the carnival festivities before Lent.

This theater has always been considered an exceptional piece of architecture. Vitruvius writes of it as the finest building of its kind, providing a model for the (now much more famous) Colosseum. It was so well conceived that the senators and the people each had their own entrances, exits, and halls. Massive enough to hold ten to fourteen thousand spectators, the structure was built of travertine and had three tiers of arches—Ionic, Doric, and Corinthian—with fifty-two columns in each. Only twelve arches from the first two tiers survive; the third tier disappeared in the course of various alterations and spoilage that is so much a part of Rome's architectural history. By the end of the first century the theater must already have been in a state of ruin since it helped provide the building material for the construction of the Ponte Cestio, the bridge between the small island in the Tiber and Trastevere on the other side. The accumulated debris of centuries created the hill now called Monte Savello and

completely covered the first tier of arcades until the theater was restored in the 1930s. The shops that Dickens
and Goethe wrote about were in fact in the second tier
of arcades.

In 1086 the ruin of the theater became the fortress of
the Pierleoni, a Jewish family turned Catholic in the eleventh century who built their base of power as bankers
and businessmen in the Jewish neighborhood of Trastevere. The Pierleoni are sometimes spoken of in contemporary Italian history books as the "Rothschilds of the
Middle Ages." Their conversion brought them a strong
political alliance with the papacy and their greatest moment was the election of a member of the family as pope.
The Pierleonis' move to the Teatro di Marcello is also
significant because from here they were able to control
the island, the main bridges to the left bank of the river,
and the entire periphery of the Capitoline Hill, which at
the time was the city's commercial center and one of its
most populated areas. The fortification they built within
the theater's ruins consisted of numerous towers, one of
which can still be distinguished in a square terrace that
rises high above the building.

In the thirteenth century the Pierleonis' power was
assumed by the Savelli family, which took over the fortress and established a very active fiefdom for themselves.
It was under their patronage in the sixteenth century that
Baldassare Peruzzi built a patrician home on the remains
of this Roman theater. In doing so he enclosed what remained of the third tier of arches and constructed a huge
palazzo that covered the full semicircle of the theater and
contained several courtyards with gardens.

Evidence of the palazzo's size and the complex network of spaces created within the original Roman design
can be attested to by the story of a Jewish countess who
hid in its secret chambers throughout the Nazi occupation of Rome. In 1712 the Orsini family became lords of
the palazzo, which is known to this day as the Palazzo
Orsini. This family first appears in Roman history in the

Fragments of marble columns around the Teatro di Marcello

early half of the twelfth century and their claim to fame, besides producing forty cardinals and two popes, is as the greatest enemy of the Colonna family, considered Rome's oldest family. Their battles were such that Pope Julius II, in his effort to bring peace to Rome, was forced to give one of his nieces in marriage to Virginio Orsini and the other to Marcantonio Colonna. At the same time he made the two heads of the families barons and prince associates to the papal throne. Today the gatekeeper at the Palazzo Orsini, now one of Rome's most elegant apartment buildings, will point to the bears standing on the gatepost as the only remains of the Orsini family.

Immediately north of the ancient theater are three marble columns with a richly carved entablature. These are the remains of the southeast corner of a building dedicated in 33 B.C. as the **Temple of Apollo**. This was the first temple in Rome dedicated to the Greek god of light and the protector of arts and letters. Apollo was also thought to have possessed healing powers and the city was being devastated at the time by a plague. The strong influence Greek culture exerted on Rome during the first century before Christ included adopting Greek gods into the Roman pantheon. The Augustan temple built by C. Sosius was on the site of a much older temple said to have been dedicated in 431 B.C. What we see now was reconstructed from fragments found during the course of excavation in 1940. Today these corniced capitals and the frieze adorned with intricate patterns of leaves, oxen horns, and branched candlesticks are one of the best examples in Rome of Augustan-period architectural decoration. Pliny described this temple's lavish interior as decorated with colored marble from Africa and containing an entablature that depicted scenes of war and triumphal procession. Fragments of this entablature can also be seen at the Capitoline Museum.

To the right of the Temple of Apollo, surrounded by a fence, are the foundations of yet another temple, the **Temple of Janus**, the porter of heaven. Janus opens the year (January) and is the guardian of gates. The ancient Romans ritualized his persona by opening the gates to this temple during times of peace and closing them during times of war. It was built to celebrate the Roman victory over the Carthaginians in 260 B.C., and the gates of the Temple of Janus were rarely open for the next two hundred years.

On the hill overlooking these two temples is an interesting thirteenth-century house surrounded by oleander trees and seasonal flowers. Recently restored as office space for the city's Administrator of Fine Arts and Culture, the structure is known as the **Albergo della Catena**, "Hotel of the Chains." The name describes the medieval street that led to it, which must have been blocked by a rope of chains.

Follow the fence enclosing the archeological site of the Teatro di Marcello; the gate is open only with a special permit. As you enter the **Via Montanara**, note the bifurcated window to the right above the door marked no. 3. Here begins a more residential section of our walk.

On our left is the **Church of S. Rita da Cascia**, which has undergone transformations since it was first built by the Buccabelli family in the eleventh century. Until 1900 when St. Rita of Cascia was canonized a saint in the Catholic Church, this church was named S. Bagio in Mercatello or in Campitello. It also stood on a narrow street at the foot of the Capitoline Hill before Mussolini made his dramatic changes to the cityscape here in the heart of Rome. Demolished in 1928, it was reconstructed on this site in 1937. The façade, designed by Carlo Fontana in 1665, was part of a restoration that completely transformed its early Christian origins.

Just beyond the church at **no. 6–7** is a building known as the **Palazzo Flaminio Panzio** after Pope Paul V's architect at the turn of the seventeenth century. It is now occupied by Rome's Cultural Ministry. Inlaid into the walls of the building are pieces of marble from Flaminio Panzio's house which was demolished in 1933 to clear the area around the Roman Forum. If the gate at no. 7 is open, go through the vestibule to the back of the building where you will find a wonderful view of the Teatro di Marcello, the three columns of the Temple of Apollo, and the front of the medieval Albergo della Catena.

We now enter the **Piazza Campitelli**, an example of the Church's plan during the Counter-Reformation to make Rome the most beautiful city of the Christian world. This movement, a period of renewal brought on by the Sack of Rome in the early sixteenth century, flourished during the seventeenth and presented a newly fortified faith with the papacy firmly established in Rome and supported by the city's nobility. It was a time of great wealth and vigor with buildings being designed on the grand scale of the baroque. Here at the foot of the Campidoglio, the symbol of secular power in Rome, the spirit of that time can be clearly seen. The piazza is a statement of nobility and grandeur with the palazzi of some of the greatest patrician families of the time facing the Church of S. Maria in Campitelli. To create this harmonious space, the church was moved and rebuilt and the façade of one of the palazzi was changed to face the church. Even the fountain was not situated in the middle of the piazza, as might usually be the case, so as to keep the church the center of attention. Designed by Giacomo della Porta, the fountain is decorated with the coats of arms of all the families whose palazzi line the piazza.

The **Church of S. Maria in Campitelli** was built by Carlo Rainaldi between 1662 and 1667 and is considered by many to be his best work. Its façade is made entirely of travertine with a leitmotif of strong vertical lines effected by placing huge columns against but not attached to the façade. These columns overpower other elements of the design and seem to reach for the sky with their double pediment. The result is similar to another of Rainaldi's churches, S. Andrea della Valle, in which the first act of *Tosca* takes place. Inside the church the same kind of trick is played: the space is given a sense of amplification, depth, and size that in fact it does not have. Baroque design aspires to startle and to create an emotional response; the architect here manages to focus attention on the high altar, which appears large and overpowering. For the price of a few coins you can listen to a tape recording in English near the entrance of the church that will give you a detailed account of the church's artistic contents.

The church was built to honor an image of the Madonna, now on the high altar, which according to legend was brought to Pope John I in 523 by two angels. At the moment of this offering all the bells in Rome miraculously started ringing. The image of this virgin was carried through the city in great penitential processions during the pestilence of 590. She was placed in the oratory of S. Gala located at the time in what is now the far end of

Courtyard of a palazzo on Piazza Margana

the piazza, and she became known as S. Maria in Portico, from the neighboring Portico d'Ottavia. In 1656 the virgin was again paraded through the streets of Rome, ending a devastating epidemic, and Pope Alexander VII declared that a new church be built in her honor with an elegant public space. To this day prayers are offered to the virgin of S. Maria in Campitelli to help fight contagious diseases.

In the seventeenth century the two palazzi flanking the Church of S. Maria in Campitelli shared the same design. In the eighteenth century, no. 10 was renovated in the style of the times and an extra story added. On the corner, the Vecchia Roma enjoys not only a fine culinary reputation but an ideal setting.

At the end of the piazza, **no. 16**, the **Palazzo Lovatelli** is the first in a series of palazzi that circumscribe the Piazza Campitelli with the grand architecture of the 1600s. Tucked between two piazzas, this palazzo opens its gate to both, giving the impression, from this entrance, of a courtyard with shops or an elegant covered arcade. Designed by Giacomo della Porta, it was completed in 1620 on the site of the original Church of S. Maria in Campitelli. Here, in the late nineteenth century, Ersilia Lovatelli

135

Caetani held a salon that was famous throughout Europe. Gregorovius, Carducci, D'Annunzio, Liszt, Zola, and Anatole France were among the many whose intellectual energies enhanced this salon's reputation.

On the other side of the piazza at **no. 1** is the **Palazzo Cavalletti**, a building of the late 1500s where Rome's last senator, Francesco Cavalletti Rondinini, died in 1870. The windows on the *piano nobile*, thus called because the reception rooms are on the second floor, are adorned in a mannered style with elegant festoons. In recent times an extra floor has been added above the cornice. This sad corruption of the original design, called the attic space, has become a necessity in modern Rome, where housing is scarce. It was also popularized during the postwar period when large numbers of foreigners moved to Rome, and their desire for fresh air, sun, and greenery was not satisfied by the local custom of merely walking in the piazza.

Since the 1600s the **Palazzo Albertoni Spinola**, at **no. 2**, has been home to an illustrious Roman family that still occupies a part of it. The palazzo was designed by Giacomo della Porta and completed by Girolamo Rainaldi with a façade that connected it to the palaces on either side. Note the lions' heads from the Albertoni family crest on the cornice and moldings. Also, above the first window on the left, observe the round tabernacle to S. Maria in Porticu, which can be seen on several buildings in this district. The tabernacle is a reference to the image of the Madonna on the high altar of the church across the way.

The **Palazzo Capizucchi, no. 3**, was designed by Giacomo della Porta. Within its walls is a famous music hall, a vestige of the strong interest in music in Rome during the sixteenth and seventeenth centuries. It is this palazzo's façade that was redesigned to face the church and the piazza. Go in the gate, which, because of the remodeling, is off-center; it opens onto a lovely ivy-covered courtyard with a view from the vestibule of the stone steps leading into the living quarters. Today the building is used by the French Cultural Center, and it is purely coincidental that the fleur-de-lis decorating the portal is part of the Capizucchi family crest.

Turn onto Via Capizucchi next to the Palazzo Capizucchi. On our right is the grim wall of the **Convent of the Tor de' Specchi**, "tower of mirrors," owned by an order of Oblates that was founded by Francesca Romana in 1425 for daughters of the aristocracy. The convent is named for a tower within its complex that was an important city landmark until it was torn down in 1750. This tower was associated with medieval legends of the Capitoline Hill and its surrounding buildings. The legend that gave it its nomenclature states that it was covered with magic mirrors through which ancient Romans could see and control their entire empire as well as protect themselves from plots of the world beyond. (If you happen to be in Rome the week following March 9, make a point of visiting this convent. It is only open to the public on the occasion of the anniversary of the death of St. Francesca Romana. In the oldest section, entered at no. 40 Via del Teatro di Marcello, you will see a fifteenth-century frescoed chapel depicting this saint's life.)

In the **Piazza Capizucchi**, at the end of the short street, you can see what was originally the main entrance to the Palazzo Capizucchi and also, on the far end behind the iron gate, an arch built to connect the Palazzo Albertoni Spinola with another family house. The attraction in this piazza is the ivy-covered fifteenth-century house on the right. Though much restored, it maintains the grace of its period architecture in the low-arched doorways and the molding of the windows. Walk around the house and look at the main entrance at **Via della Tribuna di Tor de' Specchi, no. 5**. Above the door is a crest of a harpy, the symbol of the *rione* of Campitelli, and way above along the roof line is an intricately carved stone molding. Connecting the house to the nave of the church in the Convent of the Tor de' Specchi to the left is an even older section of the house, with symbols of the Guelph cross on the window representing the medieval faction that opposed the authority of the German emperors (the Ghibellines) in Italy during the thirteenth and fourteenth centuries.

Return to the street that leads out of Piazza Capizucchi, also called Via della Tribuna di Tor de' Specchi, past nos. 28–30. In a few feet it opens onto the **Piazza Margana**, named for the Margani family who from their tower controlled this area in the fourteenth century. Immediately to the right is the **Palazzo Velli**, **no. 24**, built at the end of the seventeenth century. The building has a large, arched portal of hewn stones, and over the walled-in window on the second floor is an inscription, worn with age, that reads "Andreas Villus," probably in reference to the magistrate of Rome from 1592 until 1603. If the gate is open, walk through the portal; at the end of the vestibule, in a small enclosed courtyard, is a fountain made from a lovely sarcophagus that portrays Apollo and the Muses.

The **Palazzo Maccarani**, at **no. 19**, also has a courtyard that is worth visiting. This one is decorated, in the style of the sixteenth century, with antique fragments of sculpture, inscriptions, and columns. The fountain in the corner looks as if it were made of volcanic lava but, in fact, years of accumulated calcium from the hard Roman water have created this effect. Outside on the corner you will recognize the small tabernacle to S. Maria in Porticu protecting the house and the piazza from contagious diseases.

At the end of the piazza and toward the right are the remains of the **Marganis' tower**. In 1305 Giovanni Margani bought a house with three columns, a gate, and a side courtyard surrounded by a portico of ancient columns. He then broke with the norm by building a tower with an open loggia, one of the first examples of a less defense-oriented style of tower architecture. (Some suc-

*An ancient column embedded
in a wall on Piazza Margana*

cessive owner closed in the loggia.) Embedded in the wall beneath the street sign we can see one of the three Ionic columns; above it, a carved eagle from the family crest; and to the right, a gateway to the ancient courtyard decorated with fragments of antique cornices.

The building housing the restaurant embodies the architecture of two different centuries, primarily distinguished by the doors and the angle of its façade. At **no. 34** is the seventeenth-century section and at **no. 35** is a small entrance with molding typical of the sixteenth century. Above it is the coat of arms of the Albertoni family.

We leave the piazza on the street next to the restaurant, **Via de' Delfini**. Here for the first time on this walk is a glimpse of the small shops found in any Roman neighborhood. The bar on the right, however, is unique. Filled with pictures and busts of communist heroes, it is a hangout for members of the Italian Communist Party, now known as the Democratic Party of the Left, whose headquarters is nearby on the Via delle Botteghe Oscure.

St. Ignatius lived in a small house on the site of the elegantly conceived, late-sixteenth-century **Palazzo Delfini** at the bend in the street to your right. It was here in September 1540 that he received permission to start the Society of Jesus, or the Jesuit Order. The main entrance, **no. 16**, leads into a garden that at one time was filled with one of the world's most famous collections of antique sculpture. Today the sculptures are gone and a large part of this garden has been closed by the state to make room for the excavations of the crypt of the ancient Theater of Balbus, built in 19 B.C. by Cornilius Balbus to celebrate his triumph over the Garamantes in Africa. This theater was dedicated the same year as the Theater of Marcellus and held as many as 7,700 spectators. On the day of its opening, the Tiber flooded so badly that guests arrived in boats. The statues of Castor and Pollux at the head of the Capitoline Steps were found among the ruins of this theater in the sixteenth century.

"Get out of our neighborhood Fascists and Bourgeoisie"

Continue straight onto Via Cavalletti for one block and turn right onto **Via de' Funari**. This street is named for the ropemakers who plied their trade here. A block away on the right is the **Church of S. Caterina dei Funari**. This, one of the few examples of late-Renaissance architecture in Rome and built on the site of a monastery founded in 1000, was designed by Guidetto Guidetti, an apprentice of Michelangelo's during the construction of the Piazza del Campidoglio. The church has a lovely chapel designed by Vignola. In marked contrast to the Renaissance chapel and the façade is the bell tower that houses bells brought from Germany by St. Ignatius. Step back into the Piazza Lovatelli so that you can see it. The foundation of the bell tower was one of those simple medieval towers that were such a dominant characteristic of this neighborhood in the fourteenth century.

As part of the church, St. Ignatius founded an institution for poor and homeless girls that became a sort of finishing school providing wives for the local artisans. On the day of her marriage each girl was given an attractive dowry of fifty scudi from an endowment supported by the rich courtesans of Rome. Isabella de Luna, a famous sixteenth-century courtesan whom Bandello writes of in his novels about Rome, was one of this institution's most generous patrons.

The first intersection to our right is the **Via Caetani**. To the right we can see the spot, marked by a plaque, where Aldo Moro's dead body was found in March 1978. Italy was almost immobilized when the Red Brigade kidnapped the then-favorite candidate for election as Italy's head of state. He was held for three months and then his dead body was abandoned here. The event marked a turning point in the course of modern Italian politics and was a startling finale to any remnants of the famous *dolce vita* in Rome during the 1950s and 1960s.

On the corner of Via Caetani and Via de' Funari

stands the **Palazzo Mattei Giove**, the grandest of several built by the Mattei family, whose complex of palazzi cover an entire city block from Via Caetani to Via Paganica and from Via de' Funari to Via delle Botteghe Oscure. This family was run out of Trastevere in the 1400s, their violence having become unbearable to the local population. They then settled in this part of Rome and built their stronghold on the remains of the ancient Theater of Balbus. By the 1500s the Mattei family was again firmly established, with members holding such titles as Duchi di Giove, Marchesi di Rocca Sinibalds, Duchi di Paganica, and Principi Romani. Among their sources of wealth were the tithes they collected as the custodians of the bridges over the Tiber, and later of the gates to the Ghetto.

In the 1500s they began a massive building project including five palazzi whose construction continued until the end of the 1600s. As a consequence of a decree by Pope Gregory XII in 1574—that all new construction in the city could not be free-standing and had either to be directly attached to the adjacent buildings or connected by a wall—the Mattei palaces were separated only by interior courtyards and different styles of architecture. Since the seventeenth century this block has been known as the island of the Mattei. We will look at two of the palazzi during our walk, the first and the last to be built.

The Palazzo Mattei Giove at 32 Via Caetani, designed by Carlo Maderno between 1598 and 1618, was the last. It is a severe building except for its rich, heavy cornice decorated with the emblems of the family crest. Stand up against the building for the best view, since it is one of the most impressive cornices in town. The façade is the same on both the Via dei Funari and the Via Caetani sides, with a large entrance leading from an atrium into a vestibule. The entrance off Via Caetani faces the grand staircase while the other has a view of a classical courtyard that looks like an outdoor museum, and

The Turtle Fountain

beyond that, a garden courtyard. Walk into the palazzo. The courtyard is richly decorated with stucco and ancient reliefs of marble encased in the walls. In the vestibule is a group of marble figures, "The Sacrifice of Mitra" (the Persian god in whose name fire was adored), "Apollo and the Muses," and a Bacchanalian shrine. The first courtyard is decorated with statues and more antique reliefs, including one on the left entitled "The Hunt in the Great City of Calydrone," which was sculpted by Meleagro. There is also a beautiful "Rape of Persepine." If you go up the grand staircase you will pass more sculpture, vases, and a beautifully stuccoed vault. This leads to a loggia lined with imperial busts from the sixteenth century.

A plaque from 1616 in the first courtyard states that Astrubale Mattei was a fastidious collector who documented all of his purchases, restorations, and commissions for seventeenth-century reproductions. This is probably one of the earliest examples of collector responsibility.

Leave the building through the gate facing the Via de Funari and turn right. You will come upon the most beautiful fountain in Rome; its sensual charm soothes nerves frayed by the traffic and noise of the city. Known as the **Turtle Fountain**, it was designed by Giacomo della Porta to display the Acqua Felice, and it was sculpted by the Florentine artist Taddeo Landini. Four young boys with the limber arches of dancers stand on dolphins, and each lifts a turtle into the vase of the fountain. D'Annunzio, one of Italy's greatest poets, wrote: *"La Fontana di Giacomo—a la fresca—serenità con voce roca e pianamettea parole come una fontana-magica dell'età cavalleresca."* ("The fountain of Giacomo—in the open—serenity with a voice of rock and words of quietness like a magic fountain of the days of chivalry.")

Neighborhood folklore has it that the fountain was designed by Raphael or Bernini—who but the greatest could conceive such beauty! In fact, Bernini may have added the turtles when he restored the fountain in 1658; the original design called for dolphins to match the base. Another legend has it that the fountain was built overnight. Across the piazza, at **19 Via de' Funari**, you will see a blocked-in window. According to the legend, one of the dukes of Mattei in the 1600s gambled away his entire fortune in a night. When his prospective father-in-law heard of this he told the duke to find himself another wife. The duke, enraged by this insult, decided to prove that even without money he remained a great and powerful man, so he had this fountain built overnight in front of his house. The next day he invited his future father-in-law to the house. He opened the window exclaiming, "See what I can do in such a short time, a wretch like me." While he won the hand of the girl, she blocked the window so that standing inside her home she would never see the fountain that allowed for her sad marriage.

No. 19 is the oldest Mattei palace. Built in the first half of the sixteenth century by Nanni di Baccio Bigio, it incorporated a fifteenth-century house that was on the property. Entering through the Renaissance doorway we come upon a courtyard and what is probably the oldest wing of the palazzo with an outside staircase and an open loggia with portico. This courtyard illustrates the picturesque variety a fifteenth-century Roman courtyard can have when it unifies rustic and irregular elements with the more sophisticated, elegant sixteenth-century lines, such as the capitals and the details of the arcades. Certainly movie scouts have thought so. In the 1950s this courtyard was a favorite setting for cloak-and-dagger and spaghetti-Western movies in which the hero jumped from the staircase onto his horse.

Exit the Piazza Mattei directly across from where we entered on the **Via dei Falegnami**, the street of the carpenters. This section of Rome is part of what in the sixteenth century became known as the *calcarario*, the lime pit. Here on the site of ancient buildings, marble was excavated for reuse or reduced to lime to make mortar. The carpenters congregated here as part of the general building trade. As James Lees-Milne points out:

> It is of no ultimate consequence . . . that medieval Romans from the Pope downward systematically treated ancient monuments as quarries, whence they extracted columns and entablatures because they were too disorganized and impoverished of ideas to build with new material to new designs. Roman architecture was eventually saved by this negative iconoclasm, for gradually the spirit released out of the palaces and temples of the Emperors by the assiduous marble cutters and lime burners in the fora took refuge in the minds of these men and propagated a new offspring. The Cosmatesque art arose, phoenix-like out of the midst of the quarries and furnaces.

Along the Via dei Falegnami, to the left, with its ground floor lined with shops—including one that makes wool mattresses—is the **Palazzo Costaguti** built at the end of the sixteenth century. It contains one of the few throne rooms found in a private house. Until 1870 it was customary for the pope to call at the homes of Roman princes, dukes, and four privileged *marchesi*—the Marchesi Costaguti, Patrizi, Teodoli, and Saccheti. In order to properly receive the pontiff and, no doubt, also to underscore their privileged status, these nobles always had a throne room complete with a *baldacchino*, or canopy. The four marchesi are still known as the *marchesi del baldacchino* despite the fact that this custom disappeared with the separation of church and state in 1929. This seemingly modest though large palazzo (it occupies most of the block) is also known for its extraordinary collection of baroque art: furniture, fabrics, art objects, and frescoes by Guercino Domenichino, d'Arpino, Lanfranco, Albani, and Romanelli. The palazzo is closed to the public.

Take the first left, **Via in Publicolis**, and walk to the building occupying the second block on the left. The **Palazzo Santacroce** is a building of unusual architecture for Rome, one that also illustrates another example of city planning. The family claims direct descent from Valerius Publicola, a Roman consul during the first century. But as one writer, F. S. Burnell, states: "the historical fact that it was a Cardinal Santacroce who introduced tobacco into Italy constitutes another, and perhaps a stronger, claim on their country's gratitude."

Like that of many Roman families, their history has been a stormy one. In 1480 Prospero Santacroce stabbed Pietro Margana at the entrance to his own home, the tower on Piazza Margana. This was but one of many unruly acts leading Pope Sixtus IV to raze their house. According to the epigram inscribed over the main door of this palazzo, Antonio Santacroce rebuilt the family home in 1501. In doing so he was instructed by the pope to respect the paths of the existing streets and not disrupt habitual lines of travel. He was also told that the building should have a linear façade. The palazzo, small in dimension, has a tower on the corner and facing Via S. Maria del Pianto, a series of ground floor shops. The base of the building is covered with a decorative motif of diamond-shaped hewn stone, Catalan in origin and rarely seen in Rome. The area above the diamond points was once covered with a decorative band of travertine slabs that was said to create a wonderful light-and-shadow effect. This diamond-point decoration was originally a symbol of the warrior class, but by the sixteenth century in Rome it represented luxury and wealth.

As we end our walk, Belisarius's plea to the Ostrogoth leader Totila in 540 seems appropriate even more than 1400 years later:

Beyond all cities on earth Rome is the greatest and most wonderful. For neither has she been built by the energy of a single man, nor has she attained to such greatness and beauty in a short time. On the contrary, a long succession of emperors, many associations of illustrious men, countless years and wealth . . . have been required to gather together all the treasures she contains. She remains a monument to the virtues of the world. . . .

Walk · 3

The Artisans and the Bourgeoisie

AROUND THE PIAZZA NAVONA

The entrance to the Palazzo S. Agostino

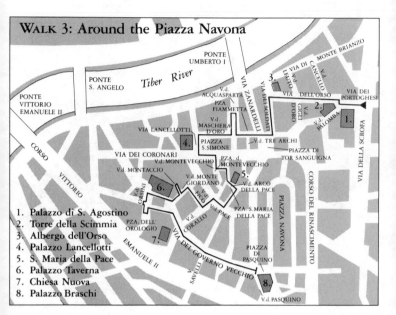

WALK 3: Around the Piazza Navona

PONTE UMBERTO I

PONTE S. ANGELO

Tiber River

PONTE VITTORIO EMANUELE II

PONTE VITTORIO EMANUELE II

V.d. ACQUASPARTA

PZA. FIAMMETTA

V.d. MASCHERA D'ORO

VIA LANCELLOTTI

VIA DEI CORONARI

V.d. MONTEVECCHIO

V.d. MONTACCIO

PIAZZA S.SIMONE

V.d. TRE ARCHI

PIAZZA DI TOR SANGUIGNA

PZA. d. MONTEVECCHIO

V.d. MONTE GIORDANO

V.d. ARCO DELLA PACE

PZA. S.MARIA DELLA PACE

VIA DEI SOLDATI

VIA ZANARDELLI

VIA DI MONTE BRIANZO

VIA DEL CANCELLO

V.d. LEUTO

VIA DELL'ORSO

V.d. GIGLI D'ORO

VIA DEI PORTOGHESI

V.d. PALOMBA

VIA DELLA SCROFA

CORSO VITTORIO

V.d. ORSINI

V.d. CORALLO

V.d. PACE

VICO

PZA. DELL' OROLOGIO

EMANUELE II

SAVELLI

VIA DEL GOVERNO VECCHIO

CORSO DEL RINASCIMENTO

PIAZZA NAVONA

PIAZZA DI PASQUINO

V.d. PASQUINO

CORSO

PONTE

1. Palazzo di S. Agostino
2. Torre della Scimmia
3. Albergo dell'Orso
4. Palazzo Lancellotti
5. S. Maria della Pace
6. Palazzo Taverna
7. Chiesa Nuova
8. Palazzo Braschi

Starting Point: Corner of Via della Scrofa and Via dei Portoghesi
Buses: 87, 94 (north on Via della Scrofa for four blocks)
Length of walk: three hours

This walk forms a wide semicircle around one of Rome's most beautiful and famous landmarks, the Piazza Navona, in a neighborhood considered the heart of the *centro storico*. Rather than visit the more celebrated Renaissance and baroque attractions, we will meander down narrow streets filled with the signposts of any city. In this case, however, modern life and business are played out within a Renaissance setting, and it is remarkable how much this prosperous bourgeois quarter still reflects its origins in the late fifteenth century, when it blossomed as a center for artisans, intellectuals, merchants, and tourists.

It is also remarkable how much life and history have been crowded into this small area, embraced by a half-loop of the Tiber River. The earliest stories document that this was the private reserve of the Tarquins, those Tuscan tyrants who were so hostile to the Roman population confined to the Palatine and Capitoline hills. When they finally drove the Tarquins out, the Romans consecrated the low-lying plain to their favorite deity, Mars, the god of war. During the Republic, the Roman legions conducted their maneuvers here, on the Campus Martius, and the population on the surrounding hills used it for sport and recreation. By the time of the Empire this expanse of open field provided the space for a new monumental quarter. The Pantheon, the Thermae of Agrippa (the first of the public baths that were to become such a rage in Rome), the Basilica of Neptune, and other structures were built in a luxurious setting of gardens and porticoes.

But fires, war, and time destroyed the grandeur of the ancient Campus Martius. After the sixth century the destruction of the aqueducts forced much of the city's population from the hills onto this plain near the river's edge, providing them with both easy access to water and predictable disaster during winter floods. Only when the Church reestablished its power and prestige after the Great Schism in the mid-1400s did the area regain some of its grandeur, reinterpreted this time in the Renaissance mode. Because of its proximity to the Vatican this became an ideal residential district for the nobility, upper-class merchants, and the clergy. It also became a tourist center with many hotels, restaurants, and shops to serve the visitors and pilgrims to the Vatican. The physical renewal initiated in the fifteenth century continued through the end of the eighteenth as blocks around the medieval street network were filled in with new residential and institutional buildings, and many remaining medieval structures were slowly replaced.

Our walk through this picturesque part of Rome begins at the corner of Via della Scrofa and Via dei Portoghesi. For a block we are in the *rione* of S. Eustachio. The rest of our walk takes place in the *rioni* of Ponte and Parione. These wards, or quarters of the city, were originally imposed by Augustus Caesar for the purpose of governing and administering and are now used only by the post office. As you walk about Rome you will see marble tablets with heraldic emblems set into the walls of houses at street-sign level identifying the *rione* you are in. These tablets were put up in the mid–eighteenth century by Pope Benedict XIV. Flags carrying the heraldic emblem were also used on public occasions from the fifteenth century on to identify people from the different *rioni*. As one might imagine, these symbols have their sources in Roman topography or history. *Ponte* means "bridge," in this case the quarter's lifeline to the Vatican. *Parione* comes from the Latin word for wall and probably refers to the barrier around the Roman port that once occupied the river's edge. S. Eustachio is a name that dates back to the early days of Christianity.

According to legend, St. Eustachius, whose name was Placidus, played an important part in the Dacian campaign as a general in the army of Trajan. One day, while hunting in the mountains between the Tiber and Praeneste, he saw a stag at bay and clearly defined between the antlers was a grave face "with eyes that penetrated his soul." (This vision of the head of the Savior between the antlers of a stag is now on the coat of arms for that *rione*.) Placidus returned to Rome and was baptized under the name of Eustachius. This act had immediate and disastrous consequences: he lost all his property and was forced to migrate to Egypt, and his wife and children disappeared during the trip. Eustachius's leadership and valor were not forgotten, however, and when Trajan faced another war, this time against the Persians, he commanded that his best general be found. Eustachius was discovered working as a hired laborer in Egypt and was brought back to Rome, where a more tolerant emperor, Hadrian, had recently taken the helm. For a short time Eustachius's life reverted to its former dignity; his campaign against the Persians was a success, his wife and children were found, and he was honored in Rome with a great triumphal procession. But when he refused to perform the traditional sacrifice of the victor to Jupiter, a ceremony held here on the Campus Martius, he was condemned to death along with all the members of his family. While this is not an unusual story of martyrdom during the early days of Christianity, it did make a very deep impression on this fledgling community: it is one of only two of the city's twenty-two *rioni* that bears the name of a Christian saint.

If you would like to fortify yourself with a quick bite before we begin our walk or just feast your eyes on sumptuous displays of food in a fancy Italian delicatessen, step into **Volpetti's**, at **32 Via della Scrofa**. It is considered one of the two or three best *rosticcerie* in town. The shelves have wine from all over Italy and the counters are piled high with gourmet delights. You don't even have to wait to sample; there is a counter where you can order a sandwich or a plate of any of the prepared items.

After enjoying these treats, return to Via dei Portoghesi. A few yards to your left at **no. 12** is the entrance to the **Palazzo di S. Agostino**, built in the sixteenth century to house the Augustine Order, whose mother church a block away is one of the earliest Renaissance churches in Rome. Incised stonework and large iron lamps provide the only decorative elements on the façade. In the portico are some reliefs and tombstones. One of the tombstones is that of Cardinal Piccolomini, nephew of Pope Pius II and a fellow humanist and patron of the arts.

This palazzo is now occupied by the Ministry of Justice and the Biblioteca Angelica, one of the best research libraries in Rome (the entrance is next to the church around the block). This library recalls that until recently, and over many centuries, this neighborhood was considered the center of Rome's intellectual life and a favorite location for printers, publishers, and booksellers. A 1526 census shows that twenty-four publishers and booksellers were located in the immediate vicinity, along with numerous writers. The publishing trade began in Rome at the end of the fifteenth century and blossomed during the seventeenth and eighteenth in conjunction with the art of engraving, which was to become one of

Rome's most flourishing trades. In this neighborhood Laf-rery printed his *Speculum Romanae Magnificentiae*, an important documentation of Roman archeological sites; de Pérac printed his famous plates; and the offices of di Rossi provided the Vatican with the basis for its collection "Calcographia Camerale" that includes, among other important engravings, the plate for the great map of Rome by Nolli published in 1748 by Giangiacomo di Rossi. Today the publishing trade is not nearly as active, but the tradition is carried on by the many antiquarian book and print shops concentrated in this section of town.

To our right, behind the iron gate and street lamps, is the national church of Portugal, **S. Antonio dei Portoghesi**. It is worth stepping back and getting a full view of the two virile figures holding up the side vaults and the heraldic angels with trumpets who seem quite capable of flying across the tile roof of the Palazzo S. Agostino. It is a façade that definitely expresses the delight and theatrical fluidity of the Italian baroque. Inside, the style continues in waves of rich autumnal marbles. Missing from the whole is a chapel in the baptistry decorated by Luigi Vanvitelli and Nicolò Salvi which was dismantled stone by stone during the eighteenth century when Rome was occupied by the French and a number of her treasures were shipped to various points in Europe. Along with the paintings and silver candelabras it now stands in the Church of S. Rocco in Lisbon.

Directly in front of us, as we exit the church, is a medieval tower from a fortress built by the Frangipane family that was later incorporated into a sixteenth-century residence. This is known to Romans as the **Torre della Scimmia**, Tower of the Monkey. Readers of Hawthorne will recognize it as Hilda's tower in *The Marble Faun*. He describes the view from where we stand:

> . . . indeed what might be called either a widening of the street, or a small piazza. The neighborhood comprises a baker's oven, emitting the usual fragrance of

sour bread; a shoeshop; a linen-draper's shop; a pipe and cigar shop; a lottery office; a station for French soldiers, with a sentinel pacing in front; and a fruit stand, at which a Roman matron was selling the dried kernels of chestnuts, wretched little figs, and some bouquets of yesterday. A church, of course, was near at hand, the façade of which ascended into lofty pinnacles, whereon were perched two or three winged figures of stone, either angelic or allegorical, blowing stone trumpets in close vicinity to the upper windows of an old shabby palace. This palace was distinguished by a feature not very common in the architecture of Roman edifices; that is to say, a medieval tower, square, massive, lofty and battlemented and machiolated at the summit.

At one of the angles of the battlements stood a shrine of the Virgin, such as we see everywhere at the street corners of Rome, but seldom or never, except in this solitary instance, at a height above the ordinary level of men's views and aspirations. Connected with this old tower and its lofty shrine there is a legend which we cannot here pause to tell; but for centuries a lamp has been burning before the Virgin's image, at noon, midnight, and at all hours of the twenty-four, and must be kept burning forever, as long as the tower shall stand; or else the tower itself, the palace, and whatever estate belongs to it, shall pass from its hereditary possessor, in accordance with an ancient vow, and become property of the Church.

I shall pause to recount the legend Hawthorne refers to because it gives the tower its Italian name. The event took place in the seventeenth century when the house was inhabited by the Scapucci family. One day the young couple's pet monkey carried their child to the top of the battlements. The infant's cries attracted attention, and the father was summoned to the scene. Standing in the center of the street he invoked the aid of the Madonna and whistled to the monkey who obediently climbed down the tower along a waterpipe, clutching the child in its arms. As an offering of thanks for this miracle the father erected the shrine to the Madonna at the summit of the tower. The lamp is still kept burning, as Hawthorne describes, and though the palace is not in the hands of the Church, it is owned by a quasireligious group.

There is also a legend dating back to the Middle Ages having to do with the origin of the name Frangipane, the family that built this tower. In 725, during an especially vicious flood of the Tiber, Flavio Anicia rowed around town in a boat dispensing bread to any stranded person. When people saw him coming, they cried out, *"Frange nobis panem,"* Latin for "break some bread with us." He and his descendants became known as Frangipane, a name they later adopted; they also added to their family crest a large loaf of bread between the feet of lions. The Frangipanes were one of Rome's most powerful families in the eleventh century.

In medieval times these towers played decisive roles in the clan fights between papal and antipapal factions. Their function is sometimes vividly described by chroniclers who make them sound like part of a Hollywood stage set with fortified walls, moats, and the strategic advantage of height. In actuality only a few of these towers were thus conceived. Many were built as status symbols; the higher the tower, the most prestige. The Torre della Scimmia was built late in the thirteenth century, and this late date, along with the remaining travertine ornamentation, indicates that it was probably constructed with status rather than warfare in mind.

From Hilda's tower we take the street to the right, **Via dell'Orso**, past the Albergo Portoghesi. Named for a famous hotel located at the far end, this street has undergone several transformations since the fifteenth century. In 1480 Pope Sixtus IV paved this road for the first time and it became known as the Via Sistina. In 1488, when another Via Sistina was built, this became the Via

Restorer's shop on Via dell'Orso

Pontificium, after the papal processions that gathered here. In 1516 it became a section of the Via Recta Papalis, again after the papal parades; and when this route was changed, it assumed the name Via dell'Orso, Street of the Bear. But it isn't just the name of the street that has changed over time. Originally known for its livery stables and hotels, in the 1800s it became a street of antique dealers. In fact, Cardinal Fesch, Napoleon I's uncle and his ambassador to the Vatican, is said to have found the first piece of Leonardo da Vinci's painting of S. Jerome in a shop on this street. Thanks to Cardinal Fesch's passion for collecting, we can now see the entire panel at the Vatican Museum. In this century the antique shops have moved to Via dei Coronari, Via Giulia, Via del Babuino, and Via di Monserrato. Today, in their place, many of the ground-floor shops belong to artisans—carpenters, jewelers, gilders, lampshade makers, furniture restorers, brass workers, and upholsterers. But this too seems to be changing. As historic Rome becomes more and more gentrified, artisans are unable to afford the rents and expensive clothing boutiques and art galleries are slowly replacing the craftsmen.

160

While it is sad to see the character of the city changing, a good deal of restoration is also taking place in the center-city, carefully supervised by the government's historic preservation commission, the Belli Arti. Two recent examples are no. 74 and no. 28. To your left, **no. 74** on the corner of Via dell'Orso and Via della Palomba, is an eighteenth-century building with a grotto and fountain in the courtyard. **No. 28** on the right is the Palazzo Antonio Massimo, which appears on Bufalini's map of sixteenth-century Rome.

A few yards to your left is the beginning of **Via dei Gigli d'Oro** (Street of the Golden Lilies). The name comes from lilies painted onto a sign that indicated a hotel or restaurant, but the street's real landmark was the women's public baths located somewhere along its short path. These baths were installed at the end of the fifteenth century to accommodate the female pilgrims and residents of the area, but they also attracted courtesans, for whom this amenity made the neighborhood an attractive place to live. Past the Vicolo del Leuto and before the door identified as **no. 87**, there is a fragment from a Roman sarcophagus with the image of a lion attacking an antelope.

To the right at the end of the street is the former hotel that gave this street its name, the **Albergo dell'Orso**. This charming structure has sheltered numerous dignitaries: Rabelais stayed here at the beginning of the sixteenth century; and when Montaigne arrived in 1581 to be made an honorary burgess of the city, this was considered the best hotel in town. (He writes of his stay at the Albergo dell'Orso in his essay on "Vanity.") Goethe is said to have found temporary lodging here when he came to Rome in 1786. Legend has it that even Dante rested here when he made his famous pilgrimage to Rome for the Holy Year of 1300, but that is unlikely because the building was not open until the Jubilee of 1475. However, numerous other foreign cardinals, nobles, ambassadors, ministers, priests, artists, scientists, and poets did pass through here and as was customary during the Renaissance, many of them commemorated their stay by having their coats of arms painted on the wall in the room they occupied.

By the end of the nineteenth century this building still functioned as a hotel, but the dignitaries had moved to more fashionable lodgings in the area around the Spanish Steps, and their cooks, maids, and coachmen found quarters here. In the 1930s the city chose to save the building from complete ruin and restored it to its sixteenth-century splendor. In 1937, on the anniversary of Rome's birthday, April 21, it was opened as an elegant restaurant/nightclub. During the restoration, the skeleton of a man was found in an enclosed medieval outhouse. Rumors spread in the neighborhood of a sinister murder and made such an impression on the immediate residents that this fact remains a much stronger source of intrigue than the many dignitaries who were once attracted to this spot in Rome.

Walk to the front of the hotel; it faces a wall and steps that lead up to the street along the river. Until the 1800s the hotel stood at the crossroads of Via dell'Orso and Via di Monte Brianzo, one of the main arteries of the medieval and Renaissance city connecting the northern section of the city to the Ponte S. Angelo and the Vatican. Some historians say that Rome's hotel industry began in this area, the Albergo dell'Orso being just one of many dating from the fifteenth century. In the sixteenth century the area around the Campo dei Fiori also picked up the lucrative business of housing and nourishing pilgrims; and by the seventeenth century, hostelries had spread to the Piazza di Spagna. Today there is hardly a section of Rome that doesn't cater to tourism, yet this neighborhood has fewer hotels than many other sections of town.

On the front of the building is an arched loggia supported by ancient marble columns and decorated with fragments of marble frescoes, traces of which are still vis-

A marble sculpture on the corner of Via dell'Orso
and Via dei Soldati

ible. A story is told that when the hotel opened, back in 1475, the owner asked a painter to decorate the façade of the building with two bears. The painter wanted six scudi to paint the bears with a chain that tied them to the portal, or four scudi to paint them without the chain. Taking the cheapest offer, the owner had a bitter surprise when after a period of rain the fresco almost disappeared. In·response to the owner's complaint the painter said, "You didn't want them chained to the wall, so they ran away."

Little is left in this part of the city to remind us of its history during the Roman Empire except for a few hints in the names of streets and some marble fragments. Here on the banks of the Tiber there was once a port used to deliver the marble so important to architectural design during and after the time of Augustus. There is no trace of the port, but embedded in the wall on the corner of Via dell'Orso and **Via dei Soldati** is a beautiful sculptured animal which some say gave the hotel and street their names. (We won't argue about whether this animal is a lion or a bear.) What we see today is unfortunately an imitation as the original, dating back to the Roman Empire, was stolen on the night of March 8–9, 1976. However, the artisans on Via dell'Orso quickly commissioned Vincenzo Piovano, a fellow shopkeeper, to carve a new one. The Via dei Soldati, which we will take, is itself a reminder of the ancient Campus Martius: it is named for the soldiers' barracks that once stood here.

During the Renaissance, Via dei Soldati was a commercial street known for its wine and woodworking shops. Today its narrow, dark length is primarily lined with the stark backs of grand baroque palazzi. An exception is the Renaissance palazzo at **no. 29** with its devilish faces decorating the windows of the *piano nobile* on the second story. To your left, beyond the Vicolo dei Soldati, is the back of the **Palazzo Altemps**, a Spanish seminary. This building is an example of the hidden treasures of Rome. It contains a collection of antique marbles, an important library, and a chapel that has the distinction of housing the only papal tomb located in a private residence, that of St. Aniceto, the eleventh pope, who reigned from 155 to 166. At one time the chapel was open to the public one day a year, on the feast day of St. Aniceto, and one could at least glimpse the impressive courtyard, the loggia with elaborate stucco work and the frescoes of Romanelli, but even that is no longer possible.

The end of the Via dei Soldati opens onto the **Piazza di Tor Sanguigna**, named after the tower on the left at the far end of the piazza, **no. 8**. This medieval tower was built by the Sanguigni family who at the time, and until the fifteenth century, controlled the immediate area. Straight ahead is a modern building that borders the northern end of the Piazza Navona. In this building, at street level, is an excavated site that allows you to see some of the stones and columns remaining from the substructure of the Stadium of Domitian (A.D. 81–96), which gave the Piazza Navona its present shape. These remains were exposed in 1938, when the avenue (Via Zanardelli) was built with the intention of opening the piazza to view from the Palace of Justice across the river. The plan so outraged most Romans' sensibilities, that the modern building was erected to replace those that had already been demolished.

Make an immediate right and cross Via Zanardelli toward the gas station and bar. Walk straight along the street, which for no obvious reason is called a piazza (Piazza Fiammetta), and make the first right onto another street, also with an inappropriate name, Via degli Acquasparta (this I would call a piazza because of the island of trees in the middle of a rectangular square). Here we see another delightful fifteenth-century house known as the **Casa di Fiammetta**. In the sixteenth century this private residence belonged to the celebrated courtesan Fiammetta Michaelis, mistress of Cesare Borgia. Fiammetta was part of a charmed circle to which Castiglione, Sadoleto, Bembo, and Raphael belonged. They entertained themselves by reading verses that were, in the spirit of the Renaissance, an extraordinary mixture of paganism and Christianity with the Virgin and the saints glorified as classical goddesses. This was a time when the classical ideal of beauty was being rediscovered, and, like the humanists, Fiammetta and her colleagues imagined that they were modeling themselves after their classical predecessors, the famous *hetaerae* of Greece and Rome. Fiammetta composed verses, studied the classical authors, cultivated the art of conversation, and surrounded herself with illustrious men. She was a very active and prominent figure in Rome, even building herself a chapel in the exclusive church of S. Agostino. This chapel, along with the tombs of other courtesans, was later removed from the church. The courtesans' contribution to the social fabric of Rome during the Renaissance cannot, however, be so quickly dismissed.

Courtesans were unusually plentiful in Rome, where a large unmarried clerical population and the guarantee of tourism ensured a clientele. Those of the highest strata were educated women, esteemed as much for their company and conversation as for their physical attributes. The greatest of them was Imperia, who lived during the reign of Pope Julius II (1503–1513). Her beauty and charm were famous throughout Europe and among her many admirers was Agostino Chigi, the most powerful Roman banker of his day. She lived in such magnificence that the Spanish ambassador, on a visit to her residence, is reported to have spat into the face of his servant because he was the only nonprecious object in the room.

Pietro Aretino, who lived in Rome during the 1520s and 1530s, delighted in depicting the low-life courtesans. In his risqué *Ragionamenti*, a wise and witty older courtesan named Nanna gives advice to a pretty young apprentice about how one rises to the top of their profession. She talks a great deal about manner, but she also tells the girl to keep some fashionable pieces of literature, such as Aristo's *Orlando Furioso* and Petrarch's poems, on her table so that her suitors will assume that she is well read. Alvigia, in Aretino's *Cortegiana*, delights in pretention and luxury. She is described as haughtily strolling down the streets in the latest of fashion accompanied by numerous servants, monkeys, and parrots.

Fiammetta shared her position in Roman society with other great courtesans who may also have lived nearby: Tulia d'Aragona, a poet prominent in the 1520s and 1530s; Camilla of Pisa, who published elegant letters to well-known literary figures; Maremma-Non-Vuole, known for her recitation of Latin and Italian poetry; and Pantha, a favorite of cardinals and one of the best-known courtesans of the time.

Back to Fiammetta's house, which couldn't be more charming despite the heavy-handed restoration. Although it has all the distinguishing features of a house built in the 1400s with arched windows and a portico, there is hardly a brick left from the original structure. Don't miss any of the details, such as the windows, gates, chimneys, and the ancient column with capital on the corner. Few such houses remain in Rome!

Retrace your steps to the Piazza Fiammetta and we will be turning right on the Via della Maschera d'Oro. But before doing that, take a quick look down the **Vicolo di S. Trifone**, which forms an angle to the left with the beginning of Via della Maschera d'Oro. After a few steps we will find ourselves on the narrowest street in the city, the **Via dei Tre Archi**, named for the three arches above. Here is another glimpse of the old medieval city.

Return to **Via della Maschera d'Oro**, street of the golden mask. This block-long street was once decorated with paintings that at one time may have seemed like golden masks on each of the otherwise austere buildings. Like all painted façades, few traces are left, although it must have been a spectacular site in the mid-1500s. To our right a miniature arch connects the Casa di Fiammetta to the huge **Palazzo Gadi**, which runs the full length of the Via della Maschera d'Oro. Now a military court, it was built as a private residence in the beginning of the sixteenth century and painted between 1524 and 1527 by the most famous duo of chiaroscuro and graffito artists, Polidoro da Caravaggio and Maturino da Firenze.

A print found at the Albertina Museum in Vienna documents what an extraordinary work of art once dressed this building. In fact, it is considered to have been the best example of Polidoro da Caravaggio's and Maturino da Firenze's work. On the ground floor, between the windows, *trompe l'oeil* niches were drawn with figures of famous men of antiquity; along the second story was a long depiction of people boarding a boat in the Orient or Egypt and landing in Lazio; next were scenes from Roman history; and, above that, allegorical figures of the gods. Unfortunately, all we see today is a rather dark and plain façade without even the architectural details of most buildings as the painting was meant to provide all the adornment.

At the far end of the Palazzo Gadi, note the large plaque which says,

> The Prince Frederigo Cesi, a Roman, who in spite of persecution and maligning statements maintained his ardor for the scientific method. A brilliant investigator of nature and the illustrious founder of the Accademia dei Lincei, gathered here in his family home the learned men of the area and his friend Galileo.

The Accademia dei Lincei (Academy of the Lynx-Eye), founded in 1603, is Italy's equivalent of France's Academie Française. We must recall that this plaque describes a courageous act, as Galileo was far from popular in Rome at the time. In fact, from 1630 to 1633 he was imprisoned in the Villa de' Medici by order of the Inquisition Tribunal.

To your left you can see faint traces of the chiaroscuro and graffito art of Polidoro da Caravaggio and Maturino da Firenze. (The most visible example of their

work today is on the Palazzo Ricci on the Via di Monserrato during Walk 1.) The first house, **no. 7**, was
painted at the request of Antonio Milesi, a literary figure
who belonged to the same group as Bembo and Castiglione and who lived in Rome just before the sack of
1527. The design on this house was so popular in late-
sixteenth-century Rome that many engravings were made
of it, and it was often used as a background in drawings.
As Vasari and other artists agree that the design on the
Palazzo Gadi across the street was by far superior, the attraction of this house may have had something to do with
the literary reputation of its owner or, more probably, its
scale, which is certainly smaller and easier to capture. Clearly
visible until the beginning of the twentieth century was the
story of Niobe, daughter of Tantalus and wife of the king of
Thebes. Niobe was punished for her motherly pride and
turned into a stone that wept continuously for her children. In 1576 a mask suspended in the hands of a cherub
and carved by Cherubino Alberti was hung in the center
of the façade. On this house even the courtyard was
painted, which, while not unusual, was rare.

The house at **no. 9** was restored in 1943 and preserves better examples of graffito than the rest. These,
however, are not by Polidoro and Maturino but by an
artist named Jacopo Ripando. We see traces of an excellent representation of the graffito style but without the
inspiration that attracted so much attention to Antonio
Milesi's house. The decoration is divided thematically by
floor: at the top are images of *putti* (cherubs) and animals;
next there are women holding vases full of fruit, cornu-
copias, and musical instruments; and on the ground floor
and the *piano nobile* were scenes from the history of
Rome. Above the series of arched windows that once
formed a loggia are images of dragons.

These monochrome paintings imparted dignity and
antiquarian flavor. They were decorative and cheaper than
travertine or colored marble and allowed the modest
builder to participate in the classical revival. This style,

which became extremely popular during the first three decades of the sixteenth century, always included scenes from mythology or Roman history.

I have often enjoyed a rest on the stone base built into the corner of Via della Maschera d'Oro and **Vicolo di S. Simone**. From here you can admire the angel "flying" off the corner of the Palazzo Lancellotti at the end of Via della Maschera d'Oro. It is also a good spot for observing Roman life as the street is not busy with traffic and there are few tourists. The sight from this corner is characteristic of the harmony and tranquility of eighteenth-century Rome. Just beyond the palace with the angel is a large area now undergoing restoration and re-habilitation. In the late 1930s those blocks were expropriated by the city government for demolition and reconstruction. The war's arrival prevented completion and the area lay abandoned until the 1970s.

Included in that area, before the construction of the river embankment, was Rome's most glamorous theater during the eighteenth and nineteenth centuries, the Teatro Apollo, more commonly known as the Teatro di Tor di Nona. Its walls were painted by Podesti, Coghetti, Capalti, and Fioroni, and it was here that Verdi's *Il Trovatore* and *Un Ballo in Maschera* had their premieres.

Walk a few more yards down Via della Maschera d'Oro and turn left onto **Via Lancellotti**, which borders the palazzo for which the street is named. Built by Cardinal Scipione Lancellotti at the end of the sixteenth century, the palazzo was constructed from a design by Francesco da Volterra and finished under the direction of Carlo Maderno. Domenichino, in the only architectural work he is known to have executed, designed the huge portal (**no. 18**) with columns supporting a balcony. This was one of the many portals that were kept closed in Rome from 1870 until the signing of the Lateran Treaty in 1929, a gesture of the "black nobility," thus called

An angel on the corner of Palazzo Lancellotti

because they were aligned with the pope against the Republic and the nobility that supported its formation. You may still see a form of protest against this antirepublican gesture on the entrance column, the letters V.V.E. for "Viva Vittorio Emanuele II."

This building, with its long line of architraved windows crowned by a beautiful cornice, is a typical example of the elegance of baroque palazzo architecture. The courtyard, though not open to the public, is one of the most interesting aspects of its design: it includes a portico, a loggia, and on one side a wall decorated with antique marble and stucco. The formal reception rooms are painted with frescoes by Agostino Tassi and del Guernico. I have been able to see small sections of this impressive work during strolls after dinner when the shutters were not closed and the lights were on. (This is something I suggest you do during your stay in Rome. Walk through any part of old Rome and keep your eyes open for the few unshuttered windows; it is the only way to see the many beautiful interiors of this city.)

Across from the entrance to the Palazzo Lancellotti is the **Piazza S. Simone**, adorned by a fountain that presents yet another example of community spirit. This piazza was created in 1939 as part of the plan I described to eliminate the shabbier buildings in the area and replace them with new ones. One of the few consolations of World War II is that it prevented Mussolini from changing the whole texture of Rome. For a long time this space lay vacant, a very noticeable discontinuity in this neighborhood of densely packed streets. When the city government decided in the 1960s to remedy the dilapidated blocks near the Lungotevere the antique dealers of Via dei Coronari organized themselves to preserve the heritage and beauty of their street. They lobbied for a fountain and got this one designed by Giacomo della Porta. Built initially for the Piazza Montanara, it stood there until that area was cleared away by Mussolini's ur-

The fountain at Piazza S. Simone

ban plans (see Walk 2). For a while it was placed in the orange garden on the Aventine Hill, but it has now found an appropriate place here, where the refreshing water of the esteemed Acqua Paola can be enjoyed by the neighborhood's residents, shopkeepers, and passersby.

The simple house now occupied by the Hosteria dell'Antiquario was probably built in the seventeenth century. While this building is of no particular interest architecturally, the restaurant distinguished itself as the inventor of *spaghetti alla checca* (spaghetti with cold, raw tomato sauce), now a standard item on most Roman summer menus. This restaurant has gone through several owners since that moment of creativity, but it remains a delightful *al fresco* dining spot.

Via dei Coronari runs along the southern side of the piazza, and while we will only cross it, its history is rather important in the development of this neighborhood. During the time of the Roman Empire, this was a section of the Via Recta, which began in the area of the Piazza Colonna and connected the Via Flaminia, leading north out of town from the Piazza del Popolo to a bridge over the Tiber River. The Via Recta traversed the entire Campo Marzio and comprised what is now Via del Collegio Capranica, Via delle Coppelle, Via S. Agostino, Via del Curato, and Via dei Coronari. The half-kilometer stretch now known as Via dei Coronari was the first straight street opened by the Renaissance papacy in its effort to impose a rational urban plan on the haphazardly developed medieval city. Under the direction of Pope Sixtus IV (1471–1484) the street was literally cut out of the medieval clutter that overran the original Roman street and paved. It became the most important access to St. Peter's Basilica and from the 1400s through the 1500s the most trafficked street in Rome.

The name of Via dei Coronari (Street of the Rosary Makers) is taken from the numerous shops that sold devotional objects and trinkets to the stream of pilgrims on their way to the Vatican. As more streets were built to connect the city to the other side of the river, commerce and traffic were dispersed and the Via dei Coronari lost its status as the most important pilgrim route. It has nevertheless remained a significant residential and commercial street since the Renaissance.

Today Via dei Coronari has a worldwide reputation as the center of Rome's antique trade, and thanks to the Antique Dealers League it continues to maintain its *cinquecento* charm. I've already commented on their successful lobbying efforts for the fountain in Piazza S. Simone. They have also made copies of the original wrought-iron lanterns which are installed and used on special occasions including the annual antique fair that is usually held in May.

Across from the fountain, at **30–32** Via dei Coronari, is a small eighteenth-century palazzo with two plaques on its façade. These tell us that on this site in 1585, Pope Sixtus V built a permanent home for the Monte di Pietà, now known as the municipal pawnshop. In 1752 the pawnshop was transferred to a new building located on the Piazza Monte di Pietà, a block away from the Piazza Trinità dei Pellegrini (Walk 1). The origins of this institution date back to 1439 when a cardinal and a Franciscan friar founded it, not for profit, but to protect the Roman population from the evils of usury. It has clearly served the city well for it is remarkable the degree to which pawning is an established means of securing cash for all Romans. In conversation, the Monte di Pietà is mostly referred to as the "Mount of Impiety" due to its high interest rates.

To the left is the **Vicolo di Montevecchio**, which leads us into an intimate residential section of this neighborhood. At the end of a short block is the Piazza di Montevecchio, a verdant oasis of slightly shabby elegance. Wind your way through this piazza toward the left as you face the restaurant. After passing several simple houses of seventeenth-century construction you will see a narrow passage at the far left-hand corner of the piazza. This leads us to **Via dell'Arco della Pace** and puts us directly in front of the entrance, at **no. 5**, to Bramante's cloister for the Church of S. Maria della Pace— a spot easier to know about than to find!

If the door is closed when you get there, you really must come back. (The hours are posted on or next to the door.) In 1855 Burckhardt called this spot "small and neglected" but added that it represented "an architectural revolution." No longer in a state of neglect, the cloister's calm and dignified atmosphere can now be appreciated without distraction. Built between 1500 and 1504 under the patronage of Cardinal Carafa, whose family emblem is above the entrance, the cloister is considered one of Bramante's masterpieces in Rome. The design illustrates a favorite theme of his early work: the simple arrangement of two spaces over one with the central pillar of the upper tier resting on the crown of the arch below. Standing in the middle of the court you can also appreciate the dome of the church to which this cloister is attached.

There is an entrance to the **Church of S. Maria della Pace** from the cloister. (Again, there will be a notice on the door to the church giving visiting hours.)

The body of the church consists of a rectangular space lined with chapels that ends in an arch leading to an octagonal, domed apse. The figures of Strength and Prudence over the arch and Peace and Justice on the entrance wall are by C. Foncelli. The Chigi chapel, the first on the right when facing the altar from the main entrance, was decorated for Agostino by Raphael with a fresco of the four Sibyls: Luma, Persia, Phrygia, and Tibur. They are depicted as each receiving a revelation from an angel. This chapel was finished after Raphael's death by Sebastiano del Piombo. Another chapel, the second on the left, the Cappella Cesi, is a superb example of high Renaissance sculptural decoration. Built by Antonio da Sangallo the Younger in 1525, the vault was later decorated with stucco and fresco designs by Sicciolante da Sermoneta. Other important works are by Peruzzi, whose paintings made Arthur Symon never tire of this church for "their strength, their gracious severity, and profound purity." There are also works by Raphael Vanni, Orazio Gentileschi, and Stefano Maderno.

When you leave, return to the cloister and back to Via Arco della Pace. To the right, as you leave the cloister gate, you will see a restored medieval house at **no. 10**. This house once had a double-arched ground-floor portico, which was probably closed in 1475 when a law was instituted that outlawed them in Rome. Today we still see the columns and the rings that were used, in conjunction with a stick of wood, to make a clothesline. In the area immediately adjacent to S. Maria della Pace are several fifteenth-century houses distinguished by their small round-topped windows. These houses are as rare today as they were abundant in Rome before 1870.

Turn left on the street and walk under the arch, the Arco della Pace. We now enter the **Piazza S. Maria della**

Pace, undoubtedly one of Rome's most picturesque. The plaque on the wall immediately to your left says: "It is forbidden for anyone to build buildings, add stories, make any changes to the exterior or any renovations in this piazza of S. Maria della Pace, or its environs, or on the adjacent streets. If anyone dares to disobey this pronouncement they will be penalized . . . June 27, 1659." This hints at the degree to which the construction of this church's façade was tied to the development of the area around it.

Walk to the middle of the piazza to a point from which you can study the entire effect of the church and the piazza. The portico accenting the front of the church is reminiscent of the antique porticoes built throughout the city by the ancient Romans. Its curved lines, both concave and convex, blend with the other façades to make this one of the most harmonious examples of baroque architecture in Rome.

Since the Middle Ages there has been a church on this site. It is said to have been the church of the *acquarellari*, "water salesmen," who delivered water from the Tiber in wooden casks to sections of town cut off from a supply of water. In this church was an image of the Virgin Mary, which, legend tells us, started to bleed after it was hit by a stone. In 1482 Pope Sixtus IV came to the church to venerate this celebrated Virgin and to give thanks for the peace he had just established on the peninsula following the assassination of Giuliano de' Medici in the Pazzi conspiracy. The pope chose to change the church's name to S. Maria della Pace and ordered a more elegant church to be built on the site. Work on it was continued by his successors. Under the reign of Julius II in the sixteenth century Agostino Chigi, the great banker, poured part of his family's wealth into the construction of a private chapel and the completion of the church. The façade was constructed by Pietro da Cortona in 1656–1661 under the reign of Pope Alexander VII.

As a result of Alexander VII's interest, the church became one of the most fashionable in town. It was also the only place where one could attend mass in the afternoon. Getting to the church, however, was not an easy task. The street leading to its main entrance was narrow, and those on either side were even worse. The passage next to the apse of the neighboring church on the right was not even wide enough for a carriage, the means of transportation that by the mid–seventeenth century was de rigueur among Roman nobility. The access on the left allowed for only one carriage, which led to many petty quarrels over procedure. This transportation problem, along with the façade, was the issue Cortona dealt with in his design for this piazza. By destroying a row of houses he created an impressive approach to the church, enough room for the carriages to turn around, and a symmetrical piazza of unusual shape. In the design for the façade he joined the church to the adjacent buildings and streets to create a single architectural unit.

"This masterly entrance," as John Gibbs called Cortona's design in the early eighteenth century, deserves a careful look. The upper part of the façade is articulated by a curved order of Corinthian columns and pilasters. Below that is the bold half-oval porch with unevenly spaced Tuscan columns. The line of the façade is extended by a wall that has outlets to the adjacent streets and two quarter-oval bays that mask the surrounding buildings.

To the right as you face S. Maria della Pace, you can see the late Gothic campanile, or bell tower, of the adjacent church, **S. Maria dell'Anima**. This is the German national church in Rome, and while its façade is on Via dell'Anima, there is an entrance on this piazza at **no. 20**. Take a quick look in the door—the high polish and cleanliness bespeak a northern temperament, quite in contrast to the atmosphere on the piazza. This church is important for its frescoes, several seventeenth-century tombs, and the tomb of Pope Hadrian VI (until the current one, the last non-Italian pope). The son of a ship's carpenter in Utrecht and the tutor of Emperor Charles V, Hadrian VI is best remembered for his efforts to reform the extravagances of the Papal Court. It is interesting to note that his reign lasted but a year, from 1522 to 1523.

Leave the piazza on the street that faces the Church of S. Maria della Pace, the **Via della Pace**, and turn right with the street, which keeps the same name. This brings us into a truly popular section of the neighborhood. On the corner is a huge building, the **Palazzo Gambirasi**, extending from Via della Pace to Vicolo degli Osti and over to Via dell'Arco della Pace. This building, designed by G. A. di Rossi, was altered by Cortona in 1656–1657 when he created the piazza of S. Maria della Pace. At the end of the seventeenth century it became the home of a priest named Donato Gambirasi who adorned the main entrance with heraldic crayfish (the Italian word for crayfish is *gambero*). Gambirasi also built a belvedere that bears his name. These seventeenth-century structures are interesting derivatives of the medieval towers in that they served the same purpose, symbolizing the family's eminence and wealth. They became popular not necessarily as a means of spying on the life of the neighborhood or for outdoor dining and sunbathing (which is the case today), but rather as perches from which a nobleman could survey his dominion.

At this point we enter a several-block section of the neighborhood that is not identified with any interesting architecture or any particularly captivating tales. During the day this section of Via della Pace is filled with fruit and vegetable stands. It is a typical small neighborhood market, unlike the large one at Campo dei Fiori, which serves all of the center-city. At the end of the street, where the wall of a house cuts the width of the passage, is an interesting *edicola* to the Virgin: it is the only one I have noticed in Rome made of wood and its charm is accented by the wall colored with graffiti and the local water tap below. This *edicola* commemorates the Church of S. Bagio

della Fossa, once the home of the confraternity of olive vendors, ringmakers, and combmakers. The church was destroyed in 1812 by the Commission of Improvements when they widened Via della Pace.

The Via della Pace ends at the **Piazza del Fico**; turn left onto the piazza. The inscription on the house to your left tells us that Marcantonio and Giambattista Fappa created this piazza at their own expense in 1634. This same Marcantonio designated a trust in his will of 1673 for the education of poor children in this neighborhood, with preference given to those who live on the piazza.

Make a right-hand turn onto **Vicolo del Fico**. It is one block long and lined with ground-floor shops specializing in making chairs. At the end of the block we make another left onto **Via di Monte Giordano**.

This area gives us an opportunity to reflect on the history of these kinds of dwellings. Early in the Renaissance the typical workman's or artisan's home was a small detached unit with two floors. The ground floor held the workshop or storeroom, and the living quarters were above. During the late Renaissance two things occurred to change this design. First, the urban scheme introduced and enforced by the papacy required orderly and aligned streets. Second, Rome's population grew so quickly that speculators were determined to get maximum use of the land, especially land near the city's business center and the Vatican. These requirements led to the standardization of building components and the appearance of a block of three-storied attached houses on a single street with a series of workshops on the ground floor. Behind the façade there was usually a small courtyard and outbuildings. On this street we see examples of small dwellings looking much as they did in the seventeenth century.

Immediately to your left, at Via di Monte Giordano, **no. 4–6**, is a typical example of a house of the 1500s. Next to it, at **no. 7–9**, is the house known as that of Teodoro

A wooden edicola *and water fountain*

Ameyden, a famous Flemish scholar who settled in Rome at the end of the sixteenth century. The house, built in the beginning of the sixteenth century, is three stories high with arched windows encased in carved travertine. Over the main door is an inscription: UNDE E OMNIA CIOE ("Where things come from they all go"). This house was recently restored and its delicate elegance is striking.

Across from this house is a dead-end street worth investigating. Called the **Vicolo del Montaccio**, this street takes its name from the steep hill you are climbing. Numerous legends explain the origin of this hill, including one that has it as the pile of earth left after digging the foundations for Hadrian's tomb across the river. A more likely explanation is that it was created by both the accumulation of silt from the ancient port at this point in the Tiber and the remains of Roman ruins. For a long time the hill was known as the *Mons Ursinorum* for the Orsini family who, beginning in 1296, controlled the area. Giordano Orsini, who gave it the name it has now (Monte Giordano), was a civic leader during the time the papacy abandoned Rome for Avignon. More specifically, he is remembered for his help in coalescing support for Cola di Rienzo's brief Republic and also as the senator who received Petrarch at the Campidoglio in 1341. If the door at **no. 9** is open you can see the apse of the ancient **Church of SS. Simone e Guida**.

Return to Via di Monte Giordano and follow its curved path. The buildings on your right, which all back onto Monte Giordano, recall a passage from Benvenuto Cellini's autobiography that, despite its bombast and narcissism, does give an interesting documentation of life in sixteenth-century Rome. Cellini tells us that he once lived in one of the houses resting on the slope of Monte Giordano. This position proved advantageous to him during the heavy floods of 1530 when he was unable to open

Sixteenth-century doorway to a house in Via di Monte Giordano

the front door; instead he climbed out a second-floor window in the back of the house with all his jewels and found safety on the top of the hill.

For centuries this hill has been an important landmark in this area, which is one of the lowest and flattest points in the city's terrain. The Orsinis seemed to have a predilection for establishing their fortresses on mounts created by the rubble of ancient Roman ruins, and this location served them as a bridgehead from which to control the only means of access to the Borgo across the river. From the top of their fortress they also had an expansive view of Monte Mario, Trastevere, and the Tiber. The fortress they built was immense, covering the entire hill and extending to the river. All around it was land controlled by them and occupied by their vassals. When Dante came to Rome in 1300 it must have made an impression on him, as it is one of the few nonreligious sites he mentions in his *Divine Comedy*:

> Just so the Romans, because of the great throng
> in the year of the Jubilee, divide the bridge
> in order that the crowds may pass along,
> so that all face the Castle as they go
> on one side towards St. Peter's, while on the other
> all move along facing towards Monte Giordano.

This site was the Orsinis' first base in Rome. From here, branches of the family moved to the Campo dei Fiori and the Teatro di Marcello, establishing themselves as one of the most powerful families in the city. Their ranks included two popes, forty cardinals, and an equal number of senators and leaders in the government of Rome and the kingdom of Naples. References to internecine warfare among nobles in Rome during the Middle Ages and later almost always mention the Orsini family and their great rivals, the Colonnas. In order to ensure the Pax Romana of 1511, the pope made a member of each family a papal prince.

For five centuries the Orsinis controlled and ruled from this hill. The huge fortress was slowly divided among different branches of the family, the dukes of Bracciano, the counts of Pitigliano, and the signori of Marino. To the right, along Via di Monte Giordano, we see the sixteenth-century façade of the building constructed by the dukes of Bracciano.

After one block, we reach the imposing entrance to the Orsini fortress, now gentrified as a palazzo, the **Palazzo Taverna**. It is hard to find a more impressive entrance. The gate, said to be created by Baldassare Peruzzi, has the family crests of both the Orsinis and the Pamphilis woven into its design. The palazzo's ponderous structure is softened both by the elegant fountain for the Acqua Paola designed in 1618 by Felice Antonio Casoni and by the monumental entrance vault built in the nineteenth century. Although this palazzo is not architecturally important, one can get an idea of its size and the various structures that create the whole by walking up the slope into the central courtyard. It is also a pleasant reprieve from the noisy streets.

There are five distinct structures inside the gate. The oldest is to the left, through an archway where we see the remains of a medieval building. There we enter a fifteenth-century courtyard with a portico, an outside staircase, and a marble portal bearing the inscription: *"Ex Olympo."* This marble may have come from an ancient tower on the site known in medieval times as the Major Tower. The building over the grand entrance facing the central court is the Palazzo dei Duchi di Bracciano. It contains a beautiful fifteenth-century portal with the Orsini emblem and shows traces of a loggia, indicated by the column embedded in the wall and dictated by the style at the time of its construction. Across from it, on the same side of the yard as the fountain, is the Palazzo of the Conti di Pitigliano with an entrance leading into its own court. Between these two buildings and opposite the oldest section of this compound is the newest wing, constructed in 1807 to connect the two palazzi. Through the arches of this new wing is the courtyard of the Palazzo degli Signori di Marino. In it is a tower, known as the tower of Augusta, built in 1880, and a third-century Roman sarcophagus now used as the bowl of a fountain. The fifth distinct structure is the ex–Church of SS. Simone e Guida, now engulfed by the various constructions and used as a residential space. Other buildings are attached to this complex, but they do not share the same main entrance and are thus not defined as part of the Palazzo Taverna.

Despite their warlike tendencies the Orsinis did make this an elegant home; in the fifteenth century it was considered one of the finest in Rome. Brutally sacked in 1527, it was well enough restored within twenty years to become the home of Cardinal Ippolito d'Este, who was known for his magnificent displays of wealth and culture and who created the Villa d'Este in Tivoli. During Cardinal d'Este's stay the poet Torquato Tasso was a frequent guest. The Orsinis stayed here until 1688, when they began to have financial problems. From 1688 to 1888 the Gabrielli family occupied the compound. They restored, modernized, and tried to unify the property, constructing the new wing with the tower of Augusta, named after Placido Gabrielli's wife. Napoleon's family was linked through marriage to Gabrielli's and Cardinal Luciano Bonaparte, Napoleon's great-nephew, lived here and entertained the Empress Eugénie during her stay in Rome. In 1888 the Gabrielli family became extinct, and the compound was purchased by a Milanese family, the Counts of Taverna. As with all huge palazzi, this one is today divided into numerous private apartments and offices.

In an article about her life in Rome for the *New York Times*, Muriel Spark had this to say about her apartment in this palazzo:

> The main room was enormous, a Renaissance Cardinal Orsini's library and the upper walls and ceilings

were painted with classical scenes and Orsini emblems. I did not try to furnish it, but made a sitting room in a remote corner while the rest of the room, with its polished Roman tiles, was for walks. (It would have made a good skating rink.) In one of the corridors a Roman pillar had been let into the wall. . . . The Palazzo Taverna, with its fountain in the great courtyard, its arches and small courtyards, was fun to live in and my echoing cardinal's room was to many of my friends one of the wonders of the world. . . . After dinner everyone in the palazzo would go down to the courtyard to take the air with the neighbors.

She goes on to comment about something that distinguishes Rome from other European cities: in its historic center there are no exclusive neighborhoods, and the rich and poor seem to live proudly next to, above, and below one another. While this is rapidly changing in Rome, this palazzo still has a medieval flavor about it, surrounded as it is by a poorer section of central Rome.

Leave the Palazzo Taverna through the main gate and walk straight onto the **Via degli Orsini**. Here to our right, at **no. 34**, is an entrance with a fountain at the end. This looks better from the street; it is meant to be seen framed by the long entry hall. On March 11, 1876, the man who was to become Pope Pius XII was born here.

To your left on the corner, with its entrance on the **Via del Governo Vecchio**, is the **Palazzo Boncompagni**. This was built in the sixteenth century by a member of an important Jewish family, Salomon Corcos, who, after converting to Catholicism, adopted the name and emblem of Pope Gregory XIII, a Boncompagni. The dragon associated with that name appears on the capitals of the columns that flank the main entrance.

Across from where Via degli Orsini intersects with Via del Governo Vecchio is the **Piazza dell'Orologio** and facing us, the **Palazzo dello S. Spirito**. This palazzo was originally begun by Borromini in 1661 at the request of Virgilio Spada but was left unfinished at the time of Borromini's death in 1663. Pope Alexander VII later ordered his nephew to buy and complete it, so now, except for an engraving by Falda, few traces remain of the great architect's design. The vestibule and courtyard probably retain more of Borromini's plan than the rest of the building, in particular the arrangement of the court with superimposed arcaded loggias, now blocked up.

The **clock tower**, to your left as you face the palazzo, gives this piazza its name. The tower was built in 1640 to embellish this intersection in a manner that befitted the papal processions that made their way up Via dei Banchi Nuovi and Via del Governo Vecchio from the Ponte S. Angelo during the high Renaissance. This was cleverly accomplished with a beveled corner and a sculptured tabernacle.

The building supporting Borromini's tower is called the **Oratorio di S. Filippo Neri**. It was built in 1572 for St. Filippo Neri by Pope Gregory XIII and Cardinal Cesi from a design of Martino Longhi the Elder. (The entrance façade is on the Corso Vittorio Emanuele II and is attached to the Chiesa Nuova.) The Oratorio institutionalized something new in the religious life of Rome; it was built as a monastery for an order of religious men, the Oratorians, who continued their careers in the secular world. The composer Pier Luigi da Palestrina was a member of this order, which attached a great deal of importance to religious music, often in semidramatic form. It is through this association that we acquired the musical term *oratorio*.

In his *Italian Notebooks*, Goethe refers to St. Filippo Neri as the "humorist saint." Neri captured the hearts of the Romans (who made him their patron saint) with his charm, kindness, and sense of humor, which was sometimes masked by eccentricity. "The church," Goethe says, "cleverly brought into its circle a man who of independent mind took his point of departure from where the holy could unite with the worldly, the virtuous with the things of everyday, and each harmonize with the other." It was this man that the Oratorians try to emulate and to his memory that this building with its elegant bell tower was erected. Today it houses the Vallicelliana Library, the first ever open to the public in Rome; the Institute of Roman Studies, which includes the Capitoline archives; and the monastery of the Oratorian Brothers.

Return to the Via del Governo Vecchio and turn right. This street was an important part of the route used to link the two major basilicas, St. John the Lateran and St. Peter's. Especially after the coronation of a new pope, a splendid procession marched along its path as the new pope went to the Lateran to take possession of his title as bishop of Rome. These parades were very elaborate and colorful; they were celebrations meant to establish the pope as the temporal ruler of Rome. Triumphal arches were constructed and decorated with hangings and figures symbolic of the cultural and political policies expected of the new pope. For Pope Leo X's procession, one of the most extravagant ever, scores of arches were erected along the Via del Governo Vecchio to symbolize Leo's role as peacemaker, as a force behind the Lateran Council, and as a patron of the arts. In the style of the time, pagan symbolism was mixed heavily with Christian. Agostino Chigi's arch included the figures of Apollo, Mercury, and Pallas to show the power, splendor, and politics Chigi expected of the new pope. Pope Paul III was depicted, during his procession, as Androcles with the lion from which he extracted the thorn of heresy representing his tasks during the Counter-Reformation. These processions included elaborate festivities such as masked dances, bullfights, showers of perfumed oranges, and floats.

In the fifteenth century this street was named Via di Parione after the *rione* it crosses. When the governor of Rome moved into a palazzo up the street in 1623, it was renamed Via del Governo. The descriptive *vecchio*, "old," came after the governor moved to the Palazzo Madama in 1741. Though it is no longer used for processions it remains a good example of a prosperous Renaissance residential quarter. Both sides of the street are lined with elegant houses whose styles, dating from the fifteenth century to the seventeenth, are vivid illustrations of the tastes of the clerical, aristocratic, and merchant circles that dominated Rome. Here merchant/artisan houses stand next to the palazzi of members of the Papal Court. While the styles may be the same, the merchant/artisan houses always had workrooms and shops on the ground floor and the nobility and clergy had elegant courtyards. These buildings, with their infinite number of architectural and decorative details, define the character of the street, which winds a curving path along what was once a medieval one. Aside from the architecture you can also enjoy some window-shopping; the street is filled with antique shops and boutiques. Along the side streets are numerous artisan shops specializing in the restoration and reproduction of antique furniture.

The house at **no. 12–13** was built in the 1400s and has the arched windows and doors typical of that period. The first and second floors are accented with travertine moldings; on the fourth floor was a loggia which is no longer open, but the iron hooks for stringing the laundry are still there. To your right continues the high spare wall of the Oratory, while at **no. 14–17**, to your left, is a house built in the sixteenth century. In contrast to the earlier house this one has a base of rusticated stone, a fashion made popular in Florence at the beginning of the fifteenth century. On the ground floor is an arched portal and three shops. The fourth level resembles a loggia with arches divided by Doric pilasters that hold an architrave of the same style, and above that is a variation on this theme that has rectangular spaces, elaborate capitals, and a much richer architrave. In the 1600s this building was attached to others along the Vicolo dell'Avila and the Via

A local knife sharpener

di Monte Giordano, forming a large unified block. At that time a belvedere was built near the corner of Via del Governo Vecchio and Via dell'Avila. Step back against the wall on the opposite side of Via del Governo Vecchio and you will see that someone still has an overview of the neighborhood. A tablet attached to this house in 1882 says that Pietro Cossa was born here on January 25, 1830. He was a playwright who used stories from Roman history in his dramas.

The section of Via del Governo Vecchio that is part of the *rione* Ponte ends at the intersection with Via del Corallo, on your left. On that corner is one of those emblematic signs put up by Pope Benedict XIV that marks the confines of this region. We now enter the *rione* of Parione. On the other side of the street by the corner of Via della Chiesa Nuova is another elaborate corner design with a painting of the Virgin, Child, and saints framed in stucco. Above that an inscription records the opening of this street in 1675. Half a block from Via del Corallo, on your left, is the governor's palace that gave this street its name, the **Palazzo Nardini, no. 39**, now in a terrible state of disrepair.

The Palazzo Nardini was constructed between 1473 and 1478 by Cardinal Stefano Nardini when Pope Paul IV called him to govern Rome. The building has the characteristics both of a fortress, with its diamond-shaped hewn-stone façade and towers from an earlier medieval construction, and of an elegant Renaissance palazzo, with its finely carved portal and large, square windows. The courtyard is probably the most interesting part of the palazzo, decorated as it is with distinctive fifteenth-century octagonal columns and graceful porticoes. This style of inner-courtyard articulation became popular in Rome, but it was still new at the time of this construction. What we see through the main entrance is only one of three courtyards encircled by this large palace, so large it covers a full block. The plaque to the left of the entrance tells us that after Cardinal Nardini's death in 1475 the building became the property of the Salvatore al Laterano hospital and the Academy of Humanistic Art. In 1624 it was deeded to Pope Urban VIII, who chose to make this palazzo again the home of the governor of Rome. After the governor moved to Palazzo Madama, Palazzo Nardini became a court of law until 1964. Since then it has mostly been abandoned.

Across from the entrance to the Palazzo Nardini is another special sight, the small sixteenth-century **Palazzo Turci, no. 123**. Its façade of Doric pilasters alternating with round-topped windows is an excellent example of the application of Bramante's architectonic principles to a small residence. In fact, such a good job was done that for a long time the design was attributed to Bramante himself. Across the façade, along the cornice at the second level, is an inscription telling us that Pietro Turci, a writer for the Papal Court, had the building constructed in 1500 for the comfort of himself and his descendants.

This palazzo, in conjunction with the next two on the same side of the street, nos. 121 and 118, gives us an easy and engaging study of the changes that took place in the design of small dwellings from the fifteenth through the seventeenth centuries. The house at **no. 118**, with its flat façade and pointed windows, was built in the 1400s; the Palazzo Turci at the turn of the century in 1500; and the house at **no. 121**, with square windows framed in travertine and topped with pediments, in the 1600s. The texture of the façades changes along with the shapes and ornamentation around the windows and doors. All these houses have ground-floor workspaces that are used as shops.

On your left at **no. 48** is the **Palazzetto Sassi**, once famous for its great collection of art and sculpture. Martin van Heemskerck (1498–1574) has left us a sketch of the courtyard when it was cluttered with important Roman and Greek marble sculpture; among them were the *Venus Genitrice, Apollo*, and *Hermes*, all of which later became apart of the Farnese family collection. An inscription on the wall of the house informs us that Fornarina, the baker's daughter who captured Raphael's heart, lived in the house. Indeed, a 1518 census tells us that a Sienese baker occupied a house belonging to the Sassi family.

Another inscription on the Palazzetto Sassi tells us that it was restored in 1867, a time when the Via del Governo Vecchio was going through a renaissance of its own. This started in 1855 when the first gaslights in Rome were hung on this street. (To commemorate this event the city government in 1966 installed copies of the original gaslights.) Later, many of the houses were restored in response to the construction of the Corso Vittorio Emanuele II, a block away, which led the residents

An ornamental drain on a cobbled street

of the Via del Governo Vecchio to believe that their property might be devalued. Both of these events helped ensure that Via del Governo Vecchio remains one of the best preserved examples of a Renaissance street in Rome.

Across the street is the Pizzeria da Baffetto, at no. 114, an eatery that I'm sure has brought more people to this street than its rich history and architecture. A favorite on the list of students coming to Rome for its cheap meals, it is also known among the residents as one of the best pizzerias. Pizza may be a national dish, but it has become even more popular these days as it combines the Romans' fancy for eating out with the possibility of a cheap meal.

A block away, **no. 95**, on the corner of Vicolo Savelli, is another 1400s house. At one time it was covered with the monochrome frescoes we saw samples of on Via della Maschera d'Oro. One of the few traces of decoration is on the corner, directly behind the traffic sign—a beveled pilaster with a carved lion's head above which is a marble bracket with carved ribbons that probably once held a sizable family emblem. The cornice is decorated with the figure of a dragon, telling us that this building once belonged to the Boncompagni family.

Next door, at **no. 104**, is a sixteenth-century house decorated with a series of medallions in stucco representing celebrated personages. On the top floor is a fading *trompe l'oeil* painted in the recess of a blocked-in window that shows the then-owner of the house dictating to his secretary. The stucco decorations around the windows and the door (including the medallions) were added in the 1700s when this house was almost completely remodeled. Don't overlook the cornice, richly decorated with rosettes, women's heads, and shells.

Across the street, at **no. 62**, is the **Palazzo Fonseca**. It is a beautifully proportioned building with an ancient well in its courtyard. Next to it, **no. 66**, is said to be the smallest house in Rome.

On the right-hand side of the street are a few more

interesting details. On the façade of **no. 96** is an *edicola* of the Virgin surrounded by stars and an oval stucco frame. A few yards farther, at **no. 91**, is a seventeenth-century house with delightful decorations: an exotic face over the door, shells on the window frames of the fourth floor, and leaves on the cornice. Walk another block and the street ends at the triangular **Piazza di Pasquino**.

Before we reach the statue for which this piazza is named, we pass a church on the left, the **Church of the Agonizzanti**. Its name hints at its mission, which from the seventeenth to the nineteenth century was to pray for the souls of those condemned to death. On their way from prison to the scaffold, prisoners were brought here for their final religious rites. A placard outside the door identified the day's victim and promised plenary indulgence to all the faithful who after confession and communion assisted at the services on behalf of the "sufferer."

Before this piazza became known as di Pasquino it belonged to the bookmakers; President de Brosses writes of the **statue of Pasquino** in the *place des librairies* in his *Lettres d'Italie*. The shops on the square were full of book-stalls, printing presses, and editors' workshops. In fact, the first guidebook to Rome in a foreign language (German) was printed here by Mauricio Bona.

We will end our walk with a story about Pasquino, a folk hero in Rome and one of that famous group of "talking statues" that have contributed so much to Rome's popular culture. I am referring to the mutilated, third-century sculpture of Menelaus supporting the body of Patroclus, to your right on the corner formed by the intersection of two streets.

This statue, which Bernini considered the finest piece of ancient sculpture in Rome, owes its fame to a reputation as critic and censor of Roman affairs. The name Pasquino comes from that of a tailor who at the turn of the fifteenth century had a shop across the way. He wove garments for the Papal Court and entertained his customers with gossip and cynical comments about the pope, cardinals, courtiers, and events of the day. After the tailor's death the statue, which had been used as a stepping-stone for crossing the nearby Via dei Leutari, was dug out and in 1501 set here by Cardinal Oliviero Carafa, just outside the shop once belonging to Pasquino. Immediately it became known as Pasquino, as if it were a reincarnation of the well-known tailor to whom all salacious criticism of the government had been attributed.

Every year on the feast of St. Mark a procession passed this way, and Cardinal Carafa had Pasquino temporarily remodeled in plaster and draped with cloth for the event. The statue assumed the character and attributions of a different deity each year: Jupiter, Mars, Apollo, Minerva, and others. A university lecturer charged with the statue's transformations also initiated among his pupils a competition of Latin epigrams for the occasion. These were posted on the pedestal of the statue. While the competition came to an end in 1517, and though these epigrams were more pedantic than witty, they set a precedent for the expression of anonymous political opposition and satire. By 1520 Pasquino had become the established mouthpiece in Rome for all popular criticism.

Once Pasquino became a popular oracle it was only natural that he should have a dialogue. It didn't take long for the people to find an appropriate partner in another statue, that of Marforio, the river god. Questions were affixed to his body to which Pasquino responded. Later, when Marforio was removed from the edge of the Forum near the Mamertine prison and locked away in the Capitoline Museum, other statues joined the ranks of "talking statues": Abate Luigi (Piazza Vidoni), Madame Lucrizia (Piazza San Marco), Babuino (Via Babuino), and Facchino (Via Lata). Pasquino is even said to have enticed the statue of Gobbo on the Rialto in Venice to participate in his discourse. These statues kept up a lively fire of wit and repartee that caused enough of a panic in the Vatican that Pope Hadrian IV proposed having the offensive statue thrown into the Tiber. He was dissuaded by Tasso who said that "like frogs, Pasquino would even croak louder in the water." Later Pope Benedict XIII imposed a "penalty of death, confiscation of property and disgrace to the family name of whomever, whatever their position, including priests, writes, prints, or disperses libels which have the character of a pasquinade." During the conclave for the election of Pope Pius VIII the environment became so tense that the statue was guarded by sentinels.

Before 1870 Pasquino acted as a substitute for a free press and scarcely an event took place in Rome about which he did not pronounce judgment. Many of these are untranslatable as they are puns on words such as the comment on Napoleon's occupation of Rome: *"I Francesi son tutti ladri"* ("the French are all thieves") to which Marforio responded, *"Non tutti—Ma Bona Parte"* ("not all, but a good many"—Bonaparte). Others have become common pasquinades (the English word comes from this statue's reputation), such as "What the barbarians didn't take the Barberini did," in reference to the stripping of bronze from the Pantheon for making the *baldacchino* at St. Peter's. Upon the death of Pope Paul III, Pasquino claimed that the pope (at the age of eighty-one) had died in childbirth having aborted two still-born cardinals. His epitaph for Queen Christina of Sweden was "Queen without a realm, Christian without faith, and a woman without shame." When Napoleon's government instituted the Legion of Honor, Pasquino had this to say:

> In fierce old times they balanced loss
> by hanging thieves upon a cross
> but our humaner age believes
> in hanging crosses on the thieves.

Many people think that Pasquino's swan song was his interpretation of S.P.Q.R. after the events of 1870: *"Sanctus Pater Quondam Rex"* ("The Holy Father Once a King").

With the establishment of the Republic and a free press, anonymity was no longer necessary and Pasquino's tongue quieted but was never silenced. You may still find a sheet of paper posted to his base. Mostly the commentary is in reference to politics, both national and local. The tradition lives on in a particularly Roman wit and cynicism that might as well be attributed to this statue's spirit.

Our walk ends here at the Piazza di Pasquino, just behind the entrance to the Museum of Rome in the Palazzo Braschi, which towers over the statue of Pasquino. If you have the stamina and time I suggest a visit. The museum contains paintings, drawings, and photographs that illustrate the life of the city from medieval times to the last century. Included in the collection are depictions of the papal processions down the Via del Governo Vecchio and the festivities held during the sixteenth and seventeenth centuries in the Piazza Navona. The entrance to the Museum of Rome is off the Via di S. Pantaleo. The Piazza Navona is just a few steps away on Via di Pasquino, where you can sit and absorb the very essence of Rome—its texture, color, and people.

Walk · 4

A Village Within the City

THE ISLAND AND SOUTHERN TRASTEVERE

The medieval Casa Mattei

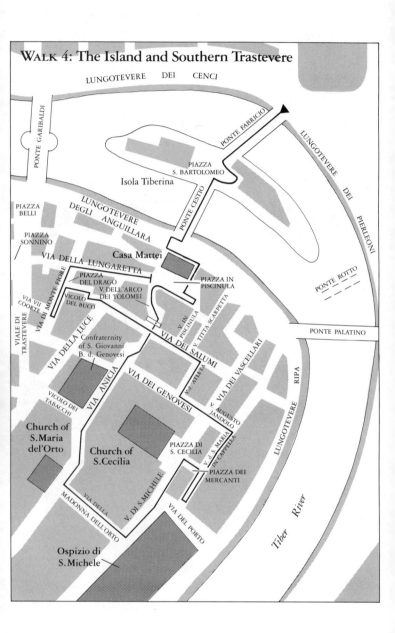

WALK 4: The Island and Southern Trastevere

LUNGOTEVERE DEI CENCI

PONTE GARIBALDI

PONTE FABRICIO

LUNGOTEVERE DEI PIERLEONI

PIAZZA S. BARTOLOMEO

Isola Tiberina

PONTE CESTIO

PIAZZA BELLI

LUNGOTEVERE DEGLI ANGUILLARA

PIAZZA SONNINO

VIA DELLA LUNGARETTA

Casa Mattei

PIAZZA IN PISCINULA

PONTE ROTTO

PIAZZA DEL DRAGO

V. DELL'ARCO DEI TOLOMEI

VICOLO DEL BUCO

VIA VII COORTE

VIA DI MONTE FIORE

VIALE DI TRASTEVERE

V. IN PISCINULA

V. TITTA SCARPETTA

PONTE PALATINO

VIA DEI SALUMI

Vlo. ATLETA

VIA DELLA LUCE

Confraternity of S. Giovanni B. d. Genovesi

VIA ANICIA

VIA DEI GENOVESI

VIA DEI VASCELLARI

V. AUGUSTO JANDOLO

LUNGOTEVERE RIPA

VICOLO DEI TABACCHI

Church of S. Maria del'Orto

Church of S. Cecilia

PIAZZA DI S. CECILIA

V. d. S. MARIA IN CAPPELLA

PIAZZA DEI MERCANTI

Tiber River

VIA DELLA MADONNA DELL'ORTO

V. DI S. MICHELE

VIA DEL PORTO

Ospizio di S. Michele

Starting Point: Corner of Ponte Fabricio and the Lungotevere dei Pierleoni

Buses: 15, 23, 96c; or four blocks down the Lungotevere dei Cenci from buses nos. 26, 44, 56, 60, 65, 75, 96, 170, 710.

Length of walk: two hours. If possible plan this walk for Tuesday, Thursday, or Sunday morning so that you can see the Cavallini fresco in the Church of S. Cecilia.

Away from the heart of imperial Rome and never a part of any of the grand Renaissance, baroque, or twentieth-century city plans, the island on the Tiber and the southern end of Trastevere retain a character all their own. Here we will find none of the more important ruins, palazzi, or piazzas. Instead of the monumental, there is an unassuming neighborhood more reminiscent of a village than any other part of Rome. It is a quarter of small houses, family businesses, and community institutions, whose façades often belie their rich heritage. Learning about it has the added pleasure of a real adventure because so many of its treasures are not readily visible. Even if you are not "treasure" hunting, there are few pastimes in Rome more enjoyable than walking down the back streets of Trastevere, absorbing the unique charm of its medieval and Renaissance architecture.

Our walk begins on the **Ponte Fabricio**, which joins the left bank of the Tiber along the Lungotevere dei Pierleoni to the small but prominent island in the middle of the Tiber River. This graceful, double-arched bridge with its narrow cobbled passage was built in 62 B.C. by Consul L. Fabricius. It is the oldest bridge in Rome. To most Romans it is known as the Ponte dei Quatro Capi, "bridge of the four heads," alluding to the two herms of the four-headed Janus on the parapet. This is the Roman deity who guards over gates, doors, and all beginnings— in this case, what was once a primary entrance to the center of the city.

Standing on this bridge in the early autumn of 1854, Gregorovius was inspired to write his *History of the City of Rome in the Middle Ages*. He suddenly realized that Rome was the crossroads where most of the major ideas that created European culture met. The buildings were relics not just of men but of the very spirit that moved them and created history. Here the Ponte Fabricio and the Ponte Rotto, the broken bridge to the left as you face the island, stand witness to the heritage of classical Rome; the Capitoline Hill rises as a hallmark to Roman Republicanism; the Catholic Church signals its dominant presence in the campaniles (bell towers) on the Aventine Hill and downriver with the dome of St. Peter's; and on the island is a church built by Emperor Otto III representing the German Empire. Looking at this, Gregorovius decided to write "something great, something that will lend a purpose to my life."

Even the muddy waters of the Tiber can elicit some historical musing. In these waters Tiberinus, king of the Etruscans, drowned, giving the ancient Romans an unexpectedly easy victory and a name for their river, which makes three dramatic curves as it winds its way around and through the city. The river springs from the same mountain ridge that feeds the Arno—Monte Coronaro, northeast of Florence—and then flows for 210 miles

The Ponte Fabricio and the island in the Tiber

through the Tuscan, Umbrian, and Lazio countryside. Twenty-two miles from this point it empties into the sea at the port town of Ostia.

Personified by the ancient Romans as a majestic old man crowned with laurel, holding a cornucopia, and supported by the she-wolf with Romulus and Remus, the Tiber nourished the fledgling city for centuries. Before the aqueducts were built this was Rome's only source of water. Again, after the sixth century, when the aqueducts were destroyed by the Goths, and until they were finally repaired in the late fifteenth century, the whole topography of the city changed as the population moved to be near the river. During this period a fascination, not unlike the contemporary Roman craze for mineral water, arose for the taste and healing power of the Tiber's water. When Pope Clement VII went to Marseilles in 1533 to marry his niece, Catherine de' Medici, to the Duke of Orleans (later Henry II), he took with him, on the advice of his physician, enough water from the Tiber to last until his return. Today it is so polluted no physician would advise you even to wash your hands in it.

The same murky yellow waters are described by Virgil: ". . . through which the Tiber flowed pleasantly, with rapid eddies and yellow from the quantities of sand, to burst forth into the sea." His allusion to the rapid stream is a reminder of yet another important trait of this river. Before the river was harnessed in 1900, Rome was devastated by major floods three or four times a century—the Corso under more than two meters of water; churches and houses on the ancient Campus Martius flooded; the Trastevere fields inundated; and the crops destroyed.

The Tiber's reputation as a great river is questionable when we see it hidden by the massive travertine embankment that was built to curb the flooding. In days past it was trafficked by international vessels. Navigable for seagoing vessels as far as Rome, it also supported a busy river business into Italy's interior; for example, most of the materials used in the construction of the Cathedral in Orvieto were carried upstream on barges. Pope Gregory XI made his triumphal return to Rome from Avignon in 1377 by way of the Tiber, as did Emperor Frederick III in 1452, Pope Sixtus IV in 1483, and Pope Alexander VI, coming from Spain in 1492 to assume the papacy. In 1464 Pope Pius II traveled the upper reaches of the river on his way to Ancona to command his fleet against the Turks. As late as 1848 the port of Ripetta was the embarkation point for the Papal Grenadiers in the campaign against the Austrians. At one time the pontiffs visited the Basilica of S. Paolo in splendid galleys, and it was the custom of many nobles to hold lavish boat parties along the river within the city walls. And, before all the bridges were built, *traghettos*, ferries, carried passengers back and forth across the river.

These days the river shows a touch of life courtesy of the rowing clubs that hold occasional regattas and the few social clubs and restaurants on boathouses anchored upriver. Recently there has been an effort by a group called the Friends of the Tiber to resurrect the river's reputation. During the summer months they encourage festivals along the quay below the embankment and there are occasional boat rides.

The island is perhaps one of the most traditional sites in Rome. According to legend it came into being when the Tarquins were expelled in 509 B.C. The Roman senate confiscated their land, which later became the Campus Martius, and, to ensure their victory, cut down the crops and threw them into the Tiber. As the river was low, the stalks of grain landed on the sandbank and soil gathered around them. In time there formed a solid piece of land that become a lasting symbol of the Roman victory over the Tarquins.

In the third century B.C., when Rome suffered a devastating plague, the senate, in response to an oracle of the Sibylline books, sent ambassadors to Epidauros in Greece to bring back a statue of Aesculapius, the god of healing. They returned with the statue, and as the ship berthed on the Tiber River a serpent slithered overboard and took refuge on the island. This was immediately interpreted by the Romans as a sign that the god himself had come to them. To commemorate this blessing they built a temple on the island to Aesculapius, and in remembrance of the ship that carried the snake (or, perhaps, because the island is shaped like the hull of a boat) the island itself was encased in marble and travertine to look like a ship with an obelisk as the mainmast.

Three temples were eventually built by the ancient Romans. The Temple of Aesculapius was the first, erected on the tip to your left as you face the island. It was adorned with paintings brought from Greece, and on the threshold of the *cella* was inscribed Antiochus the Great's recipe for curing snakebites. It was a large temple with porticoes where the sick could sleep in hopes that the god would visit them in their dreams and prescribe a cure. According to Ovid the Temple of Faunus (god of fields and shepherds) was to the right, at the other end of the island. The Temple of Jupiter, the father of gods and men, adjoined that of Aesculapius and was erected by Lucius Furius Purpureo, a Roman consul, in fulfillment of a vow made during the Gallic wars. In that temple stood a statue of Caesar, and it is said that his head turned from west to east during the reign of Vespasian. As Georgina Masson observes, "Sacred statues that move are no new thing in Italy." The obelisk was erected at the height of the Empire, after the reign of Augustus, who introduced obelisks to Rome. These Egyptian symbols of the sun's rays are but another example of the Romans' engineering prowess. Pliny tells us that huge vessels had to be constructed specifically for their transport, and then they were installed with the aid of massive wooden scaffolding, special pulleys, and the labor of thousands of men.

Straight ahead is the square medieval tower with a small marble head embedded in the brick (look straight up from the edge of the bridge). This head may be in memory of Matilda Canossa, who gave the tower its name, **Torre della Contessa**. In 1087 she drove the antipope factions off the island and later gave protection to both Pope Victor III and Pope Urban II.

Walk to the end of the bridge. To your right is the **Church of S. Giovanni Calibata**, built in 1640 on the site of an earlier church to St. John the Baptist. The baroque façade was designed in 1711 by the architect Romano Carapecchia. The church is named after a recluse of the fifth century, a member of a rich noble family in Constantinople who secretly left his home to become a monk. He earned his place on the Catholic Church's Mount Olympus when, after six years, he returned disguised as a beggar and lived in a hut near his family's mansion. Only upon his deathbed did he disclose his real identity to his mother.

A marble head embedded in Torre della Contessa

Since 1584 the church has been a part of the hospital that belongs to the Order of the Fatebenefrattelli, which covers the entire right side of the island. The hospital, along with the pharmacy on the corner, derives its eccentric name from a sign on an almsbox in the Church of S. Giovanni Calibata with the exhortation *"Fate Bene, Frattelli,"* "Do good, brothers." Established by a brother of the Order of St. John of God, who arrived in Rome with Don John of Austria after the victory of Lepanto in 1571, the hospital has carried on the tradition started with the Temple of Aesculapius. Today it is one of the most popular obstetrics hospitals in Rome and certainly a distinctive location to have as one's birthplace.

A few steps ahead, on your left, is the picturesque **Piazza S. Bartolomeo**. In the center rises a pillar surrounded with the statues of St. Bartholomew, St. Paulinus of Nola, St. Francis, and St. John of God. This pillar was commissioned by Pope Pius IX to commemorate the opening of the Vatican Council in 1869. It was here that the obelisk once stood, the only one in Rome of unknown origin. The remaining fragments are now in the ducal palace of Urbino.

The **church** with a medieval porch at the end of the piazza is now dedicated to **St. Bartholomew** in another example of the medieval passion for the saints' relics. Originally founded at the end of the tenth century by Emperor Otto III, it was consecrated to his friend St. Adalbert, who had been killed by the Prussians in 998. When the church received the body of St. Bartholomew, poor St. Adalbert was upstaged by this apostle's dedicated following. Despite later claims that the body was actually that of St. Paulinus of Nola, the church retains its association with St. Bartholomew.

Walk through the piazza to the church, which has gone through numerous restorations and remodeling because of damage from the flooding river. The bell tower dates back to 1118, as do many of the marble fragments embedded in the walls of the portico. This medieval portico has also survived a seventeenth-century restoration during which a new façade was added. The modern sculpture, in rather sharp contrast to its surroundings, is the work of one of the brothers now residing in the attached monastery. Inside is a typical basilica with the nave and aisles divided by red granite columns, which are said to be relics from the Temple of Aesculapius. On the whole, however, the impression is that of a much later church including frescoes by Carracci in three of the side chapels (the second to the right and the third and second to the left). An especially fine piece is the small carved marble well-head of the twelfth century set in the chancel steps. An inscription in Latin states that "One here sees the saints arranged in a circle around the mouth of the well," and another, now illegible, concluded, "Let him who is thirsty come to the fountain to draw from the spring of health-giving draught." In the past people came from all over to drink the miraculous water. The dream cure of the ancient Romans, akin to the Greek practice of drugging or hypnotizing, was thus replaced in time by the Christians' faith in the healing power of the water from this well. This island's healing tradition was reinforced further by a legend that said that Henry II's court jester, Rahere, had a vision here that led to the founding of the Hospital of St. Bartholomew in London.

Return to the piazza with its busy traffic of pregnant women and young parents with infants piling in and out of cars. In the evenings, as the sun sets behind the Gianicolo and suffuses its rich light against the ocher tones of these buildings, this becomes one of the most unforgettable spots in Rome. To the left, as you face the church, is the **Oratory of the Sacconi Rossi**. This was a confraternity whose mission was to provide a Christian burial for all bodies drowned in the Tiber. A subterranean cemetery, not easily accessible to the public, contains a curious design made of human bones—these designs are similar to those in the Church of S. Maria dell'Orazione e

The serpent of Aesculapius

Morte on Via Giulia and the Capuchin church on the Via Veneto. (Go to the Capuchin church if you want to see an example of this macabre baroque decor.)

Near the beginning of the bridge that connects the island to the Trastevere mainland, on the right toward the hospital, is a staircase that leads to the river's edge.

Go down these stairs and when you reach the bottom, turn left and walk under the bridge toward the Ponte Rotto and the office of the river police, who, along with the monks and patients of the hospital, comprise all of the island's residents. From here there is a fine view of the **Ponte Rotto**, which was built in 179 B.C. by M. Aemilius Lepidus. Because of its slanting position across the river and the pressure of the flooding waters against its side piers this bridge was carried away four times—in 180, in 1230, in 1557, and in 1598. After the last disaster it was never repaired, and only one arch now stands in the middle of the running current. At the end of the island, against the base of the buildings on the Ponte Fabricio side, you can still see a fragment of the old Roman travertine wall that represents the prow of a ship; carved on it is the familiar symbol of the Aesculapius serpent. From here you also have a good view of the structure of the Ponte Fabricio.

In days past the barges of millers and fishermen surrounded the banks of the island. For whatever reason, this was considered the best place along the Tiber to fish—a fact attested to by the ancient fish markets nearby at the Portico d'Ottavia and the Piazza in Piscinula. It is an opinion that must still hold true because a few fishermen are always on the Ponte Palatino. The floating river mills are said to be the clever invention of Belisarius following the destruction of the aqueducts; before that they were located on the Gianicolo Hill. They remained here on the river until the last century and were a colorful addition to the scenery around the island, as well as being the city's source of flour.

Retrace your path back up the stairs to the **Ponte Cestio**. This bridge was originally built in the first century A.D. but has been restored many times. It takes us to Trastevere, that part of town "across the river," a boundary that is more than merely physical. The native residents of Trastevere consider themselves descendants of the purest Roman stock: Horatius, Scaevola, and other early patriots who defended the Republic against the assaults of Lars Porsena and the exiled Tarquins. Through the centuries the Trasteverini have maintained a self-sustaining community isolated from the rest of Rome. That isolation has given the people a character all their own as well as their own dialect, immortalized in the nineteenth century by the poet Giuseppe Gioacchino Belli and in this century by Carlo Alberto Salustri, known as Trilussa. (Both have been honored with commemorative fountains in piazzas named for them: Trilussa's opposite the Ponte Sisto and Belli's opposite Ponte Garibaldi.) The Trasteverini's sense of independence was only encouraged by the Romans on the left bank, who looked upon them as uncivilized neighbors. Augustus Hare's description of the Trasteverini—"more hasty, passionate, and revengeful as they are a stronger and more vigorous race"—would probably have satisfied the citizens on both sides of the Tiber. Since World War II the differences have become less apparent, especially as Trastevere has become a chic place to live and a favorite night spot. No longer will you meet a Trasteverino who has never gone to Rome or vice versa. Still, no other quarter in the city preserves its identity so strongly.

The first bridge connecting Trastevere to Rome was probably built by King Ancus Martius, who was motivated by reasons of both commerce and defense. Ancus was the legendary founder of Ostia, at the Tiber's mouth, and there lay the salt beds that formed the basis of a prosperous trade with all of central Italy. To protect this trade Rome needed to control both sides of the Tiber. In addition, the hill beyond Trastevere became an important military outpost against the frequent attacks of the Etruscans. The land near the river was farmed, and it was nearby that the legendary farmer Cincinnatus had his fields.

During the Empire the sailors for the imperial fleet, largely drawn from the Adriatic, were settled in Trastevere in what became known as the city of the Ravennatti. When Hadrian's harbor of Portus eclipsed the older port

A view of the Tiber Island

of Ostia, commercial agents from many lands filtered into this community of "pure Roman stock," including the first Jewish immigrants to settle in Rome. A maritime trade mingled with such small industries as leather workers and tanners, potters, carpenters, fishermen, and the millers from the barges on the river. For centuries the high seas molded the character of this neighborhood, and while the port is gone, its memory continues in the street names and the institutions.

Cross the busy Lungotevere degli Anguillara at the traffic light and take note of the picturesque medieval house in front of you with its small, walled garden, cross-mullioned windows, and tower. Walk a few yards to your left till you see a staircase that leads to the sunken **Piazza in Piscinula**. Here we plunge right into the quiet atmosphere of the southern end of Trastevere, which contrasts sharply with the busier and better known section across Viale di Trastevere. This is a neighborhood of old-world charm, narrow streets, and institutions. While a bit dated, Roderick Hudson's experience of Trastevere as described by Henry James still resonates:

He was particularly fond of this part of Rome, though he could hardly have expressed the sinister charm of it. As you pass from the dusty swarming purlieus of the ghetto you emerge into a region of empty, soundless, grass-grown lanes and alleys, where the shabby houses seem mouldering away in disuse and yet your footsteps bring figures of startling Roman type to the doorways. There are few monuments here, but not a part of Rome seemed more oppressively historic, more weighted with ponderous past, more blighted with the melancholy of things that had their day.

The name "in Piscinula" along with the topography of this piazza indicates that it may have been the site of one of ancient Rome's famous baths. This area, however, has never been excavated and the two important buildings are from the Middle Ages. The first of these is a house, part of which we saw crossing the Lungotevere, the **Casa Mattei**. This block of handsome masonry still shows some traces of its twelfth-century origins, but there are many details from later centuries, including some of the fancies of its owner/restorer in the 1930s. At that time it was rescued from years of abuse as a cheap inn, called the "Spendthrift." Even if far from authentic, many details—the windows, fragments of Roman marble, iron bars and rings to harness horses, the *edicola* to the Virgin Mary, and the egg and billet moldings—create a captivating and suggestive building. Certainly it is a wonderful introduction to this neighborhood, where the medieval is most insistent.

For several centuries and until the fifteenth century, the Matteis were one of the most powerful families in Trastevere. As was the case with most of this quarter's baronial families, their history was one of arrogance, murder, and intrigue. The Matteis, however, went too far, and in a rare example of democratic power were forced by the community to flee across the river after an appalling series of murders that culminated in a homicidal brawl during a family wedding. Settling on the edge of the Jewish Ghetto, they saw their fortunes turn around. Within a century they joined the ranks of the Roman nobility, becoming masters of three grand palazzi near the Turtle Fountain. A member of the family even became one of the greatest collectors of Roman antiquities, which led to quips by some of the nobility that the Matteis' move to Rome obviously saved them from the bad influences of Trastevere's environment.

Across the piazza, next to the snack bar, is the other medieval building, the **Church of S. Benedetto in Piscinula**. Its claim to fame is as the smallest Romanesque church in Rome with an equally minute campanile housing the oldest bell in the city. This church, built in the eleventh century, rests on the site of the house where St. Benedict lived as a boy. Here he pursued his studies before leaving for Subiaco where, at the age of thirteen, he founded a monastic order that within a hundred years spread over Europe from Italy to Britain. The façade of the church was renovated during the seventeenth century. The older interior, as is so often the case in Rome, is not open to the public without special permission—but check the door for a sign in case that policy has suddenly changed. There one would see an atrium with ancient Roman columns, a vaulted ceiling, and interesting *cosmatesque*, or inlaid tile, pavement of unusual arabesque patterns in dark green serpentine marble. This is said to be the cell where St. Benedict lived. The main part of the church also has ancient columns dividing its small nave and aisles. On the altar is an early fifteenth-century Venetian Madonna and Child and, on the walls, fragments of ancient frescoes.

Try to get a good view of the tiny campanile, or bell tower, by going around the corner and making a left onto Via Titta Scarpetta. There you can easily see the brick structure intersected with terra cotta moldings. Returning to the piazza there is a small marble plaque with a fish, to the left above the garage doors. This is in reference to the fish market that existed for many centuries in the

Piazza in Piscinula. Next to the church is the local snack bar with a sign showing that it also serves as a *tabacchi*, or "cigarette shop." This means more than is immediately apparent; aside from the sandwiches, light snacks, coffee, and liquors, they sell all state-controlled items—cigarettes, matches, legal sheets with government stamps printed on them, postage stamps, and salt. Many of these products are clearly legacies of the rationing that took place during and after World War II. Fresh milk is also bought at this bar. Even ten years ago it was not always easy to find fresh milk in Rome. The substitute was not dry milk but a reconstituted milk that sits out of the refrigerator for months and resembles milk as much as it does chalk. Next door is a restaurant. At one time *ristorante* meant that it was more elegant and expensive than a *trattoria* or an *osteria*, but in Italy's big cities these distinctions no longer mean anything. As with many of the restaurants in Trastevere this one specializes in fish.

The changes that have taken place in Rome during the 1980s are nowhere quite as disturbing as they are here in the Piazza in Piscinula. Gentrification has replaced the intimacy of neighborhood stores such as the bakery and the *alimentari* (dry-goods shop), with restaurants, one more expensive than the next. As you turn left onto **Via dell Arco dei Tolomei**, you will notice an outside staircase leading to the door at **no. 9**. The wall of this house used to be covered with fragments of ancient marble all of which have recently been removed and an iron gate placed at the bottom of the stairs.

Walk up the steep incline that is another of Rome's *montes* created by the accumulation of dirt and rubble over an unexcavated archeological ruin. Ahead at **no. 1** is a building whose structure spans centuries and reflects architectural styles from the medieval to the baroque. In ancient times this was the home of the Anici family, a

The Arco dei Tolomei

wealthy clan who in the sixth century produced Pope Gregory the Great, the first pope of the Middle Ages in Rome. The original medieval structure with its tower and arch was built by the Tolomei family of Siena, who claimed to be descendants of the Ptolemies of Egypt and came to Italy with Charlemagne. Today it is a Jewish orphanage, one of the few reminders of the community that originally established itself in southern Trastevere during the time of Augustus.

The street curves and is soon engulfed by a dark stone arch, the **Arco dei Tolomei**. In the far left corner is a rare example of a more practical relic of the city's past, an open urinal. These public conveniences are known as *Vespasiani* after the Roman emperor Vespasian (from whom the statue of Caesar on the island turned in disgust). According to Suetonius's account as related by Georgina Masson:

> The emperor would have been the first to regret the disappearance of the Vespasiani, as the reason why they are called after him is that he derived a consid- erable income from this unexpected source. Again, according to Suetonius, this first of the Flavians was very attached to money. Suetonius's story casts an amusing light on the characters of both the emperor and his son, Titus. Apparently Titus complained to his father about the tax which he had placed on the sale of the contents of the city's urinals (this was used for fulling woollen cloth), Vespasian handed his son a coin, which had been part of the first day's takings, and asked if it smelt. "No, Father," came the sur- prised reply. "That's odd," said the emperor, "it comes straight from the urinal."

We leave the Arco dei Tolomei and head straight along the **Via Anicia**, an area filled with the institutions that are such a feature of this neighborhood. To the left is a school; farther down are the high walls of a convent. At the end of the block, on the corner of Via dei Genovesi, is a captivating view of the medieval campanile and Romanesque apse of the Church of S. Cecilia behind the bare convent wall. In July this otherwise lifeless street is festooned with arches of multicolored lights decorating the parade of *Noantri*, "We others." For an entire month the Trasteverini celebrate their heritage with a mixture of religious, cultural, and commercial fanfare that ends with an explosion of fireworks on top of the Gianicolo Hill.

Halfway down the next block of Via Anicia, to your right at **no. 12**, is a plaque that identifies the **Confraternity of S. Giovanni Battista dei Genovesi**. While the door is always closed, it is open to the public from October to April from 2:00 P.M. until 4:00 P.M. and April through September from 3:00 P.M. until 4:00 P.M., except for the month of August when it is closed. Ring the button on the lower left-hand corner for the *guardiano*. He will open the door to the most beautiful fifteenth-century cloister in Rome. This is one of those hidden spots in Rome that gives this already well-endowed city such a special place in the hearts of romantics. The cloister and its adjoining convent were built in 1481 for the colony of sailors from Genova who resided near the river's port. Conceived by Meliaduce Cicala, Pope Sixtus IV's treasurer, it was dedicated to St. John the Baptist, protector of the city and port of Genova. The lush garden is circumscribed by stately octagonal columns supporting a double loggia designed by Baccio Pontelli, one of the pre-Bramante architects of the early Renaissance in Rome. In the center, surrounded by orange trees and fragrant jasmine, is a well framed by two marble columns. Within this protected space Antonio Lanza planted Rome's first palm tree in 1588.

The church attached to the cloister is usually closed. Inside, the simple design of a nave without a transept has been completely restored, meaning, as it usually does in Italy, that it was altered during the last century. It is interesting to note that the money to pay for this work came from Rome's Genovese community, who still have a strong attachment to their ancestral home. Among the few remains of the ancient church is the fine tomb of the founder, Meliaduce Cicala, which is an example of the work done in the shops of Mino da Fiesole and Andrea Bregno. The principal tabernacle is from the eighteenth century, as are the altarpiece and other objects in the sacristy. An inscription on the wall commemorates the birth in this hospice of the baritone Antonio Cotogni, 1831–1914.

Continue down Via Anicia and you will pass the **Vicolo dei Tabacchi**. This street refers to the tobacco factory around the corner that was founded in 1863 by Pope Pius IX. The factory was part of his plan to industrialize Rome, which, unlike other Italian cities, never developed a vigorous manufacturing economy. The factory was also an effort directed specifically at the population of Trastevere, who had never enjoyed the economic prosperity of their neighbors across the Tiber. **No. 11 Via Anicia** is an example of more contemporary planning measures—a recreation center for the unemployed and the retired.

Follow this seemingly lifeless street for another block until you reach (on the right) the **Church of S. Maria dell'Orto**, with its curious series of obelisks across the top. The church harks back to the days when this part of Trastevere and beyond was a large field cultivated by truck farmers who supplied the city with fruits and vegetables. Built under the auspices of the Corporation of Fruit Growers, the church is a tribute to the economic and social power of guilds in fifteenth-century Rome. These guilds were at once trade organizations, social networks, and religious sodalities with origins dating back to the empire. However, it wasn't until the fifteenth century that they became an integral part of the city's social fabric. They were local organizations that, aside from setting strict requirements for the exercise of their particular craft, served important welfare functions, such as financing the dowries of poverty-stricken members, paying for members' funerals, and funding orphanages and hospitals. On the whole they were autonomous organizations, but ultimate control was held by the Vatican.

S. Maria dell'Orto and the hospital attached to it included among its patrons a large cross-section of the population of Trastevere: the delicatessen workers, the shoemakers, the millers, the merchants and brokers of the court of Ripa, the pastamakers, the grape growers, the chicken sellers, the fruit vendors, and the lemon growers. The church was dedicated to a Madonna who was painted on the wall of one of the gardens. In the sixteenth century the reputation of this "Madonna of the Gardens" spread beyond the confines of Trastevere to, of all places, Japan. The story is told that on the occasion of Rome's first Japanese visitors, a group of recently converted Catholics coming to pay their respects to Pope Gregory XIII, the Vatican organized a trip for them down the Tiber to Ostia. It was a splendid flotilla meant to impress and entertain the guests, but halfway the journey was interrupted by a terrible storm. Only when the captain, a Trasteverino, invoked the Madonna dell'Orto did the storm subside, leaving these tourists with a lasting impression of the miraculous powers of this Virgin of the Fields.

The construction of the church began in 1419, and until its completion in 1579 a number of Rome's architects were involved. Guidetto Guidetti is generally credited with the body of the church; Vignola, with the façade. Other names associated with various stages of the church's construction are Raphael and Francesco da Volterra. The obelisks, which are such a distinguishing feature of the church, were probably added in 1762. The interior is only open for Sunday morning services, but it is worth a special trip to see the opulence of its decor. Between the vestry and the altar is an area covered with stucco work of the Neapolitan-Roman school, and in it is a splendidly carved wooden turkey donated in the eighteenth century by the chicken sellers' guild to commemorate the arrival of the first turkey from America. The sumptuous baroque decor includes frescoes by Bartolo di Taddeo, Frederico Zuccari, Giovanni Baglioni, Corrado Giaquinto, and, on the main altar, Giacomo della Porta. The vault is wrapped in the stucco and gilt work of the eighteenth century. On the back wall is an impressive organ. When you enter on a Sunday morning, you join a congregation still associated either as descendants or current members of the trade guilds that created this church. Today, however, they are nothing more than religious sodalities.

To the right of the church is an attached building with a lone tree standing in the courtyard. This used to be the hospital and pharmacy associated with the church; they were built in 1739 by Valvassare, the confraternity's architect at the time. The *edicola* in the wall across from the church to your left is reminiscent of the original shrine in the 1400s that sparked the Trasteverini's following for the Madonna dell'Orto.

We continue our walk on the **Via della Madonna dell'Orto**, straight ahead from the entrance to the church. The building to our left is a high school named after Italy's first queen, Regina Margherita, who inaugurated it herself in March 1888. In Italy children start specializing in the ninth grade; they may choose a classical college preparatory course, a scientific and technical one, or a trade school. This is one of the professional trade schools.

On the right behind the wall is a military unit encamped in one of the former gardens, which until the turn of the century still produced fruits and vegetables. This military camp is suggestive of days in ancient Rome when troops camped in the fields of Trastevere to defend the city from the threat of the Etruscans. Here also was the sacred grove of the goddess Furina, where Gaius Sempronius Gracchus was killed in 123 b.c. after his reforms failed. Protected by his friends, Gracchus escaped from the Aventine and crossed the Tiber on the Pons Subblicius with his servant Philocrates. When they were unable to find a horse to continue their escape Philocrates killed his master and then himself. In the meantime, the senate issued a proclamation stating that anyone who brought them the head of Gracchus would receive its weight in gold. When he found the bodies, Septimulenus cut off Gracchus's head and filled it with lead. He walked into Rome with the head on the top of his spear and was paid the promised reward.

Beyond, looming directly in front of us, is the **Ospizio di S. Michele**. This immense complex occupies 27,000 square meters and encompasses several buildings around courtyards and two churches. Its construction spans a period of 150 years, from 1672 to the beginning of the nineteenth century. Originally founded by Cardinal Odescalchi, nephew of Innocent XI, this was a refuge for vagabond children. Here they were properly housed and taught a trade. Later a variety of papal assistance programs were added for the aged poor, juvenile delinquents, lone women, and mendicants.

Out of this institution's mandate to train their charges in the industrial arts rose the city's most important craft schools and workshops in tapestry, typography, bookbinding, weaving, etching, woodcarving, sculpting, welding, tailoring, etc. Among the alumni were etchers Pietro Mercuri and Luigi Colamatta and the sculptor Ercole Rosa.

On the whole the complex is purely functional with little architectural character, even though Carlo Fontana worked on the design. To him is attributed the first prototype of a juvenile correctional facility that for a long time was the basis, both in concept and design, for all such facilities in Europe. Ferdinando Fuga also worked on this complex, unifying its long façade along the river's edge.

This institution, once central to the city's social welfare and artisan endeavors, was slowly dismantled at the beginning of this century and dispersed among various government bodies. Then for decades it stood abandoned. In 1970, the government began renovations for use by the Ministry of Cultural Affairs and Restoration.

Turn left at the end of the street onto Via di S. Michele. To your right in a building of the Ospizio di S. Michele is the entrance to ICCROM, the International Center for the Study and Preservation of Cultural Property, an institute started in the 1960s after the disastrous flooding in Florence. Since then ICCROM has contributed greatly to the preservation of art works in Italy and throughout the world. Continue down the street for a block to Piazza di S. Cecilia. Here we return to a more residential section of the neighborhood.

A large iron gate marks the dramatic entrance to the **Church of S. Cecilia**, set behind a garden courtyard adorned with a magnificent classical vase. As we walk through the gate we step into the equivalent of the neighborhood's park, accented with the season's blooming flowers and the gentle sound of the water flowing down the vase's brilliant white contour. A bench offers some rest and time to read about the life of St. Cecilia.

Stories of the saints' lives were once the basis of the earliest guidebooks to Rome, written for the pilgrims whose visit to this capital of Christianity was intended solely as a religious experience. The details of St. Cecilia's life seem appropriate here because of the important inspiration she has been to Western art: in poetry from Chaucer to Dryden and Pope; in art from Raphael to Cimabue, Tintoretto, and Rubens; and in music as its patroness. Furthermore, the church is built on the site of her home and naturally evokes the drama of Christianity's struggle in ancient Rome. Ruins from her home can be seen in the basement of the church, but here, in the *cortile*, the vase suggests the fountain that may once have adorned the peristyle of the Valerii family.

St. Cecilia is said to have lived during the time of Marcus Aurelius. She was the daughter of one of Rome's noble families and in marrying Valerianus became a member of another illustrious family. When she became

Entrance to the Church of S. Cecilia

a Christian she apparently took a vow of virginity, which despite her marriage, she upheld. Instead, she converted both her husband and brother-in-law to the then very dangerous and subversive concepts of Christianity. The story is told that when her husband returned from his baptism he found her singing triumphant hymns, though his conversion was meant to be a surprise. Her rejoicing, however, soon ended in a series of tragedies. Valerianus and his brother, Tiburtius, were beheaded for refusing to worship the Roman gods. When Cecilia inherited the fortunes of both men, becoming one of the wealthiest women in Rome, she also became the object of great resentment. It wasn't long before the prefect of Rome, Almachius, condemned her to death as well.

She was locked in the *sudatorium*, "steam room," of the baths in her own house and kept there for three days with the fires blazing. According to the story in the *Lives of the Saints*, "God sent a cooling shower" and when the door was finally opened she sang "with a voice of such sweetness" that there was no doubt she was still alive. Fearing the consequences of the news of this story, Almachius immediately sent one of his guards to behead her. After three blows of an ax, the most allowed by law, she remained alive for three days. During that short time she converted more than four hundred people to Catholicism and bequeathed her palace to the Church for the construction of a chapel. She, "who sang to God in her heart with the sound of musical instruments," is remembered on November 22 with concerts. The Academy of Music in Rome is named for her.

Pope Urban I, who reigned from 222–230, founded and consecrated a church in her palace. This was rebuilt by Pope Pascal I in 821 when, according to an account in the Vatican archives, St. Cecilia appeared in his dreams and revealed her burial site in the catacombs of St. Calixtus. The remains of her body were then transferred to the new church. In 1599 the saint's legend entered the domain of verified history. Then Cardinal Sfondrati opened the tomb and found her body absolutely intact and dressed in a shimmering golden robe. Led by Pope Clement VIII, all of Rome came to see this miracle, including the sculptor Stefano Maderno, who carefully sketched Cecilia's graceful pose. In celebration of this event the church was restored and Stefano Maderno was asked to complete a sculpture for the high altar.

In the convent adjoining the church a fascinating medieval ritual continues. Here the nuns weave the papal pallia, narrow bands of white wool decorated with six black crosses, which the pope wears around his neck over the chasuble. Every year on January 21, the feast of St. Agnes, two lambs are carried into the Church of S. Agnese on the Via Nomentana during the singing of the "Agnus Dei" (Lamb of God). The lambs lie on the altar in wicker baskets decorated with blue ribbons and, after the pope has blessed them, they are sent to the convent of the Church of S. Cecilia. Here they are specially cared for until Holy Thursday when their wool is shorn for the twelve pallia that are made every year. After the pallia are woven the nuns present them to the subdeacons of St. John the Lateran, who hand them to the subdeacons of St. Peter's, who, in turn, hand them to the canons. They are then placed in a golden casket beneath the high altar at St. Peter's, which is built above the traditional tomb of the apostles.

In the early days of the Church the pallium was worn only by the pope; even today only he may wear it on all occasions. This, one of the most ancient of ritual vestments, is older than the papal tiara and far more significant. In fact, during the papal coronation the most solemn moment comes when the new pope is vested with the pallium, a symbol of his role as the shepherd of Christ's flock.

Now look at the exterior details of the church. The bell tower and the portico were built in the twelfth century. This bell tower, to the right as you face the church, stands out amidst the thirty-eight Romanesque campaniles left in Rome as one of the most impressive. The atrium incorporated into the eighteenth-century façade by Fuga has antique marble columns from ancient Roman ruins and a mosaic frieze with medallions of the heads of Cecilia, Valerianus, Tiburtius, Urban I, and other saints. Along the walls are several medieval tombs and inscriptions, as well as fragments of crosses and sculpture.

Walk through the portico into the church. This transition is rather shocking, as what we encounter inside matches the eighteenth-century façade and not the Romanesque campanile nor the story of its early Christian foundation. The ancient marble columns have been encased and a fresco of the *Apotheosis of S. Cecilia* by Sebastiano Conca covers the ceiling. A further restoration in 1822 almost concealed every medieval feature but a more discerning look will show us marvelous examples from this period and others.

To the right of the main door is the fine tomb of Adam Easton, titular cardinal of the church, who died in 1398. The tomb bears the coat of arms of the Plantagenets, members of the English royal house founded by Geoffrey, Count of Anjou. To the left of the door is another tomb by Mino da Fiesole, which is noteworthy for its simplicity and delicacy; buried here is Cardinal Forteguerri who died in 1473. Passing the first chapel on the right, enter a narrow passage decorated with landscapes by Pomarancio and Paul Brill. This leads into the *sudatorium* where Cecilia survived the first attempt on her life. Lining the walls are fragments of the ancient terra-cotta pipes used to conduct the steam from the boiler. On the wall is Guido Reni's *Marriage and Martyrdom of St. Cecilia*. Returning to the aisle of the church we see through a grille the Ponzani family chapel with frescoes of the school of Pinturicchio and Antonio da Viterbo. Beyond that is a chapel of relics designed by Vanvitelli, and further still, a *Madonna and Child* by Perugino. At the end of the aisle is a twelfth- or thirteenth-century fresco representing the discovery of St. Cecilia's body.

The apse of the church is decorated with fine Byzantine mosaics from the ninth century. The Savior stands in a golden robe; at his side are Saints Peter, Paul, Cecilia,

Valerianus, Pascal carrying the model of his church, and Agatha. Also represented are the mystic palm trees and phoenix, symbols of eternity, and beneath that, the four rivers and twelve sheep that represent the apostles walking through the gates of Bethlehem and Jerusalem to the adoration of the lamb. If you are lucky you will see the nuns moving silently like giant white butterflies against this mosaic and, in the tradition of St. Cecilia, hear them singing their prayers in a lovely a cappella that resonates throughout the church.

Above the main altar stands Arnolfo di Cambio's noble canopy dating from 1283, and below that lies Stefano Maderno's inspiring representation of St. Cecilia as he saw her when the coffin was open—lying on her side in a state of peaceful and elegant repose, her robe gracefully molding her body and limbs, and her neck showing the wounds from the three blows. So impressive is the masterpiece of this Lombard sculptor that Gregorovius said, "Hardly a more gracious figure was created by the imagination of Christian art."

The rather stiff Byzantine qualities of the background mosaic stand in pointed contrast to Maderno's work, and both these pieces must be compared to Pietro Cavallini's fresco, which at the end of the thirteenth century forever buried the Byzantine style and paved the way for the Renaissance. This important fresco is in the back of the church in an upper gallery once used by women (a custom brought to Rome by the Eastern Church) and is now part of the convent. You really should make every effort to see the Cavallini frescoes, but it isn't easy! The gallery is open after Sunday mass at about 11:00 A.M. and on Tuesday and Thursday mornings between 10:00 and 11:30 A.M. Don't arrive at the last moment since only a certain number of people are allowed in the gallery at any one time and it is closed at 11:30 on the dot, if not earlier.

Ghiberti wrote of Cavallini, with an enthusiasm one cannot help but share, "This most learned and noble of artists." While only two of his major works exist—the

A restaurant on Piazza dei Mercanti

Last Judgment here in S. Cecilia painted about 1293 and his mosaic of the story of the Virgin at S. Maria in Trastevere—they are enough to confirm Cavallini's genius. In the fresco Christ sits enthroned and surrounded by angels with outspread wings dressed in jeweled robes. They are depicted in deep pastel colors in an array of tones and shades that even Missoni has not been able to duplicate. Above this are the apostles and saints painted in grays and blues. This is one of the most beautiful frescoes in Rome and is especially remarkable for its age and for the fact that it predates Giotto.

Ask the person at the desk where you pay to see the Cavallini frescoes about a visit to the crypt. There you will see a good imitation of the Byzantine by Giovenale, the sarcophagi of the saints, and some older underground structures including the pavement of a bath house and some Republican columns.

Leave the church and courtyard as you entered and return to the Piazza di S. Cecilia. Across from the entrance of the church is another medieval house, the **Casa dei Ponzani**, whose family chapel we saw in S. Cecilia. What these houses actually looked like in medieval Rome is hard to visualize because most, like this one, have been heavily restored. This house is an example of several structures fused into a single complex; the raised corner gives the impression of an ancient tower, and across the façade are signs of an ancient portico constructed to unify the various parts.

Walk toward the house. Along its side is the beginning of the **Piazza dei Mercanti**, which more than any other part of the neighborhood evokes the spirit of the old port of Ripa Grande. In the past this piazza was busy with the activities of Syrian porters carrying litters, Jewish moneylenders, sailors and bargemen of the Tiber, dockworkers, tradesmen, and brokers. Here corn was unloaded from Sicily and Africa, wine from Chios, marble from Paros and Luna, and all kinds of luxurious merchandise from the East. It was anything but this now quiet and charming space, carefully restored to give a flavor of the medieval and flanked by restaurants.

At the far end of the **L**-shaped piazza is a small, picturesque medieval house at **no. 18**. On its exterior staircase there is little distinction between inside and out—it is an entry, a stand for flowerpots, a storage area, an extension of the living room, and a place to hang the laundry. Ten steps farther is the intersection with the Via del Porto and a place from which we get a splendid view of the Aventine Hill. From here we see none of the new constructions, just the high wall covered with vegetation and crowned with churches and bell towers—S. Sabina, S. Alessio, S. Maria del Priorato, and S. Anselmo. At the end of the street once stood the Tiber's most important port, and in the fourteenth century we would have seen surrounding the port a number of churches and watchtowers. Within the monotonous façade of the Ospizio di S. Michele is the Church of S. Maria della Torre, better known to the users of the port as the Church of the Madonna del Buon Viaggio, Madonna of the Safe Trip. The tower that gave the church its name, of which there is only a trace (not visible to us standing on this street), corresponded with another on the opposite bank of the Tiber. Both were built in the middle of the ninth century and between them a chain was stretched to close the river to traffic and to protect the city against an attack by the Saracens. This pair of towers was but one of a series along the river, some of which can still be seen outside the Porta Portese.

Retrace your steps past the ocher "stage-set" Renaissance house and walk straight ahead to the narrow **Vicolo di S. Maria in Cappella**. This street framed by a string of dangling ivy is typical of what remains of medieval Rome. Its small houses, low dark entrances, small windows, and arched wooden doors preserve the look, if not all the habits, of this ancient quarter. We mustn't forget that in the days when everything was thrown into the gutter, it was a wise precaution to have as few windows as possible looking outward. Instead, attention was directed to the inner courtyard or garden, something that most if not all of these houses have behind their workshops. While this street may look as it did centuries ago, work habits have changed; now we have a carpenter making custom furniture and a movie production house. To the right is a single building combining an old-age home with a public shelter.

At the end of the block to your right is the entrance to the miniature Romanesque **Church of S. Maria in Cappella**. Here there is no elaborate iron gate or beautiful garden, just a spare desolate square. Still, it has a charm all its own: petite, adorned with a blue and white della Robbiaesque image of the Virgin, and a bell tower said to be the smallest in Rome. This church dates back to 1090 and was one of the many associated with the merchant community of the old port. In the fifteenth century it became the headquarters for the barrelmakers' guild, which controlled some of the most important monopolies in the city, those of wine and transport.

In the seventeenth century Donna Olimpia Pamphili, Pope Innocent X's sister-in-law and the power behind the throne, turned the garden behind this church into a riverside playground. Two hundred years later, in 1860, her descendants decided that instead of the garden the community needed a home for the elderly. The building to the right of the church was the first old-age home for the poor in Rome and continues as such.

Leaving S. Maria in Cappella we follow the **Via Augusto Jandolo**. Within a block it intersects with the Via dei Vascellari, named for the boat builders who for centuries kept up a busy trade in this neighborhood. Past this intersection, the street becomes the **Via dei Genovesi**, and suddenly we have a lively section of shops, grocery stores, a bar, and a restaurant.

As you may have guessed walking the streets of Rome, the concept of one-stop shopping has not taken hold here. There are a few supermarkets; in fact, nearby on Viale Trastevere is a Standa, but most supermarkets are on the outskirts of the city and in the suburbs. In the center of the city, the morning cappucino is followed by a daily visit to a number of stores and to the open market for fresh fruits and vegetables. The pretext for this daily event is the need for fresh food, but in reality it is also a very social time of the day. With the produce and the bread come all the intimacies that draw people's lives into a community.

Turn right at the next street, just beyond no. 33, onto the **Vicolo dell'Atleta**. Once again, this is a charming medieval street. In the few meters of its length the street curves, bifurcates into an upper and lower walk, and at one point is so narrow that the travertine post placed at the curve to protect the building is almost worn through. Where the street widens and divides, at **no. 13–14**, stands a fine example of an early medieval house with a loggia, one of the few of its kind left in Rome. Many think this may have been built as a synagogue for the Jewish community, which at the time lived in this part of Trastevere. Some suspect that it is in fact the synagogue built by Nathan ben Yeihiel Anav (1035–1106), author of the first compendia of Talmudic regulations called the "Sefer Arukh." This is the most impressive of a series of very old houses along this street, many of which have been recently restored. Under the cobblestones of this street in 1849 was discovered the *Apoxyomenos*, a sculpture of an athelete using a stigil, copied from an original by Lysippus. The statue was taken to the Vatican Museum where it remains on view and the street was given its present name, "street of the athlete."

This *vicolo* leads us to the **Via dei Salumi**, where once sausage makers had their warehouses for storing salami. This trade is not typically Roman but rather that of people from the mountain regions of Tuscany, Umbria, and the Abruzzi. They, along with the Syrians, Greeks, Jews, and Genovesi, help disprove the Trasteverini's age-old claim of descendence from "pure stock." In this neighborhood, more than elsewhere in Rome, the population fits the more modern criteria for a true Roman—that forefathers should be established here no later than 1850. The city's population of 200,000 in 1870 was doubled by 1900, augmented by another million by 1946, and since then by more than two million. Without belaboring the statistics it is clear that most of Rome's citizens are Johnny-come-latelies, hailing from all over Italy but primarily from the south. While the Trasteverini have helped accommodate this huge influx, true to their parochial character they have been less willing to share their neighborhood than the Romans across the river. Only in the 1960s, with the help of the expatriate American community, did Trastevere become a fashionable bohemian quarter. This southern end was spared that onslaught except for some scattered artists' studios.

Today, however, there is a shortage of housing in Rome, and over the last twenty years living in any part of the historic center has become the ambition not just of foreigners attracted to the beauty of Rome's center-city, but of any Roman who can afford it. This recent interest in restoring and living in old Rome can no doubt be traced in part to the ever-worsening traffic conditions. Rome is still a small enough city that walking is a reasonable alternative if one lives in the *centro storico*.

Turn left onto Via dei Salumi. The first intersection to your right is the Via Titta Scarpetta. It was originally named simply Scarpetta, after a carved marble foot that stood along its path. After the foot was stolen the city government found the street's name, which means "shoe," unseemly and, in any case, no longer appropriate. With the cunning resourcefulness often attributed to the Trasteverini, one of its residents remembered Scarpetta Giovambattista, called Titta, who fought for the defense of Malta against the Turks in 1559. Thanks to this vague historical figure a compromise was reached and the residents were able to keep their street name.

To your left is a junior high school, Goffredo Mameli, named for a Genovese compatriot, poet, and soldier who died in combat for the Republic in 1849. He wrote several martial hymns and is best remembered for his song "Fratelli d'Italia," "Italian Brothers."

At the end of the block occupied by the school we find ourselves once again at the intersection of Via Anicia and Via Arco dei Tolomei. From this perspective we can better admire the remains of an ancient medieval tower at **no. 32** and some of the detailing on the ancient Tolomei family residence. Continue another block down Via dei Salumi until you come to the **Via della Luce**.

Walking the streets of Rome you may occasionally see a cage with a canary just outside a window or door. For many years there was one on this block. This is a custom from southern Italy where one sees canaries outside most houses in hopes that if a curse is put on a house it will fall on the smallest member of the family— in other words, the canary and not the children.

We will take a small detour to our right down Via della Luce. Immediately to your left is a **Casalinga** with

its colorful display of household items pouring out onto the street and hanging around the entrance. Here one finds almost anything needed for the home, ranging from disposable diapers and children's toys to a garlic press, a broom or a *bombole*, a gas tank used for cooking and heating. It is the one store in every Roman neighborhood with the largest variety of items, almost equivalent to a five-and-dime.

Across the street at **no. 34** is a shop specializing in stucco—capitals, columns, moldings, masks, reliefs, etc. This is the kind of craftsmanship that remains in Italy but is disappearing, as it has elsewhere. Now this is the only shop of its kind in the center-city.

Across the street is the **Church of S. Maria della Luce**. Both the church and the street take their name from a miracle that took place on March 28, 1730. The story is told that a young unemployed man was about to commit suicide by throwing himself into the Tiber near Ponte Cestio when he saw the image of the Virgin Mary against the peeling paint of an ancient wall. This apparition caused him to forget his anxieties, and within a few days, he was even able to find a job. Later a blind man recovered his sight thanks to the same image, which became known as St. Mary of the Light. The miraculous image was transferred to this church, which was originally built in the twelfth century and named S. Salvatore in Corte. The church was both renamed and rebuilt with only the apse and the campanile remaining from the earlier structure. The façade, designed by Gabrieli Valvassari, was never completed.

Retrace your path back to the intersection with Via dei Salumi and make a right-hand turn onto the small **Vicolo del Buco**, which winds its way around the Church of S. Maria della Luce. As you round the curve beyond the restaurant you can admire a small medieval house and the elegantly simple Romanesque apse of S. Maria della Luce. This brings us to the Piazza del Drago. Straight ahead, toward the modern buildings, is the **Via di Monte**

The stucco shop on the Via della Luce

Fiore. Turn left down this street, whose name recalls the period in Trastevere's history when the area was full of flowering gardens. Walk one block.

On the corner to your right behind the brick and iron wall are the ruins of a large building. This was the **Coorte dei Vigili**, the ancient Roman fire station for the region of Trastevere, dating back to the first century. These ruins were discovered only in 1866 beneath other construction. You can see the atrium covered with ancient graffiti and the *impluvium* used to catch rainwater.

Return to the Via di Monte Fiore. At the intersection is a picturesque grouping of medieval houses, one with an outside staircase. It was here in 1656 that the first case of the plague that devastated all of Europe was discovered.

Return to the Piazza del Drago and make a right turn onto **Via della Lungaretta**, once an important route for pilgrims between St. Peter's and St. Paul's Outside the Walls. While Pope Julius II is responsible for paving this street we do not find here the examples of papal opulence and control that are so visible in other neighborhoods of the historic center. The houses that line this street continued to be of the same dimensions and type as their predecessors, inter-rupted occasionally by a compact baronial house and not a palazzo. Even the churches are scattered about the neigh-borhood and not focused along a particular path.

Today this is a commercial street lined with a bakery shop, a dry cleaner, a restaurant, a shoe repair shop, bars, and a lottery and off-track betting stand. On your right, halfway down the first block, **no. 25** is the Open Book Shop, which specializes in new and used English-language books. Farther down to your left, at **no. 161**, is an old-fashioned *latteria*, "milk bar," with its black-and-white tiled floors, white marble counter and tabletops, and white tile walls. Not many of these *latterie*—where you can sit and enjoy a drink as well as buy eggs and milk products—are left. In fact this *latteria* is so old-fashioned that it is now styl-ish. If you step inside you can see old photographs of this shop, which is still owned by the same family. In times past, cows were brought from a field on the edge of the city to a shed behind the shop to be milked. As you leave, notice the crenelated design across the front of the building and the outside staircase on the side.

As we continue down the next thirty yards of Via della Lungaretta there is one final observation to be made about Roman life from the street—the shutters. If you haven't already noticed them you will see that every window has a pair of shutters that is usually closed. The most common assumption is that Romans love their privacy, but more than that, these shutters are simply a means of temperature control. During the summer they are open only in the early morning and again as the sun sets to capture the cool breeze. In the winter (and you can't imagine how cold and damp these old houses get) they are open only when the sun is shining in order to capture some heat and then are bolted tight to keep the wind and rain out. The rules are so stringently observed by all Romans that, whenever one sees a window whose shutters are not conforming to the routine of the others, it is safe to assume that the apartment is inhabited by foreigners.

In the nineteenth century Roesler Franz documented in watercolors the street life of Trastevere. There is one painting of a scene on the Via della Lungaretta that shows what a depressed area this was at that time. Large pools of water formed in the street where the cobblestones were missing, and in place of horses and carriages he saw two oxen pulling a cart. Around that were slums and destitution. This was a typical street scene in the Trastevere of pre-1870.

The Via della Lungaretta returns us to the Piazza in Piscinula, where our walk ends. You can have a great plate of pasta at the Ristorante La Gensola, to your left at 15 Piazza della Gensola; or just grab a sandwich at a bar here or on the Viale di Trastevere, while you wait to go back to the cloister of the Confraternity of S. Giovanni Battista dei Genovesi, 12 Via dei Genovesi.

Walk · 5

The Church
and the Jews

THE OLD JEWISH GHETTO

The gates to the Jewish Synagogue

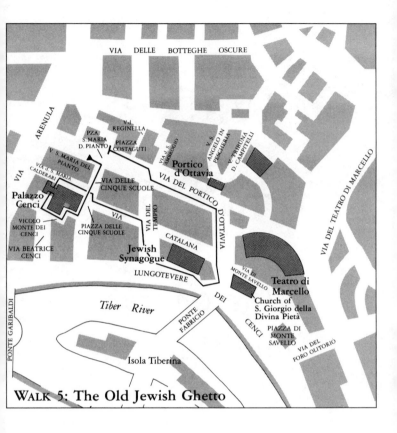

VIA DELLE BOTTEGHE OSCURE

VIA ARENULA

V.d. REGINELLA

PZA S.MARIA D. PIANTO

PIAZZA COSTAGUTI

V. S. MARIA DEL PIANTO

VIA S. MARIA CALDERARI

Palazzo Cenci

VIA DELLE CINQUE SCUOLE

VICOLO MONTE DEI CENCI

VIA BEATRICE CENCI

PIAZZA DELLE CINQUE SCUOLE

VIA

VIA DEL TEMPIO

VIA S. AMBROGIO

Portico d'Ottavia

VIA DEL PORTICO D'OTTAVIA

V. S. ANGELO IN PESCHERIA

V. TRIBUNA D. CAMPITELLI

Jewish Synagogue

CATALANA

LUNGOTEVERE

DEI

CENCI

Tiber River

PONTE GARIBALDI

PONTE FABRICIO

Isola Tiberina

VIA DEL TEATRO DI MARCELLO

Teatro di Marcello

VIA DI MONTE SAVELLO

Church of S. Giorgio della Divina Pietà

PIAZZA DI MONTE SAVELLO

VIA DEL FORO OLITORIO

WALK 5: The Old Jewish Ghetto

Starting Point: The Piazza S. Maria del Pianto, two blocks down Via Santa Maria del Pianto from the Via Arenula.
Buses: 26, 44, 56, 60, 65, 75, 96, 170, 710
Length of walk: One and a half hours. Plan this walk in the morning if you want to visit the Jewish Museum or the late afternoon if you want to witness the street life.

The **Piazza S. Maria del Pianto**, which is little more than an intersection, is still popularly known as the Piazza Giudea because it was once the main entrance to the Jewish Ghetto. From here we will explore a small section of Rome which has been associated for centuries with its Jewish population. Like many foreigners in the city, the Roman Jews always had their own neighborhood. Initially they lived on the right bank of the river in Trastevere, but after the pillage of Rome in 1084, they migrated first to the island and then to this area on the left bank of the Tiber.

In the mid–nineteenth century, when Gregorovius was busy studying and writing his great survey of civic and cultural life in medieval and Renaissance Rome, he became fascinated with the Jews and their ghetto, writing both a poem, "Lament of the Children of Israel in Rome,"

245

and an essay. "Because of the historical relation of the people of Israel to the Romans who destroyed Jerusalem and dispersed the Jews over the world, the ghetto of Rome is the most remarkable of all the Jewish communities of Europe," writes Gregorovius. He goes on to praise their courage for having made "their home in what for them was the most dangerous spot in the world because it was in sight of their enemies, the Romans . . . and afterwards the popes. . . ." The story of the Jewish community in Rome reflects a long and difficult tenure going back to ancient times.

The first diplomatic encounter of the Jews with the Roman senate was in 160 B.C., when a mission was sent by Judas Maccabeus to seek out the friendship of Israel. In 139 B.C. a treaty of commerce was signed, and by 50 B.C. the Jewish community in Rome seems to have been flourishing. At that time Cicero wrote of the Jewish influence on the city, and Caesar proclaimed an edict that granted them religious freedom. Only after the conquest of Jerusalem in 70 A.D., when Jews were brought back as slaves, were there any real problems for Jews living in Rome. (That event was memorialized by the Arch of Titus in the Forum, which depicts the plunder of the Temple of Jerusalem. For centuries no pious Jew would walk through it.) Nevertheless, the Empire did give Jews some protection, both civil and religious, and their numbers flourished to 40,000 with as many as ten synagogues.

As Christianity became more powerful after the fourth century, the differences between Jews and Christians became more conspicuous. Before that, Jews and Christians were considered part of the same sect and persecuted equally. It was after the consolidation of the authority of the pope and the choice of Rome as his seat that the conflict between Christians and Jews became a reality. In the late Middle Ages their position worsened considerably as their fate depended less on established dogma than on the whim of various pontiffs.

In the thirteenth century, sumptuary laws were imposed on all Jews and heretics, forcing them to wear a mark of distinction. This was at various times a large circle of yellow cloth, a scarlet mantle, and an orange cap. Only physicians, some of whom were doctors to the Vatican and considered public benefactors, were exempt. Other humiliations included carnival races from the Piazza Navona to the Corso in which Jews were pursued by jeering crowds. This practice began in 1468 and got progressively worse until it finally stopped in 1668 when Pope Clement IX instead accepted a tax of thirteen hundred scudi. The real turning point for the Roman Jewish community was in 1555 when Pope Paul IV rescinded all the privileges enjoyed by the Jews and established the Ghetto based on ghettos in Prague and Venice.

The word *ghetto* in fact comes from the Venetian word for "foundries," which occupied the quarter relegated to the Jews in Venice. Before 1555, Jews were at liberty to live anywhere in Rome, though they seldom chose to do so. The ghetto assigned them a secluded area that embraced a few narrow streets along the Tiber enclosed by walls through whose gates every Jew entered at sunset and could not leave until sunrise. In some part, the decision by the Vatican to segregate the Jews was reinforced by the general tone of physical and intellectual defensiveness brought on by the Counter-Reformation.

An event that took place in 1559, when Pope Paul IV died, gives a hint of the Jewish population's sentiments toward this segregation. At the announcement of his death a mob of Jews broke through the gates of the Ghetto and stormed into the Conservatory Palace on the Capitoline Hill. They overturned the statue of the pope and dragged its head through the streets back into the Ghetto, crowning the pontifical tiara with the same hateful orange cap they were forced to wear.

The Ghetto wall was built by Galvestro Peruzzi, son of the famous architect Baldassare Peruzzi, and was paid for by the Jewish community. It extended from the Ponte Fabricio to the Portico d'Ottavia, across to the Piazza

A balcony overlooking Piazza S. Maria del Pianto

Giudea, or S. Maria del Pianto, and back down to the river. In 1555 it was 270 meters long and 150 meters wide, and it housed 3,500 Jews. The main entrance here on the former Piazza Giudea had a large ornamental gate and a fountain by Giacomo della Porta, which Pope Paul IV commissioned to "relieve the misery of the Jews." The other gate was across from the Church of S. Giorgio della Divina Pietà near the bridge to the Tiber Island. In 1577 a third gate was added at the Portico d'Ottavia. The boundaries of the wall were enlarged from time to time and the number of gates eventually increased to eight. These gates were closed at seven o'clock in the evening in the winter and at eight in the summer.

In some respects the Ghetto provided the Jews with

some degree of safety. Late in the eighteenth century Moses Mendelssohn, grandfather of the composer, wrote to a friend in Berlin complaining bitterly that his movements were circumscribed in this city of self-styled tolerance by cries of "Jew" raised against him and his children.

The Ghetto Gregorovious visited in 1853 was both exotic and depressing:

> They sit in their doorways or outdoors on the street which affords scarcely more light than their damp and dismal rooms, and tend their ragged merchandise or industriously patch and sew. The chaos of patching and mending [called *cenci* in Italian] is indescribable. All the world seems to lie about, . . . pieces of junk of every kind and color are heaped high before the doors: scraps of golden fringe, pieces of silk brocade, rags of velvet, patches of red, scraps of blue, orange, yellow, black, white, old, torn, threadbare, badly worn scraps and tatters. I have never seen the like. The Jews might patch all creation with it and make the whole world as varicolored as a harlequin.

He describes astrologers, diviners, magicians, witches, and crystal gazers who were often frequented by grand Roman ladies. But this fascinating texture of color was against a miserable background. "What most horrifies the spectator in the ghetto is the narrowness and filth of these tortuous streets and alleys and the narrow houses which reach high above them. In them Jewish families live as in a Roman columbarium [pigeon house], stacked one over the other in rows." A population of over four thousand lived in an area that could really only accommodate half that many. During the rainy season, the constant flooding of the Tiber made for a perilous web of narrow, muddy streets. The upper part of the Ghetto, where we now stand, was less prone to floods and was inhabited by wealthier Jews who made their money in banking, as physicians, or trading silk.

Under Napoleon (1798–1815) and again under Mazzini and the Roman Republic (1848–49) Roman Jews enjoyed, at least in theory, full professional and religious liberty, but the actual end of the Ghetto only came in 1870, when the Papacy was stripped of its temporal powers. In 1885 a new city plan was adopted that built up the embankments along the Tiber to control flooding. Many of the houses in the old Ghetto were demolished and the streets widened, and a large number of Jewish families were forced to seek housing in other parts of the city. In 1904, when a huge modern synagogue was built on the ruins of the ancient Ghetto, the king made a point of being present at the opening ceremonies. The persecution of Rome's Jews did not, however, end with the creation of the Kingdom of Italy. Their position before and during World War II has been relatively forgotten in the face of the Nazi murders in Germany and Poland. Nevertheless, it is estimated that between 1938 and 1944 a quarter of the Jewish population in Rome lost their lives. The centuries-long tension between the popes and the Roman Jewish community was only reconciled in April of 1986 when Pope John Paul II came to pray for brotherhood and love with the Jews in their synagogue.

The Piazza S. Maria del Pianto is named for a peculiarly designed church to your right as we face the old Ghetto. It has no real façade, though its entrance is around the corner, and this side is blocked by an apartment house. If you step back you can see the octagonal-shaped dome rising from the top of the building. The church's name, "St. Mary in Tears" is explained by a couple of legends. One is that the image of the Virgin on a picture that once overlooked this piazza burst into tears after witnessing a particularly gruesome murder. Another story tells of the Virgin's despair and tears at the failure of the Jews to convert to Christianity. Gregorovius also tells an interesting story about the church during the height of

the Counter-Reformation. At that time contests of cate-
chetical knowledge were held here, and boys from all over
Rome participated. The winner was then taken trium-
phantly to the Vatican where he could ask any one favor
of the pope. Invariably, the boys asked for bread and
wine for the rest of their lives, giving us some hint of the
economic state of Rome during the seventeenth century.

Turn right onto the **Piazza delle Cinque Scuole**. This
piazza was carved out of the old Ghetto at the turn of
the century when so much of it was demolished to build
new apartment houses, to widen the roads, and to create
more public spaces. As is the case all over modern Rome,
this piazza has become a large parking lot for the patrons
of the many wholesale shops in this neighborhood and
their owners, many of whom no longer live in the old
Ghetto. On hot summer days after the shopkeepers and
their customers had left, Gregorovious might have recognized an element of the scene he described so vividly:
families from the adjacent apartments laying claim to the
piazza with chairs, tables, and dinner.

At **30 Via di Santa Maria de Calderari** is one of
the few remaining authentic Roman *osterie*, or simple
neighborhood restaurants. The fountain, barely visible
behind all the cars, is the one commissioned by Pope
Paul IV of Giacomo della Porta that once stood at the
main entrance to the Ghetto. Beyond that is the impressive entrance, no longer in use, to the Palazzo Cenci, a
huge many-sectioned structure that covers a full block.

While the **Palazzo Cenci** was just outside the Ghetto
walls, it evokes another tragedy I can't resist recounting,
and it deserves a quick detour from the main focus of
our walk. The building itself is worth some attention as
it represents that intrinsically Roman phenomenon of a
fortress that is built on the remains of an ancient ruin
and which with each passing century acquires more re-
finement and additions much like a child's Lego project.

Cross the piazza and wander around the building up
the narrow **Vicolo dei Cenci**. This hill was created by

An almsbox on Vicolo Monte dei Cenci

ancient ruins, probably those of the Circus Flaminius, constructed in 221 B.C. and standing until the fourth century. For a long time there were arguments about the precise location of the circus, but the discovery of the Severan Marbles, an architectural design of Rome during that emperor's reign, establishes the circus's site as extending from the Piazza S. Carlo Cairoli to the Teatro Marcello and from the Portico d'Ottavia to the river.

The Cenci family held a prominent position in Rome as early as 914, when one of them became Pope John X. Later, four cardinals came from this family, but it was in the sixteenth century with Francesco Cenci that the family gained the reputation it still bears. This was a man with such a serious record of evil that the pope banished him from Rome in the 1590s. Francesco Cenci moved to Petrella where, lacking a larger audience, he vented his cruelty on his wife and two sons, Giacomo and Bernardo, and even tried to violate his daughter Beatrice. Exhausted and demoralized by his treatment, the family plotted murder. In 1598 with the help of a servant, Giacomo killed his father and threw the body over a wall pretending that Francesco had accidentally fallen.

Unfortunately, the investigators did not believe this story and arrested the whole family. During the trial only Beatrice would respond to questioning and Giacomo accused the others of murder. It is said that Pope Clement VIII might have pardoned the Cencis, given Francesco's turpitude, except that a similar crime by another prominent Roman family forced him to set an example. The entire Cenci family was decapitated except for Bernardo, who because of his youth was forced instead to witness the deaths of his mother and siblings and then imprisoned for life. The family's property was also confiscated, which at the time included a good part of what is now the Villa Borghese Park. Beatrice's tragedy especially captured many people's imaginations and empathy. Her remains are buried under the high altar at S. Pietro in Montorio, on the Gianicolo Hill. A portrait of her by Guido Reni can be seen in the Corsini Picture Gallery, and Shelley created a play based on her story.

The **Church of S. Tommaso** to the left as you go up the Vicolo Monte dei Cenci is the Cenci family church. When it was built in the twelfth century it was known as the miller's church because of the wheat mills working near here on the Tiber River. In 1575 it was restored by Francesco Cenci and became the family's chapel. For centuries the Confraternity of Coachmen said mass here on the anniversary of the Cenci executions, but the church has recently been deconsecrated and now houses a social welfare agency.

Next to the church is a famous restaurant, **Piperno's**, which serves a number of dishes particular to the cuisine

of the Roman Jewish community, including crispy-fried artichokes, stuffed zucchini flowers, and cod fillets fried in batter. This spot, secluded from the traffic and congestion of this neighborhood, is an especially attractive, though not inexpensive, choice for a pleasant meal.

As you reach the end of Vicolo Monte dei Cenci, turn right, and you can see what is now the front of the Cenci Palace. After the Ghetto walls were built a new façade and entrance were created on this side of the building allowing the residents and guests at the Palazzo Cenci to ignore their proximity to the Ghetto. A medieval arch in the distance connects the main wing, decorated with a curious Spanish baroque-style portal, to a smaller more elegant structure built in the early sixteenth century. The Palazzo Cenci is now divided into numerous residences and among the tenants is the Rhode Island School of Design.

Walk under the dark Cenci arch, which may evoke a few impressions of medieval times, and return to Via di S. Maria de Calderari. There toward Via Arenula at **no. 23** against the building is an arch of brickwork flanked by two travertine columns, probable remnants of the ancient Circus of Flaminius. Today it is the entrance to this neighborhood's firehouse. The relative safety of a city constructed largely of brick and concrete makes this a fairly minor institution in the fabric of the city, but it was not always so. In ancient times, fires were a major problem in the residential neighborhoods where houses were made of wood. In fact, twice a year at the Circus Flaminius sacrifices were offered to the god of fire, Vulcan.

Turn around and return on Via S. Maria de Calderari to the Piazza delle Cinque Scuole and the old Jewish Ghetto. The piazza's name refers to the five different schools of prayer within the Ghetto community, reflecting a bit of its cultural diversity. The Scuola del Tempio

The Arco dei Cenci

enjoyed the greatest prestige as it was made up of the descendants of the ancient Roman colony who came as prisoners under Titus and Septimius Severus. The Scuola Siciliana was formed by those who came from Sicily, and the Scuola Nuova included all other Roman Jews including many from communities in Lazio. Two were of the Spanish rite, having come to Rome following the Spanish Inquisition, and they distinguished themselves geographically: the Scuola Catalana and the Scuola Castigliana. In the late 1400s and early 1500s, these different backgrounds caused great internal friction within the Jewish community but during this century they have united in a single synagogue.

Cross the piazza, bear toward the right, and there you will see the **Via Catalana**, named for the large population of Spanish Jews who settled in Rome from that Spanish province. The street is flanked with apartment buildings built at the turn of the century and at the end of the block is the new synagogue.

Designed by Costa and Armanni, the **synagogue** was consecrated in 1904. In an effort to avoid any possible resemblance to a Christian church, its structure and decor echo the East, in particular Assyrian-Babylonian motifs. It is a solid-blocked complex with a centralized symmetry and a heavy square base graduating to a large square metal dome. This massive structure is a prominent feature on the Roman skyline, joining St. Peter's and the Pantheon as points of focus. In the early 1900s visitors, no doubt not used to its presence, wrote that the dome was almost blinding when it reflected the sun.

The synagogue houses the permanent exhibition of the Jewish community of Rome, and it is open every weekday morning from 10:00 A.M.–2:00 P.M. and on Sundays until noon. Among its manuscripts and religious objects are prints that display a map of the old Ghetto. During the Nazi occupation in 1943, the contents of the synagogue's library were confiscated. Until then it was considered the richest and most distinctive collection of its kind.

You will have noticed the police guards and barricades around the synagogue. Go to the gatepost on the corner of Via del Tempio and Via Catalana, and you can see a plaque (facing Via Catalana) commemorating the most recent attack on the Jewish population in Rome. "On October 9, 1982, after prayers, Stefano Tachi Gay, two years old, was killed in front of this temple and forty Jews injured by anti-Semitic gunmen." Since then, security in and around the Jewish temple has been highly visible.

Walk around to the front of the synagogue onto the **Lungotevere de Cenci**. There you will see the entrance to the museum and several memorial plaques in honor of Jews killed during World Wars I and II. The first was dedicated in 1921 honoring Jewish soldiers who died in the First World War. Another plaque recounts that on October 16, 1943, German soldiers captured 1,024 Jews, and in the following days the number rose to 2,091. (This number is but 30 percent of the total number of Jews deported from Italy by the Nazis.) All were sent to Auschwitz, Dachau, or Bergen-Belsen and only 15 returned. Another plaque is in memory of the 75 Jews shot to death at Fosse Ardeantine (near the Via Appia Antica) on March 24, 1944.

Walk the full length of the temple and its grounds to the **Via del Portico d'Ottavia**. Across the Lungotevere dei Cenci you will see a bridge that leads to the Tiber Island. Today that bridge, officially known as the **Ponte Fabricio**, is popularly called the Ponte dei Quatro Capi (bridge of the four heads) for the two herms of the four-headed Janus on the parapet. In the sixteenth century, however, the bridge's popular name was dei Giudei (bridge of the Jews) because it linked this part of the left bank occupied by Jews with a section of Trastevere and the island itself where Jews lived before the Ghetto walls were built. Next to the bridge once stood the Synagogue of the Arbace Roshim, Synagogue of the Four Heads, which was closed in 1558.

Here at the end of the Via del Portico d'Ottavia (and

Casa dei Vailati

we must remember that the embankments along the Tiber River and the Lungotevere did not exist) stood one of the gates to the Ghetto. The small church, which has become an island between the busy Lungotevere and Via Monte Savello, stood just outside the gate. Built in the seventeenth century, **S. Giorgio della Divina Pietà** has a painting on its façade of the crucifixion with an inscription in bold Hebrew and Latin letters clearly addressing its audience. The inscription is from Isaiah: "All day long I have stretched out my hands to a disobedient and gainsaying people."

Turn left onto Via del Portico d'Ottavia. We will walk past the synagogue's verdant side garden accented with palm trees and, on our right, the backside of the **Theater of Marcellus**. This is another ancient Roman ruin turned fortress, then palazzo. In this case, the transformation from ruin to fortress was done in 1086 by a Jewish family, the Pierleonis, who built their base of power and wealth as bankers and businessmen in the Jewish neighborhood of Trastevere. Having acquired their fortress overlooking the Tiber, they converted to Catholicism, which brought with it a strong political alliance with the papacy. Their greatest moment was the election of a Pierleoni as Pope Anacleto II. Although this occurred during a schism and he is now referred to as an antipope, this event signaled the acme of power for this Jewish family and a period of great hope for the Roman Jewish community. The Pierleonis' fortress in the Teatro di Marcello gave them control over the island; the main bridges to the left bank of the river and the roads leading out of town to the southeast; and the eastern periphery of the Capitoline Hill, which at the time was the city's commercial center and one of its most populated areas. (Walk 2 includes a more detailed discussion of the Teatro Marcello.)

Soon we will come to a gate through which we can see the ruins of the Theater of Marcellus and the three elegant columns from the Temple of Apollo. If you walk across the Via del Portico d'Ottavia for some perspective you will see a small but provocative view that captures so much of what is the essence of Rome. Amidst the ancient ruins at the end of the street (to the left and across the street) are a jumble of architectural styles, periods, and forms. This vista reflects the dense texture that only Rome with its long and varied history can produce: on the one hand haphazard, yet very much part of a dynamic whole.

Back to the other side of the street at **no. 28–29** is one of the few free-standing medieval houses left in Rome, the **Casa dei Vailati**. Built in the thirteenth century, this house is a good example of the architecture of that period when most buildings were irregular in shape and occupied spaces defined by narrow, crooked streets. On the ground floor is a small portico covered by what was once an outside staircase leading to a loggia. Inside is an open courtyard to bring in the light and some fresh air, and a small tower for protection. The portico on the ground floor, with its iron gate, was probably used for mercantile purposes. Today this building houses offices for the Belli Arti, which is charged with preserving Rome's architectural heritage.

While the Casa dei Vailati was just outside the Ghetto wall, a marble plaque under the bifurcated window memorializes the more than two thousand Jews rounded up and exterminated by the Nazis in 1943. Every year on October 16, the anniversary of that event, the street is cleared for a sundown service to honor the dead.

Straight ahead are the ancient ruins of the **Portico d'Ottavia**. This too was just outside the Ghetto wall but was the setting for some dramatic events in the history of the Jewish community. First built in 149 B.C. by Quintus Metellus after his triumph in Macedonia, the portico was in the form of a parallelogram 118 meters by 135 meters, surrounded by a double arcade of 270 columns and enclosing the Temples of Jupiter Stator and Juno. In front of these temples, Metellus placed a group of twenty-five bronze statues by Lysippus commissioned by Alexander the Great. Augustus completely reconstructed the portico with richly carved marble and dedicated it to his sister, Ottavia, next to the theater named for her son, Marcellus. In Augustus's time the portico enclosed Greek and Latin libraries, as well as the two temples, and more Greek sculpture including a cupid by Praxiteles (later destroyed by fire) and the famous Medici *Venus* (now at the Uffizi). The complex had two entrances, each with a double atrium and monolithic columns of white marble between two Corinthian pilasters supporting the tympanum. Before us, and all that is left of the original, is the principal entrance. It was reconstructed by Septimius Severus following a fire in A.D. 203, and since then the second pediment seems to have been rebuilt in a collage of fragments including bits of fluted columns.

According to Pliny, the architects employed by Augustus were two Greeks named Batrachos and Sauros. Because they were not allowed to sign their work they carved lizards and frogs on the fluting of all their columns, thus leaving us the personal touch of the artisan in this age of emperors. One such column, with a lizard and a frog clearly visible on the capital, was used to decorate the Church of S. Lorenzo Fuori le Mura, "Church of St. Lawrence Outside the Walls," and many of the other two hundred-odd columns are now preserved in the monuments of Christian Rome.

It was here at the Portico d'Ottavia that Vespasian and Titus met the Roman Senate in a triumphal procession following their victory over Israel which brought the first Jewish slaves to Rome. The description of this extravagant affair by the Roman historian, Flavius Josephus, creates a vivid picture for us:

> It is impossible adequately to describe the multitude of those spectacles and their magnificence . . . for almost all the objects which men . . . have acquired

A view from under the arch of the Portico d'Ottavia

one by one—the wonderful and precious productions of various nations—by their collective exhibition on that day displayed the majesty of the Roman Empire. Silver and gold and ivory . . . might be seen, not as if carried in procession, but flowing, so to speak, like a river . . . there were carried images of their gods . . . and beasts of many species. . . . The numerous attendants conducting each group of animals were decked in garments of true purple dye, interwoven with gold. . . . Even among the mob of captives none was to be seen unadorned, the variety and beauty of their dresses concealing from view any unsightliness arising from bodily disfigurement.

But nothing in the procession excited so much astonishment as the structure of moving stages; indeed their massiveness afforded ground for alarm and misgiving as to their stability, many of them being three or four stories high, while the magnificence of the fabric was a source at once of delight and amazement. For many were enveloped in tapestries interwoven with gold, and all had a framework of gold and wrought iron. The war was shown by numerous representations, in separate sections, affording a very vivid picture of its episodes. . . . For to such sufferings were the Jews destined when they plunged into the war, and the art and magnificent workmanship of those structures now portrayed the incidents to those who had not witnessed them, as though they were happening before their eyes. On each of the stages was stationed the general of one of the captured cities in the attitude in which he was taken. A number of ships also followed.

The spoils in general were borne in promiscuous heaps; but conspicuous above all stood out those captured in the Temple at Jerusalem. . . . After these, and last of all the spoils, was carried a copy of the Jewish law. Then followed a large party carrying images of victory, all made of ivory and gold. Behind them drove Vespasian, followed by Titus; while Domitian rode beside them, in magnificent apparel and mounted on a stead that was itself a sight.

The **Church of S. Angelo in Pescheria**, whose entrance is behind the gate across the right-hand side of the portico, is an example of the manner in which the city has constantly adopted its edifices to the cultural mores and taste of the times. Literally inserted into the ruins of the portico in 770, the vestibule of the ancient structure forms the porch of the church. In the fifteenth century the church was rebuilt in conjunction with restoration of the ruin, and then in the seventeenth century it was decorated in the style of that time. The entrance arch, which substitutes for two of the original columns, still bears faint traces of thirteenth-century frescoes of the Archangel

Michael (for whom the church is named) and of the Virgin Mary and St. Paul. In the twelfth century the church added *in pescheria* to its name when the portico became the site of the central fish market. Later, in the sixteenth century, the appellation was reinforced when the Confraternity of Fishmongers adopted this church as their place of worship.

The plaque in the brickwork by the entrance to the church is a Latin ordinance prescribing that the head and the body up to the first fin of any fish larger than the plaque were to be delivered to the city magistrates. These fish were supposedly used in the soup kitchens of the poor. It was a form of tax, which, the population complained, took the best part of the fish, and was repealed only after the French Revolution in 1798.

Old engravings depict the portico and church surrounded by large marble slabs that were rented by local nobles to the fishmongers so that they could cut and clean their fish. Until 1880, when the fish market was moved, this spot was one of Rome's picturesque attractions, frequently depicted by its community of foreign artists and often described in visitors' journals.

One of the most dramatic moments for the Church of S. Angelo in Pescheria was in 1347 when Cola di Rienzo gathered his forces to conquer the city. Born in 1313 just a few blocks from here, Cola di Rienzo grew up the son of a poor family during a time when Rome had been abandoned by the pope and had become a private battleground for the nobility. In keeping with the spirit of the times, Cola studied the classics and history and took great pride in his heritage. He yearned for the lost glory of Rome and after his brother was killed in a factional fight, Cola di Rienzo decided to conquer Rome. With the help of Pope Clement VI he impressed people with his charisma and his grandiose schemes for the reestablishment of a Rome free from the petty feuds of the barons. He insisted that the pope return to St. Peter's, that the Eternal City be once again the world's metropolis, and, above all, that the people be sovereign subjects only to God. What is so remarkable about Cola di Rienzo is that he not only dreamed of a revolution, but he achieved it—if only for a short time, from May to December of 1347. He is recognized today as the first of the Italian liberators.

This was also the site of further humiliation of the Jews of Rome beginning in the sixteenth century. Pope Gregory XIII, with the encouragement of a converted Jew, issued a decree forcing the Ghetto population to hear Christian sermons. For over two hundred years S. Angelo in Pescheria was filled every Saturday with Jews desperately dreaming the time away while being lectured about the true faith.

Via Portico d'Ottavia curves to the left as you face the ruin. Across the street, where the curve forms an angle, is the entrance to **Limentani's**, one of the better-known wholesale shops in the old Ghetto specializing in kitchen equipment and tableware. The restaurant **Da Giggeto**, on the right, is a neighborhood landmark, serving Roman Jewish cuisine. When the weather allows, tables are set up next to the granite columns jutting from the sidewalk. Here you can gaze at the Portico d'Ottavia and the pockmarked travertine arcades of the Teatro di Marcello and contemplate the grandeurs of ancient Rome over a plate of pasta. In 1982 the city dug up the Via del Portico d'Ottavia to put in new pipes for methane gas and, as if to confirm our knowledge of what existed here over the last two thousand years, numerous fragments of marble were uncovered, including a marble slab from the old fish market.

Next to the portico at **no. 25** is a medieval house, the only one of its era remaining in the old Ghetto. It is undoubtedly the base of a thirteenth-century tower and the ground-floor shop entrance is framed with ancient fragments of ornate molding. Further up the street at **no. 13** on the right is a house with an evocative court-yard. It was built by the Fabi family who briefly lived in the ruins of the Teatro Marcello and whose family tomb is in the church of S. Nicolà in Carcere, next to the ancient theater. The next house at **no. 8–11** is a solid but graceful structure from the fifteenth century whose top floor was once an open loggia.

The Via del Portico d'Ottavia is the heart of the present-day Jewish neighborhood. Most of the shops are owned by Jews. **Bar Toto** down the street is the community meeting spot, and it is along this street that the early evening *passeggiata* takes place. Nowhere else in Rome is the traditional evening's walk taken so seriously. Every generation finds its group, and the crowds spill onto the middle of the street arm-in-arm, blocking traffic from about 5:00 P.M.–7:00 P.M. every evening.

Only the buildings on the right side of the street and along the Via della Reginella remain from the days of the Ghetto. Then the Via del Portico d'Ottavia was a mere lane and an entire block of houses and yet another street stood between these medieval and Renaissance houses and what is now the other side of the street. The final extension of the Ghetto was up the **Via della Reginella**. When Pope Leo XII effected this in conjunction with the abolition of liquor in bars and restaurants, it inspired a clever *pasquinade*, or lampoon:

> *Fior de mu ghetto*
> *Papa Leone e diventato matto*
> *Ha chiuso le osterie e allargato il ghetto.*

> Lilies of the valley
> Pope Leo has gone mad
> He has closed the bars and enlarged the ghetto.

Between Via di S. Ambrogio and Via della Reginella, and parallel to the line of houses, once stood the Portico di Filippo, built by Augustus's brother-in-law Filippo. This, like the Portico d'Ottavia, was ornately decorated in marble, was filled with important sculptures, and surrounded a temple.

*Fragments of antique sculpture on Lorenzo
Manili's house*

Continue to the end of Via del Portico d'Ottavia to
where it joins the Piazza S. Maria del Pianto, where we
began our walk. On our right is a house that dates back
to 1497 and is known as the **Casa di Lorenzo Manili.**
The house consists of three sections, one with windows
from the 1600s, another with arched windows, and the
third with the remains of a crossed window. Lorenzo
Manili covered the façade of his house with antique fragments taken from the Appia Antica. The fine sculpture of
a lion attacking a doe, the relief of a dog and a rabbit,
and the four busts from funerary stelae (near Bar Toto)
are particularly impressive. Built by a man of modest fortune, this house is a wonderful, rare example of the humanistic and archeological fervor that seized Rome at the
end of the fifteenth century. After three centuries during
which Rome was reduced to a shabby battlefield, the late
fifteenth century brought a period of relative tranquility
and affluence. Romans turned with pride to their classical
heritage and this renewed spirit manifested itself in all
aspects of the city's cultural life.

Lorenzo Manili seems to have taken great pride in his
house. Not satisfied with an inscription bearing his name

five times in Latin, he had it repeated as many times in Greek. The inscription also bears the date of the founding of Rome and the year, according to the ancient Roman calendar, of the building's dedication, 2221. Around the corner on the frieze of the window overlooking Piazza Costaguti, a descendant of Lorenzo Manili carved the words HAVE ROMA to salute the reascendence of his city to its former splendor, "Urbe Roma in Pristinium formam rinascente . . . HAVE ROMA."

The small, rounded iron construction attached to the building next to the Casa Manili on Piazza Costaguti is known as the **Tempietto del Carmello**, built in 1759. This was the only chapel within the confines of the Ghetto walls and here too Jews came to listen to the Christian sermons required of them by Pope Gregory XIII.

This ends our walk through the old Jewish Ghetto. If you are interested in pastries you might try the shop on the corner of Lorenzo Manili's house. This Jewish bakery is famous throughout Rome for its ricotta pies and turnovers. A pleasant light lunch with a selection of wine by the glass is available at the wine store half a block down Via S. Maria del Pianto, at no. 9–11. Bar Toto, of course, has sandwiches, mineral water, coffee, liquor, and lots of gossip.

Restaurants, Hotels, and Shops

Restaurants

It is hard to find a bad meal in Rome, so don't hesitate to walk into any of the many *trattorie*, *ristoranti*, or *osterie* that may catch your eye. Below is a short list of some of my favorites. All restaurants close one day a week so it is wise to call beforehand to make sure they are open. Many restaurants also close for the month of August.

Elegant and More Expensive
(Reservations a must, $75 to $100 per
person for three courses including wine)

Alberto Chiarla, 40 Piazza San Cosimato, tel. 581-6068. At this elegant seafood restaurant, which serves only dinner, you will be greeted with a glass of sparkling wine. The menu includes fresh oysters, lobster, an assortment of grilled fish, and, of course, pasta. There is no meat dish. (In Trastevere, not far from Walk 4.)

Carmelo alla Rosetta, 9 Via della Rosetta, tel. 656-1002. This restaurant, in a more casual setting, claims to have the freshest fish in town; they, too, serve only fish. Try the risotto made of squid in its own ink. (Near the Pantheon.)

Coriolano, 14 Via Ancona, tel. 855-1122. You will dine in an atmosphere more reminiscent of Switzerland than of Italy, but the food is Italian at its best. They also have one of the largest wine cellars in Rome. (A cab ride away in the northern section of town.)

Girarrosto Toscano, 29 Via Campania, tel. 482-1899. Highlighting Florentine cuisine, this is the best place in town for grilled steak. (Near the Via Veneto.)

Papa Giovanni, 4 Via dei Sediari, tel. 686-5308. Here they pride themselves on nouvelle Italian cuisine, and their huge cellar is stocked with the best of Italian and French wines. (Near the Piazza Navona.)

Patrizia e Roberto del Pianeta Terra, 95 Via Arco del Monte, tel. 686-9893. One of the most talked-about restaurants of the *cucina nuova*. Located in an old palazzo with limited seating, dinner only. (Near the Campo dei Fiori.)

Piperno, 9 Piazza Monte Cenci, tel. 654-6029. The best of the Roman Jewish restaurants, it specializes in such dishes as fried artichokes, fried mozzarella, and salt cod. It is also pleasantly located and some of its back rooms are the most elegant in town; be sure to ask for a table in the rear if you are not dining on the piazza. (In the old Jewish Ghetto.)

Taverna Giulia, 23 Vicolo dell'Oro, tel. 686-9768. This is a Genovese restaurant with the one of the best pestos in town. They also have that tasty, creamy walnut sauce used to coat oversized tortellini. (At the beginning of Via Giulia.)

Vecchia Roma, 18 Piazza Campitelli, tel. 686-4604. Many of my friends consider this the best restaurant in Rome; certainly you will enjoy a magnificent meal in a pleasant setting. (At the foot of the Capitoline Hill.)

Moderate
($50 per person for three courses
including house wine)

Buca di Ripetta, 36 Via di Ripetta, tel. 361-9391. Run by a family, this is the kind of restaurant in which you would feel happy to eat all of your meals. Highly recommended, cash only. (Near the Piazza del Popolo.)

La Campana, 18 Vicolo della Campana, tel. 687-5273. This is not the prettiest restaurant in Rome, but it is recognized for its good food at good prices. (Near the beginning of Walk 3.)

Colline Emiliane, 22 Via Avignonesi, tel. 481-7538. Specializing in the cuisine of Emilia Romagna, the chef prepares some of the best tortellini and boiled meats I have ever had. You come here not for the decor, but for the excellent food in a friendly atmosphere. (Near Piazza Barberini.)

Il Drappo, 9 Vicolo del Malpasso, tel. 687-7365. Sardinian food is served in a warm intimate setting with draped ceilings and flowers on every table. You will enjoy every bite of your meal, which is carefully prepared by the brother and sister who run this establishment. (Near Via Giulia.)

Da Giggeto, 21A Via del Portico d'Ottavia, tel. 686-1105. This restaurant serves *trattoria*-style Roman and Roman-Jewish cuisine. During the summer you can sit out and eat in the shadow of the Portico d'Ottavia and in view of the Theater of Marcellus. (In the old Jewish Ghetto.)

Nino, 11 Via Borgognona, tel. 679-5676. A favorite lunch place near the Spanish Steps, this one is also good for a quiet dinner.

La Tana di Noantri, 1–3 Via della Paglia, tel. 580-6404. Another favorite restaurant in Trastevere, this is always crowded with Romans as well as tourists. The food here is good and reasonably priced. (In the heart of Trastevere.)

Restaurants, Hotels, and Shops

Relatively Inexpensive
(An average of $35 per person)

La Carbonara, 23 Piazza Campo dei Fiori, tel. 686-4783. You can sit out on the piazza in nice weather. (Walk 1.)

La Gensola, 15 Piazza della Gensola. Good Sicilian pasta, closed Sundays. (In Trastevere, Walk 4.)

Grappolo d'Oro, 138 Via dei Baullari, tel. 686-4118. (Near the Campo dei Fiori.)

Hostaria dell'Aquila, 58 Via Natale Grande. Specializing in Roman cuisine. (In Trastevere.)

Da Pancrazio, 92-94 Piazza del Biscone, tel. 686-1246. In the ruins of the Theater of Pompey. (Near the Campo dei Fiori.)

La Pollarolo, 24-25 Piazza Pollarola, tel. 654-1654. (Near the Campo dei Fiori.)

Ristorante Pierluigi, 144 Piazza de' Ricci, tel. 686-1302. A good place to sit outside. (Near the Campo dei Fiori.)

Trattoria Armando, 31 Salita dei Cescenzi, tel. 654-3034. (Near the Pantheon.)

Cheap (Less than $35 per person)

Alimentari, 28 Via del Governo Vecchio. They make their own *pizza bianca* here, and you can select the filling for a very inexpensive but delicious sandwich. Take it to the Piazza Navona and get a *tartufo* from Tre Scalini for dessert. (Walk 3.)

Buffet Savoia, 11 Via Ludovisi. A step up in elegance from ordinary *tavola calde*. (Near Via Veneto.)

Fiaschetteria Beltrame, 39 Via della Croce (no phone). At this family-run establishment you sit wherever there is a seat, sharing your table with shopkeepers at lunch and with an artistic crowd at dinner. (Near the Spanish Steps.)

Osteria, 15 Via G. Bovio. (Somewhat near the Vatican.)

Osteria, 30 Via di Santa Maria de' Calderari. (In the old Jewish Ghetto, Walk 5.)

Paneformaggio, 7 Via de Ripetta. A bread and cheese store that doubles as a snack bar for lunch. (Near the Spanish Steps.)

Pizza da Loreto, 296 Corso Vittorio Emanuele. (Closed Mondays, near the Campo dei Fiori.)

Pizzeria da Baffetto, 114 Via del Governo Vecchio. (Near the Piazza Navona, Walk 3.)

Pizzeria ai Balestrari, 42 Via dei Balestrari. (Closed Mondays, Walk 1.)

Pizzeria La Faschetta, 234 Via di S. Francesco a Ripa. (Trastevere, near Walk 4.)

Pizzeria Er Grottino, 32A Campo dei Fiori. (Closed Thursdays, Walk 1.)

Pizzeria-Trattoria Galleria Sciarra, 76 Piazza dell'Oratorio. (Closed Mondays, near the Spanish Steps.)

Trattoria-Pizzeria da Mario, 12 Via della Chiesa Nuova. (Closed Wednesdays, near the Campo dei Fiori.)

Wine Bars

Antica Enoteca Capranica, 100 Piazza Capranica. (Near the Pantheon.)

La Bottega del Vino, 9–11 Via S. Maria del Pianto. (Light lunch in the old Jewish Ghetto.)

Bucione, 19 Via di Ripetta. (Near the Piazza del Popolo.)

Enoteca Cul de Sac, 73 Piazza Pasquino. (Near Piazza Navona, light lunch and dinner.)

Enoteca al Parlimento, 15 Via dei Prefetti. (Near the Pantheon.)

Cafés and Ice Cream Parlors

Alemagna, 181 Via del Corso. This is one of the biggest bars in Rome with a busy hot and cold lunch counter. (Near the Spanish Steps.)

Alfredo Pica, Via della Seggiola. Go into this small bar for some of the best ice cream in town and they also have a *tavola fredda* for lunch. (Located off Via Arenula, across from the Ministry of Justice, just a few blocks from Walk 5 and the old Jewish Ghetto.)

Babington's Tea Room, 23 Piazza di Spagna. If you are in the mood for a cup of tea and scones this is the place, but be prepared to pay an exorbitant price. (At the foot of the Spanish Steps.)

Bar San Filippo, 8 Via San Filippo. Out of the way in the northern Parioli section of town, but if you are an ice cream fanatic you will have to give it a try. (North of Piazza Hungaria.)

Caffè Greco, 86 Via Condotti. In the nineteenth century this café attracted a crowd of writers, musicians, and artists; today it attracts a very fashionable set. Walk in if only to see its 1860s environment. (Near the Spanish Steps.)

Europeo, 33 Piazza San Lorenzo in Lucina. Visit this bar for ice cream and Sicilian pastries. (Near the Spanish Steps.)

Giolitti, 40 Via Uffici del Vicario. A visit here is a must; it is the most important ice cream parlor in Rome. You can have anything from a variety of chocolate flavors to watermelon with bits of chocolate made to resemble seeds. (Between the Via del Corso and the Pantheon.)

Mella Stregata, 1 Piazza Pasquale Paoli. This bar has the best *cornetti*—crescent-shaped breakfast rolls—in town. For me it was worth a long walk every morning. It is on your way to the Vatican. Their ice cream also has a good reputation. (Near Ponte Vittorio Emanuele II.)

Rosati, 4 Piazza del Popolo. This fashionable café has been a favorite of Roman society for several generations.

Its liberty-style decor competes with a view of one of the finest baroque piazzas in Rome. (On the Piazza del Popolo).

Tre Scalini, 30 Piazza Navona. Its view of the Bernini fountain and the *tartufo*—a ball of chocolate ice cream with bits of chocolate and a cherry in the middle—makes this a special hangout for both Romans and tourists. (On the Piazza Navona.)

For the Best Cup of Coffee

Sant'Eustachio, 82 Piazza Sant'Eustachio. Here you will find the creamiest cappuccino in town. Their *granita di caffè*, chips of iced coffee, is also superb. (Near the Pantheon.)

La Tazza d'Oro, 84 Via degli Orfani. This bar serves only coffee, and they take their product very seriously. Supposedly they are located here in order to make their brew with the Acqua Virgine, considered the best of Roman waters. They also have a great *granita di caffè* during the summer months. (Near the Pantheon.)

Hotels

Cheap (Under $100)

The cheapest accommodations in Rome are as a paying guest at a convent where you will usually find a room with a bath at the end of the hall. There may also be a curfew restriction and a meal included in the daily rate. Listed below are three such convents where English is spoken:

Fraterna Domus, 62 Via di Monte Brianzo, tel. 656-2727. (Near the Piazza Navona.)

Santa Brigida, 96 Piazza Farnese, tel. 686-5263. (Near the Campo dei Fiori.)

Sisters of the Immaculate Conception, 113 Via Sistina, tel. 474-5324. (Near the Spanish Steps.)

Another cheap category is small hotels that used to be *pensiones*. While the rooms are very simple, they are clean, centrally located, and you can choose to have one with or without a bath.

Albergo della Lunetta, 68 Piazza del Paradiso, tel. 686-1080. (Near the Campo dei Fiori.)

Casa Kolbe, 44 Via di S. Teodoro, tel. 679-8866. (Quiet, with a small garden at the foot of the Palatine Hill.)

Hotel Arenula, 47 Via S. Maria dei Calderari, tel. 688-06251. (Near the old Jewish Ghetto.)

Hotel Piccolo, 32 Via dei Chiavari, tel. 689-2330. (Near the Campo dei Fiori.)

Inexpensive (Around $100)

Below are four small hotels popular for their location and their relatively inexpensive rooms. You must book early to find a room.

Hotel Cisterna, 7 Via della Cisterna, tel. 581-7212. (In the heart of Trastevere.)

Hotel Margutta, 34 Via Laurina, tel. 679-8440. (Near the Piazza del Popolo, view from the top floor.)

Hotel Portoghesi, 1 Via dei Portoghesi, tel. 686-4231. (Near the Piazza Navona.)

Pension Suisse, 56 Via Gregoriana, tel. 678-3649. (At the top of the Spanish Steps.)

Moderate (Around $150)

Within this category you are guaranteed a private bath and a comfortable room.

Carriage, 36 Via delle Carroze, tel. 679-3152. (Newly renovated thirty-room establishment near the Spanish Steps.)

Condotti, 37 Via Mario de' Fiori, tel. 679-4661. (Near the Spanish Steps, owned by a family that runs one of Rome's most luxurious hotels.)

Gregoriana, 18 Via Gregoriana, tel. 679-4269. (A nineteen-room hotel at the top of the Spanish Steps.)

Hotel Due Torri, 23 Vicolo del Leonetto, tel. 687-6983. (On a narrow, quiet street near the Piazza Navona.)

Hotel Teatro di Pompeo, 8 Largo di Pollarola, tel. 687-2812. (This small hotel is my choice in Rome, near the Campo dei Fiori.)

Pensione Scalinata di Spagna, 17 Piazza Trinità dei Monti, tel. 679-3006. (At the top of the Spanish Steps, fourteen rooms with a great view and a devoted clientele.)

Expensive ($200 to $350)

Albergo del Sole, 63 Piazza della Rotonda, tel. 678-0441. (Overlooking the piazza in front of the Pantheon, one of the oldest hotels in the city but recently renovated, can be noisy.)

Forum, 28-31 Via Tor de' Conti, tel. 679-2446. (In a medieval section of the city near the Roman Forum and the Colosseum.)

D'Inghilterra, 14 Via Bocca di Leone, tel. 672-161. (An elegant small establishment near the Spanish Steps.)

Hotel Raphael, 2 Largo Febo, tel. 683-8881. (With a dining room on a quiet square next to the Piazza Navona.)

Hotel Santa Chiara, 21 Via Santa Chiara, tel. 654-1700. (Recently modernized on a quiet street near the Pantheon.)

De La Ville-InterContinental, 67-71 Via Sistina, tel.

67-331. (Deluxe accommodations at first-class prices, next to the Hassler at the top of the Spanish Steps.)

Deluxe (Over $400)

Crowne Plaza Minerva, 69 Piazza della Minerva, tel. 684-1888. (In a newly renovated eighteenth-century palazzo near the Pantheon.)

Hassler-Villa Medici, 6 Piazza Trinità dei Monti, tel. 678-2651. (Swiss-owned and operated, this hotel at the top of the Spanish Steps has long had the reputation as Rome's best.)

Apartment Hotels

Rome also offers apartment hotel accommodations with kitchens called *residenzas* for visitors planning longer stays of at least two weeks.

Palazzo al Velabro, 16 Via del Velabro, tel. 679-2985. (At the foot of the Capitoline and Palatine Hills.)

The Residenza di Ripetta, 231 Via di Ripetta, tel. 678-141. (Centrally located near the Piazza del Popolo.)

Shops

Leather Goods and Shoes

Alexia, 76 Via Nazionale. Moderately priced leather bags and accessories.

Amadeo Perrone, 92 Piazza di Spagna. Specializes in gloves.

Bottega Veneta, 16 Salita San Sebastianello. Expensive purses and accessories.

Fendi, 36 Via Borgognona. Expensive leather bags

and suitcases all marked with the *F* trademark of the Fendi sisters.

Ferragamo, 66 Via Condotti, for men's shoes, and 73-74 Via Condotti, for women's shoes.

Fratelli Rosetti, 51A Via Borgognona. Stylish shoes for men and women.

Gucci, 8 Via Condotti. The main shop in Rome for this respected designer's products.

Lily of Florence, 38C Via Lombardia. Specializes in narrow, American-size shoes for men and women.

Raphael Salto, 34 Piazza di Spagna. Men's, women's, and children's shoes.

Sac Joli, 154 Via del Corso. Purses and an assortment of belts.

Santini e Dominici, 120 Via Frattina. Stylish shoes for the younger set.

Skin, 41 Via Crispi. The best in town for leather jackets, coats, and suits.

Tanino Crisci, 4 Via Borgognona. Probably the best-quality handmade shoes in Rome.

Tradate, 176 Via del Corso. Shoes and boots for men and women.

Men's Clothing

Battistoni, 61A Via Condotti. An expensive and classic men's clothing store in the courtyard of a Renaissance palazzo.

Borsalino, 157B Via IV Novembre. The best hats—possibly in the world.,

Carlo Palazzi, 75 Via Borgognona. An ancient Roman palazzo turned into one of the most elegant men's shops in town.

Emporio Armani, 140 Via del Babuino. Needless to say, carries clothes by the designer of the same name.

Roxy, 110 Via Veneto. Silk ties at bargain prices.

Testa, 13 Via Borgognona. A reasonably priced shop especially noted for its suits and pants.

Women's Clothing

Elsy, 106 Via del Corso. Good buys in ready-to-wear clothing.

Max Mara, 28 Via Frattina. One of the best moderately priced but stylish shops.

Missoni, 38B Via Borgognona. The best knitwear in Italy.

Valentino's Boutique, 15 Via Bocca di Leone. This famous designer's ready-to-wear shop.

Vanita, 70 Via Frattina. The most luxurious undergarments and nightwear.

Gifts and Household Items

Bises, 93 Via del Gesù. An old established name in retail fabric.

Bulgari, 10 Via Condotti. One of the world's greatest jewelers.

Caesare, 1 Via Barberini. Linens, towels, and lingerie, including custom-made terrycloth robes.

Cereria Pisoni, 127 Corso Vittorio Emanuele. Candlemakers to the pope since 1803.

Fornari, 71 Via Frattina. This is Rome's store for contemporary Italian silver.

Frette, 10 Piazza di Spagna. The most elegant and expensive bed linen in the world.

Laboratorio Scatoli, 27 Via della Stelletta. Decorative boxes in all sizes and to order.

Myricae, 36 Via Frattina. Latin for "little gracious things," ceramics from around the world.

Pineider, 68 Via Due Marcelli. Beautiful stationery and desk accessories.

Richard Ginori, 87 Via Condotti. The best porcelain, china, glass, and crystal.

Vertecchi, 38 and 70 Via della Croce. Beautiful wrapping paper, desk accessories, and artist's supplies.

Drawings and Prints

Galleria Carlo Virgilio, 9 Via della Lupa. Nineteenth- and twentieth-century drawings and watercolors.

Giuseppe Tanca, 10–12 Via Salita de Crescenzi. High quality antique drawings.

Roberto Boccalini, 61 Via del Banco di Santo Spirito. Inexpensive to expensive engravings and lithographs.

Books

The Economy Book and Video Center, 136 Via Torino. A large selection of new and used paperbacks. It also rents English-language videos.

The Lion Bookshop, 181 Via del Babuino. The largest English-language bookstore, carrying a selection of books on all subjects, including many recent publications.

Postcards

69A Piazza della Rotonda. This minuscule shop (across from the Pantheon) has the biggest and best selection of new and old postcards and trinkets.

Index

Academy of Music, 228
Accademia dei Lincei, 168
Accademia di S. Cecilia, 14
Accommodations, 18–19
    see also Hotels
Ackerman, James, 102
Acqua Alessandrina, 120–21
Acqua Felice, 121, 145
Acqua minerale, 25–26
Acqua Paola, 51, 98, 173, 185
Acqua Virgine, 98, 276
Acquis, De (Fontinius), 50
Adalbert, Saint, 210
Aeneas, 35
Agrippa, Marcus Vipsanius, 88
Aida (Verdi), 13
Airports, 19–20
Albani, Francesco, 147
Albergo della Catena, 132, 133
Albergo della Lunetta, 277
Albergo dell'Orso, 161–64
Albergo del Sole, 69–70, 278
Alberti, Cherubino, 169
Alberto Chiarla, 270
Albertoni family, 136, 140

Aleagar, 14
Alemagna, 275
Alexander VI, Pope, 79–80, 83,
    100–101, 206
Alexander VII, Pope, 135, 177–
    78, 188
Alexander the Great, 261
Alexia, 279
Alfredo Pica, 275
Alimentari, 273
Almachius, 228
Amadeo Perrone, 279
American Embassy, 31
American Express, 15, 29
American Hospital, 31
Ameyden, Teodoro, 181–83
Anacleto II, Pope, 259
Anav, Nathan ben Yeihiel, 236
Anchises, 35
Ancus Martius, king of Rome,
    35, 214
Andrea del Sarto (Andrea
    d'Agnolo), 62
Aniceto, Saint, 165
Anicia, Flavio, 159

Index

Anici family, 218–20
Antica Enoteca Capranica, 274
Antiquarian book and print
    shops, 157
Antique Dealers League, 174
Antique shops, 30, 82, 95, 160,
    174
Antonio del Grande, 92
Apartment hotels, 279
Appian Line, 15
Aqueducts, 49–50, 51, 88,
    120–21, 154, 205, 213
D'Aragona, Tulia, 167
Ara Pacis, 37
Architectural terms, glossary of,
    33–35
Architecture, books on, 9–10
Arch of Janus Quadrifons, 112–
    13, 114
Arch of Septimius Severus (Arco
    dei Argentari), 38, 112
Arch of Titus, 246
Arcioni, Battista, 65
Arco dei Argentari (Arch of
    Septimius Severus), 38,
    112
Arco dei Cappellari, 81
Arco della Pace, 176
Arco dei Tolomei, 219, 220
Aretino, Pietro, 166–67
Armellini, 42
Arnolfo di Cambio, 231
Arpacata, 68
Art, books on, 9–10
Auditorio di Via della
    Conciliazione, 14
Augustine Order, 156
Augustus, Roman emperor, 37,
    68, 109, 129, 154, 208,
    261
Aurelian Walls, 38, 113
Aurelius, Marcus, 38
Azienda Tramvie Autobus
    Comunali (A.T.A.C.), 21,
    22

Babington's Tea Room, 275
Baglioni, Giovanni, 224

Balbus, Cornilius, 140
Ballet, 13
Banco di Santo Spirito, 29
Bandello, Matteo, 142
Banking, 29
Bars, 57, 140
Bar San Filippo, 275
Bartholomew, Saint, 210
Bartolo di Taddeo, 224
Bar Toto, 266, 268
Basilica Julia, 37
Basilica of Neptune, 154
Basilica Thermae, 38
Baths, public, 154, 161, 216
Baths of Caracalla, 13, 38, 100,
    103
Batrachos, 261
Battistoni, 280
Beaches, 14–15
Belisarius, 148–49, 213
Belli, Giuseppe Gioacchino, 96,
    214
Bembo, Pietro, 165–66, 169
Benedict, Saint, 217
Benedict XII, Pope, 198
Benedict XIII, Pope, 63, 92
Benedict XIV, Pope, 155, 191–
    92
Bernini, Gian, 17, 86, 94, 96,
    145, 196
Biblioteca Angelica, 156
Bigio, Nanni di Baccio, 86,
    146
Bises, 281
Black Virgin, 83
Blado, Antonio, 76
La Bocca della Verità, xvi, 98,
    117–18
Bona, Mauricio, 196
Bonaparte, Luciano, Cardinal,
    186
Boncompagni family, 195
Boniface VIII, Pope, 55
Books:
    on Rome, 8–10
    shopping for, 157, 282
Borgia, Cesare, 79, 165
Borgia, Lucrezia, 79

Borromini, Francesco, 57, 59–
60, 61–62, 96, 188
Borsalino, 280
Bottega Veneta, 279
La Bottega del Vino, 274
Il Botteghino, 13
Boundary stones, 90, 91
Bramante, Donato, 77, 92, 94,
175, 192–93
Breakfast, 23–24
Bregno, Andrea, 222
Breughel, 62
Bridges, 50–53, 122–23, 129,
143, 204, 205, 212–14,
257
sacrifical tradition and, 52–53
Brill, Paul, 230
Brosses, President de, 196
Bruno, Giordano, 74–76
Brutus, Decimus, 112
Brutus, Marcus (1st century
B.C.), 68
Brutus, Marcus (3rd century
B.C.), 112
Buca di Ripetta, 272
Buccabelli family, 133
Bucione, 274
Bufalini, 76, 161
Buffet Savoia, 273
Bulgari, 281
Burckhardt, Jakob, 70, 175
Burial chambers, 97
Burnell, F. S., 148
Buses, 20, 21, 22
Byron, George Gordon, Lord,
62, 126
Byzantine Empire, 38, 40, 113,
118

Caesar, Julius, Roman emperor,
36–37, 62–63, 68, 112,
208, 220, 246
Caesare, 281
Caetani, Ersilia Lovatelli, 135–
36
Cafés, 275, 276
Caffè Greco, 275

Calcarario, 146–47
Calipius, Saint, 53
Calixtus III, Pope, 83
Camilla of Pisa, 167
La Campana, 272
Campidoglio, 38, 125, 133, 183
Campo dei Fiori, 3, 70–76, 89,
98, 162, 184
history of, 73–76
inscription at, 65–66
market at, 67, 70–73
name of, 73
neighborhood of, 45–105
Campus Martius, 37, 49–50, 78,
88, 103, 120, 154, 155,
164, 206, 207
Cancellieri, Francesco, 98–99
Canossa, Matilda, 208
Capalti, 170
Capitoline Hill, 121, 204
foot of, 2–4, 74, 107–49
Capitoline Museums, 16, 52,
132
Capitoline Picture Gallery, 16
Capitoline Steps, 140
Capizucchi family, 137
Capo di Ferro, Cardinal
Girolamo, 60, 61, 63
Cappuccino, 24
Carafa, Oliviero, Cardinal, 175,
197
Carapecchia, Romano, 208
Caravaggio (Michelangelo
Merisi), 17
La Carbonara, 273
Carcere Mamertinus, 36
Carcere Nuovo, 92
Carcopino, Jerome, 104
Carducci, Bartolommeo, 136
Carlo Palazzi, 280
Carmelite Order, 84–86
Carmelo alla Rosetta, 271
Caro, Annibale, 79
Carracci, Annibale, 104, 211
Carriage, 277
Casa dei Crescenzi, 122, 123
Casa dei Fiammetta, 165–66,
167

Index

Casa Kolbe, 277

Casalinga, 237

Casa di Lorenzo Manili, 267–68

Casa Mattei, 200, 216–17

Casa dei Ponzani, 233

Casa dei Vailati, 258, 260

Casoni, Felice Antonio, 185

Castel S. Angelo, 38

Castiglione, Baldassare, 165–66, 169

Catholic Church, 3, 4, 47–48, 55, 77–78, 113–14, 133, 154, 204
  see also Papal Court; Vatican

Cato the Censor, 36

Cattanei, Vanozza, 79–80

Cavallini, Pietro, 5, 116, 231–32

Cecilia, Saint, 227–29, 230

Cellini, Benvenuto, 88–89, 90, 93, 100, 183–84

Cenci family, 252–53

Cereria Pisoni, 281

Cesi, Cardinal, 188

Cesi, Prince Frederigo, 168

Chamber music, 14

Charlemagne, 40, 41, 220

Chiavica de Santa Lucia, 88–89

Chigi, Agostino, 166, 176, 177, 189

Chigi family, 82

"Childe Harold's Pilgrimage" (Byron), 62, 126

Christina, queen of Sweden, 104, 198

Christmas fair, 14

Church of the Agonizzanti, 196

Church of S. Agnese, 229

Church of S. Agostino, 166

Church of S. Andrea della Valle, 134

Church of S. Angelo in Pescheria, 263–65

Church of S. Antonio dei Portoghesi, 157

Church of S. Bagio della Fossa, 179–81

Church of S. Bartholomew, 210–11

Church of S. Benedetto in Piscinula, 217–18

Church of S. Caterina dei Funari, 142

Church of S. Caterina da Siena, 95

Church of S. Cecilia, 5, 221, 226, 227–33

Church of S. Eligio degli Orefici, 94

Church of S. Filippo Neri, 90–91

Church of S. Giorgio della Divina Pietà, 259

Church of S. Giorgio in Velabro, 112, 114–16

Church of S. Giovanni in Ayno, 86, 87

Church of S. Giovanni Calibata, 208–10

Church of S. Ivo, 96

Church of S. Lorenzo in Damaso, 65, 79

Church of S. Lorenzo Fuori le Mura, 261

Church of S. Marcello, 57

Church of S. Maria dell'Anima, 178–80

Church of S. Maria Campitelli, 134–35

Church of S. Maria in Cappella, 234–35

Church of S. Maria della Concezione, 97

Church of S. Maria in Cosmedin, 117, 118–20, 121

Church of S. Maria della Luce, 239

Church of S. Maria in Monserrato, 83–84

Church of S. Maria dell'Orazione e Morte, 96–97

Church of S. Maria dell'Orto, 222–24

Church of S. Maria della Pace,
    175–76, 177–78
Church of S. Maria della
    Quercia, 63–64
Church of S. Maria della Torre,
    233–34
Church of S. Maria della
    Vittoria, 84–86
Church of S. Nicolà in Carcere,
    125–27, 266
Church of S. Pietro in Montorio,
    253
Church of S. Rita da Cascia,
    133
Church of SS. Giovanni e
    Petronio dei Bolognesi,
    99
Church of S. Spirito, 93–94
Church of SS. Simone e Guida,
    183, 186
Church of SS. Trinità dei
    Pellegrini, 56–57
Church of S. Tommaso, 253
Church visits, 8, 12, 18
Ciampino, 20
Cibo, Franceschetto, 77
Cicala, Meliaduce, 221, 222
Cicero, 37, 246
Cincinnatus, 214
Circus Maximus, 36
Circus of Flaminius, 3, 252,
    255
Cisterna, Eugenio, 95
CIT, 15
Clark, Eleanor, 3
Claudius, Appius, Roman
    emperor, 125–27
Clement V, Pope, 41
Clement VI, Pope, 264
Clement VII, Pope, 88,
    205–6
Clement VIII, Pope, 229, 253
Clement XI, Pope, 121
Clement IX, Pope, 247
Climate, 7–8
Cloaca Maxima, 36, 110, 117,
    118, 122
Cloaca di Ponte, 88

Coffee, 24
  best cup of, 276
Coghetti, 170
Colamatta, Luigi, 225
Collegio Ghislieri, 92–93
Colline Emiliane, 272
Colonna, Marcantonio, 131
Colonna family, 131, 184
Colosseum, 3, 38, 63, 111–12,
    129
Column of Marcus Aurelius, 38
Compagnia Italiana Autoservizi
    Turistici (C.I.A.T.), 21
Conca, Sabastiano, 230
Concerts, 14
Condotti, 278
Condulmer, Cardinal, 68
Confraternity of Butchers, 63,
    64, 65
Confraternity of S. Caterina da
    Siena, 83
Confraternity of S. Giovanni
    Battista dei Genovesi, 5,
    221–22
Constans II, Byzantine emperor,
    114
Constantine I, Roman emperor,
    38–39, 112, 113
Constantine's Arch, 38
Convent of the Tor de' Specchi,
    137–38
Coorte dei Vigili, 240
Copernicus, 74
Corcos, Salomon, 187
Coriolano, 271
Corsini Picture Gallery, 253
Corso Vittorio Emanuele II, 193
Cortegiana (Aretino), 167
Corte Savello, 81, 92
Cosmati School, 119–20
Cossa, Pietro, 191
Costanza, 69
Cotogni, Antonio, 222
Council of State, 60
Counter-Reformation, 56, 121,
    133, 189, 247
Courtesans, 70, 90, 161, 165–
    67

Index

Credit cards, 29
Crime, 32, 83
Crowne Plaza Minerva, 279
Crucifixion of the Hatmakers,
    81
Cultural Ministry, 133

Damascus I, Pope, 79
D'Annunzio, Gabriele, 136, 145
Dante Alighieri, 161, 184
D'Arpino, Cavaliere (Giuseppe
    Cesari), 147
Delicatessens, 156
Democratic Party of the Left, 140
Deodatus, Cosma, 120
Diaconiae, 114, 118
Dickens, Charles, 128, 130
Dinner, 23, 25–26
    see also Restaurants
Diocletian, Roman emperor,
    38
Divine Comedy (Dante), 184
Doctors, English–speaking, 31
Domenichino, Guercino, 147,
    170
Domitian, Roman emperor, 129,
    263
Domus Augustiana, 37
Doria Pamphili Gallery, 17
Drainage system, 88, 110, 117–
    18
Il Drappo, 272
Drawings, shopping for, 282

Easton, Adam, 230
Eating and drinking, 23–27,
    235
    best cup of coffee, 276
    cafés and ice cream parlors,
        275–76
    Campo dei Fiori market, 67,
        70–73
    wine bars, 274
    see also Restaurants
Economy Book and Video
    Center, 282
Edicole, 53–54, 80, 179–81,
    196, 216, 224

Electricity, 8
Eligio, Saint, 94
Elsy, 281
Emergencies, 31–32
Emporio Armani, 280
Enoteca Cul de Sac, 274
Enoteca al Parlimento, 274
Entertainment, 13–15
Esposizione Universale (EUR),
    43
Espresso, 24
D'Este, Ippolito, Cardinal, 186
Etruscans, 204, 214, 224
Eugene IV, Pope, 68
Eugénie, empress of France,
    186
EUR, 15, 21, 22
Europeo, 275
Eustachio, Saint (Placidus),
    155–56
Exchange rates, 29
Executions, 74–76, 117, 228,
    253
Exultation of the Cross, feast of,
    81

Fabi family, 265–66
Fabricius, L., 204
Fairs, 14
Falconieri, Orazio, 96
Falda, 188
Fappa, Giambattista, 181
Fappa, Marcantonio, 181
Farnese, Alessandro (later Pope
    Paul III), 100–102, 189,
    198
Farnese, Giulia, 100–101
Farnese, Pietro, 96
Farnese bathtubs, 100
Farnese family, 98, 100–102,
    104, 193
Farnesina, 97, 102
Faustulus, 110
Fendi, 279–80
Ferragamo, 280
Ferrante, king of Naples, 57
Fesch, Joseph, Cardinal, 96,
    160

Festivals, 14, 93, 129, 207
Fiammetta Michaelis, 165–66, 167
Fiaschetteria Beltrame, 273
Fioroni, 170
Fiumicino Airport, 19–20
Flaminius, Titus, 112
Flavian dynasty, 38
Foix de Montoya, Monsignor Pietro, 94
Foncelli, C., 176
Fontana, Carlo, 57, 133, 225
Fontana, Giovanni, 51
Fontana, Luigi, 86
Fontinius, 50
Food and drink, *see* Eating and drinking
Fornari, 281
Forteguerri, Cardinal, 230
Forum, *see* Roman Forum
Forum of Augustus, 37
Forum Boarium, 109, 110–12, 117, 118, 120, 121
Forum Olitorium, 109, 127
Forum of Trajan, 38
Fountains, 51–52, 53, 59, 60, 98, 120–21, 138, 144, 145–46, 172–73, 179, 185, 251
France, Anatole, 136
Francesci, Pietro Paolo, 89
Frangipane family, 113, 157, 159
Franz, Roesler, 17, 97, 241
Fratelli Rosetti, 280
Fraterna Domus, 276
Fredrick III, emperor of Austria, 90
Fregene, 15
French Cultural Center, 137
French Embassy, 103–5
Frescoed façades, 80, 195
Frette, 281
Friends of the Tiber, 207
Fuga, Ferdinando, 96, 225, 229

Gabrielli family, 186
Galileo, 168

Galleria Borghese, 16–17
Galleria Carlo Virgilio, 282
Galleria Spada, 17–18, 60, 62
Gambirasi, Donato, 179
Garibaldi, Giuseppe, 42, 56
Gay, Stefano Tachi, 257
La Gensola, 273
Gentileschi, Orazio, 176
Ghetto:
origin of word, 247
see also Jewish Ghetto
Ghibellines, 138
Ghiberti, Lorenzo, 231–32
"Ghost architect," 64
Gianicolo, 96
Giaquinto, Corrado, 224
Gibbs, John, 178
Gifts, shopping for, 281–82
Da Giggeto, 265, 272
Giolitti, 24, 275
Giovenale, Giovanni, 232
Girarrosto Toscano, 271
Giuseppe Tanca, 282
Gladiators, 68, 112
Glycon of Athens, 103
Gnoli, Domenico, 80
Goethe, Johann Wolfgang von, 3, 128, 130, 161, 188–89
Goths, 205
Gracchus, Gaius Sempronius, 224–25
Grappolo d'Oro, 273
La Grechetta, 70
Green Squadron, 78
Gregoriana, 278
Gregorovius, Ferdinand, 40–41, 97, 136, 204, 231, 245–46, 249, 250–51
Gregory I (Gregory the Great), Pope, 40, 113, 220
Gregory XI, Pope, 41, 206
Gregory XII, Pope, 143
Gregory XIII, Pope, 99, 187, 188, 223, 265, 268
Gucci, 280
Guelphs, 138

Del Guernico, 172
Guidetti, Guidetto, 142, 223

Hadrian, Roman emperor, 38, 155, 183
Hadrian I, Pope, 118, 119, 121
Hadrian IV, Pope, 197–98
Hadrian VI, Pope, 178–79
Hall of One Hundred Columns (Hectostylon), 68, 78
Hall of One Hundred Days, 78
Hare, Augustus, 56, 118, 214
Hassler–Villa Medici, 279
Hawthorne, Nathaniel, 157–58, 159
Hectostylon (Hall of One Hundred Columns), 68, 78
Heemskerck, Martin van, 193
Henry II, king of England, 211
Hilton Hotel, 15
History of Rome, 35–43
  books on, 9
Holy Roman Empire, 40, 42
Horatius, 213–14
Horse–drawn carriages, 23
Hospitals, English–speaking, 31
Hostaria dell'Aquila, 273
Hosteria dell'Antiquario, 173
Hotel Aldrovandi, 15
Hotel Arenula, 277
Hotel Cisterna, 277
Hotel Due Torri, 278
Hotel Margutta, 277
Hotel Piccolo, 277
Hotel Portoghesi, 277
Hotel Raphael, 278
Hotels, 18–19, 161–64, 276–79
  apartment, 279
  cheap, 276–77
  deluxe, 279
  expensive, 278–79
  inexpensive, 277
  making reservations in, 7, 11, 19
  moderate, 277–78
  oldest, 69–70
  tipping in, 27

Hotel Santa Chiara, 278
Hotel Teatro di Pompeo, 278
Household items, shopping for, 281–82

Ice cream, 24
Ice cream parlors, 275–76
Ignatius, Saint, 140, 142
Imperia, 166
D'Inghilterra, 278
Innocent I, Pope, 39
Innocent VI, Pope, 84
Innocent X, Pope, 81
Innocent XI, Pope, 225
Inquisition, 3, 74–76, 168, 256
Institute of Roman Studies, 189
International Center for the Study and Preservation of Cultural Property (ICCROM), 227
International Daily News, 13
International Herald Tribune, 13
International Horse Show, 14
Isabella de Luna, 142
Italian Government Travel Office, 7

James, Henry, 1, 117, 215–16
Jewelry, crime and, 32
Jewelry shops, 79
Jewish Ghetto, 5, 143, 243–68
  wall around, 247–48
Jewish Synagogue, 243, 250, 256–57, 259
John I, Pope, 134
John X, Pope, 252
John the Baptist, Saint, feast of, 14
John Paul II, Pope, 250
Josephus, Flavius, 261–63
Jubilee of 1300, 55
Jubilee of 1450, 50
Jubilee of 1475, 51
Jubilee of 1550, 56
Judas Maccabeus, 246

Julius II, Pope, 41, 83, 92, 131, 166, 177, 240
Julius III, Pope, 17, 60, 61, 63
Juvenal, 124

Laboratorio Scatoli, 281
Lafrery, 157
Lancellotti, Scipione, Cardinal, 170
Landini, Taddeo, 145
Lanfranco, Giovanni, 147
Lanza, Antonio, 221
Largo Moretta, 88–92
Lateran Council, 189
Lateran Treaty (1929), 43, 78, 170
Latterie, 240–41
Leather goods, shopping for, 279–80
Lees-Milne, James, 116, 118–19, 147
Leo I (Leo the Great), Pope, 39, 40
Leo III, Pope, 40
Leo X, Pope (formerly Giovanni de' Medici), 41, 68, 77, 95, 189
Leo XII, Pope, 266
Leonardo da Vinci, 160
Leonardo da Vinci airport, 19–20
Lepidus, M. Aemilius, 122, 213
Liceo Galileo, 92–93
Lily of Florence, 280
Limentani, 265
Lion Bookshop, 282
Listz, Franz, 136
Literature, set in Rome, 10
Lombards, 116
Longhi, Martino, the Elder, 56, 188
Ludovisi, Bernardino, 57
Lunch, 23, 26
    see also Restaurants
Lungotevere dei Cenci, 257, 259
Lysippus, 236, 261

Maderno, Carlo, 17, 84, 94, 143, 170
Maderno, Stefano, 176, 229, 231
Madonna of the Oak Tree, 63
Male, Il, 76
Mameli, Goffredo, 56, 237
Manili, Lorenzo, 267–68
Marble Faun, The (Hawthorne), 157–58
Marcellus, Marcus Claudius, 129
Marchesi del baldacchino, 147
Maremma–Non–Vuole, 167
Margana, Pietro, 148
Margani, Giovanni, 138
Margani, Ludovico, 65
Margani family, 138
Martin V, Pope, 41, 48, 50, 105
Mascarino, Ottaviano, 99
Mascherone fountain, 98
Masson, Georgina, 208, 220
Mattei, Astrubale, 145
Mattei family, 143, 145, 146, 216–17
Maturino da Firenze, 80, 86–87, 168–69
Mausoleum of Augustus, 37
Max Mara, 281
Mazzini, Guiseppe, 42, 250
Mazzoni, Giulio, 60, 61
Medical Diagnostic Center, 31
Medici, Giovanni de' (later Pope Leo X), 41, 68, 77, 95, 189
Medici, Giuliano de', 177
Meleagro, 145
Mella Stregata, 275
Mendelssohn, Moses, 249
Men's clothing, shopping for, 280–81
Mercuri, Pietro, 225
Messaggero, Il, 13
Metastasio (Pietro Trapessi), 81
Metellus, Quintus, 260
Metropolitan, 13
Michelangelo, 94, 97, 102, 142
Mignanelli family, 60

Index

Milesi, Antonio, 169
"Milk bars," (latterie), 240–41
Ministry of Cultural Affairs and Restoration, 225
Ministry of Justice, 156
Mino da Fiesole, 222, 230
Mirabilia, 123
Missoni, 281
Money, 29
Montaigne, Michel Eyquem de, 161
Monte Cassino, 50
Monte Giordano, 183–87
Monte di Pietà, 174–75
Monte Savello, 129
Moro, Aldo, 142
Mosaics, 119–20, 230–31
Movies, 14
Museo Nazionale Romano, 16
Museo Nuovo, 16
Museum of Rome (Museo di Roma), 17, 199
Museums, 12, 15–18, 62
Mussolini, Benito, 18, 43, 90, 110, 122, 133, 172–73
Myricae, 281

Napoleon Bonaparte, 42, 186, 198, 250
Nardini, Stefano, Cardinal, 192
National Gallery of Ancient Art, 17
National Gallery of Modern Art, 18
National Museum of Naples, 101, 103
National Museum of the Villa Giulia, 17
Neri, Saint Filippo, 56, 188–89
Nero, Roman emperor, 37–38, 67
Newspapers, 13
Nicholas, Saint, 125
Nino, 272
Noantri Festival, 14
Nolli, 157
Norceria Viola, 73

Odescalchi, Cardinal, 225
Open Book Shop, 240
Opera, 13
Oratorian Brothers, 188–189
Oratorio di S. Filippo Neri, 188–89, 190
Oratory of the Sacconi Rossi, 211–12
Order of the Fatebenefrattelli, 210
Orsini, Giordano, 183
Orsini, Virginio, 131
Orsini family, 66, 68, 73, 130–31, 183, 184–87
Ospizio di S. Michele, 17, 225, 233–34
Osteria (Via G. Bovio), 273
Osteria (Via di Santa Maria de' Calderari), 274
Ostia, 14, 22, 205, 214, 215, 223
Ostiense Air Terminal, 20, 21, 22
Ostrogoths, 148–49
Otto III, Holy Roman Emperor, 204, 210
Ovid, 208

Paese Sera, Il, 13
Palazzetto Sassi, 193–95
Palazzetto Spada, 58, 59
Palazzo Albertoni Spinola, 136, 137
Palazzo Altemps, 164–65
Palazzo Antonio Massimo, 161
Palazzo Boncompagni, 187
Palazzo Caffarelli, 16
Palazzo della Cancelleria, 76–79
Palazzo Capizucchi, 136–37
Palazzo Capponi, 84
Palazzo Cavalletti, 136
Palazzo Cenci, 251–53, 255
Palazzo Cisterna, 95
Palazzo dei Conservatori, 16
Palazzo of the Conti di Pitigliano, 185
Palazzo Corsetti, 87–88

Palazzo Costaguti, 147
Palazzo Delfini, 140
Palazzo Doria, 17
Palazzo dei Duchi di Bracciano, 185
Palazzo Falconieri, 96
Palazzo Farnese, 96, 97, 98, 100–105
Palazzo Flaminio Panzio, 133
Palazzo Fonseca, 195
Palazzo Gadi, 167–68, 169
Palazzo Gambirasi, 179
Palazzo Giangiacomo, 83
Palazzo Lancellotti, 170–72
Palazzo Lovatelli, 135–36
Palazzo Maccarani, 138
Palazzo Mattei Giove, 143–45
Palazzo Montoro, 82
Palazzo Nardini, 192
Palazzo Orsini, 130–31
Palazzo Ossoli, 64
Palazzo Pallavicini, 84, 87
Palazzo Pio, 68–69
Palazzo Ricci, 86–87, 93, 169
Palazzo Sachetti, 93
Palazzo di S. Agostino, 150, 156
Palazzo Salmoni Albertischi, 54–55
Palazzo Santacroce, 148
Palazzo degli Signori di Marino, 186
Palazzo Spada, 44, 59–63, 96
Palazzo dello S. Spirito, 187–88
Palazzo degli Stabilimento Spagnoli, 94
Palazzo Taverna, 185–87
Palazzo Turci, 192–93
Palazzo Varese, 94–95
Palazzo al Velabro, 279
Palazzo Velli, 138
Palazzo Venezia Museum, 18
Palestrina, Giovanni Pier Luigi da, 93, 188
Pamphili, Donna Olimpia, 235
Pamphili family, 185
Da Pancrazio, 69, 273
Paneformaggio, 274

Pantha, 167
Pantheon, 37, 38, 51, 125, 154, 198
Panzio, Flaminio, 133
Papa Giovanni, 271
Papal audiences, 15
Papal Court, 42, 47–48, 92, 179, 190, 196–97
  moved to Avignon, 41, 116
  see also Catholic Church; Vatican
Pascal I, Pope, 228
Pasquino, 14, 196–99
Passeggiata, 5
Passports, 7, 31
Patrizi, Maria Verginia, 82
Patrizia e Roberto del Pianeta Terra, 271
Paul III, Pope (formerly Alessandro Farnese), 100–102, 189, 198
Paul IV, Pope, 192, 247, 248, 251
Paul V, Pope, 51, 98, 133
Pawning, 174–75
Pazzi conspiracy, 177
Pensione Scalinata di Spagna, 278
Pension Suisse, 277
Pepin, 40, 47
de Pérac, 157
Perugino (Pietro Vannucci), 58, 176, 230
Peruzzi, Baldassare, 58, 94, 130, 176, 185, 247
Peruzzi, Galvestro, 247
Petrarch, 47, 56, 183
Pharmacies, 31–32
Philocrates, 224–25
Piazza del Biscione, 66–69
Piazza Bocca della Verità, 117, 120–22
Piazza Borghese, 30
Piazza del Campidoglio, 142
Piazza Campitelli, 133–37
Piazza Campo dei Fiori, 79
Piazza Capizucchi, 137–38
Piazza Capo di Ferro, 59–60

Index

Piazza dei Cinquecento, 21

Piazza delle Cinque Scuole, 251, 255–56

Piazza Farnese, 80, 98, 100

Piazza del Fico, 181

Piazza Lovatelli, 142

Piazza Margana, 138–40

Piazza dei Mercanti, 232, 233–34

Piazza Montanara, 128

Piazza Navona, 4, 165, 199, 247

neighborhood around, 151–99

Piazza dell'Orologio, 187–89

Piazza di Pasquino, 196–99

Piazza in Piscinula, 215–18

Piazza della Quercia, 63

Piazza della Repubblica, 21

Piazza Ricci, 86–87

Piazza S. Andrea della Valle, 81

Piazza S. Bartolomeo, 210–12

Piazza di S. Cecilia, 227, 233

Piazza di S. Ignazio, 63–64

Piazza S. Maria della Pace, 176–79

Piazza S. Maria del Pianto, 245, 248, 250–51, 267

Piazza di Spagna, 162

Piazza S. Simone, 172–73

Piazza di Tor Sanguigna, 165

Piazza Trilussa, 52, 53

Piazza della Trinità dei Pellegrini, 55–57

Piccolomini, Cardinal, 156

Pickpockets, 32

Picnics, 26

Pierleoni family, 130, 259

Pietro da Cortona, 57, 96, 177, 178, 179

Pilgrims, 50, 55–56, 109, 114, 154, 161, 162, 174, 240

guidebooks for, 123

stories of saints' lives written for, 227

"Pilate's House," 123

Pineider, 282

Pinelli, Achilli, 84

Pio di Carpi family, 68

Piombo, Sebastiano del, 176

Piovano, Vincenzo, 164

Piperno, 253–55, 271

Piramide Metro Station, 20

Pisano, Guidotto, 127

Piscina Rose, 15

Pius II, Pope, 76, 156, 206

Pius VI, Pope, 42, 103

Pius VIII, Pope, 198

Pius IX, Pope, 77, 210, 222

Pius XII, Pope, 187

Pizza da Loreto, 274

Pizzeria da Baffetto, 195, 274

Pizzeria ai Balestrari, 274

Pizzeria Er Grottino, 274

Pizzeria la Faschetta, 274

Pizzeria–Trattoria Galleria Sciarra, 274

Plague, 240

Platina, 48

Pliny, 67–68, 69, 88, 110, 125–26, 132, 208, 261

Podesti, 170

Podocatori, Monsignor, 88

Poggio Bracciolini, Gian Francesco, 50

Polidoro da Caravaggio (Polidoro Caldara), 80, 86–87, 168–69

La Pollarolo, 273

Pomarancio, 230

Pompey, 66, 73, 78, 89

statue of, 62–63, 69

Pons Janiculensis, 50, 52–53

Ponte Cestio, 129, 213–14

Ponte Fabricio, 204, 205, 213, 257

Pontelli, Baccio, 221

Ponte Rotto, 204, 213

Ponte S. Angelo, 50

Ponte Sisto, 50–52, 92, 98

Ponzani family, 230, 233

Porsena, Lars, 214

Porta, Giacomo della, 96, 98, 102, 126, 134, 135, 136, 145, 172, 224, 248, 251

Porta, Guglielmo della, 95

Porta Portese flea market, 31
Portichetto de Via della
    Consolazione, 127–28
Porticoes, 57–58, 127–28
Portico di Filippo, 266
Portico d'Ottavia, 3, 260–63,
    265
Portogallo, Elenora di, 90
Posi, Paolo, 95
Postal services, 19, 28
Postcards, shopping for, 282
Praxiteles, 261
Prints, shopping for, 157, 282
Prisons, 92, 117, 125–26
Pronto Spettacolo, 13
Publicola, Valerius, 148
Publishing trade, 156–57, 196
Purpureo, Lucius Funus, 208

Quinquatrie, 129
Quirinal Hill, 121

Rabelais, François, 161
Ragionamenti (Aretino), 166–67
Raguzzini, Filippo, 63–64, 92
Rainaldi, Carlo, 134–35
Rainaldi, Girolamo, 136
Ramanelli, 147
Raphael, 17, 93, 94, 145, 165–
    66, 176, 223
Raphael Salto, 280
Raymond, John, 6
Rea Silvia, 35
Red Squadron of Charioteers,
    103
Regina Margherita, queen of
    Italy, 224
Remus, 35, 110, 205
Reni, Guido, 230, 253
Repubblica, La, 13
Residenza di Ripetta, 279
Restaurants, 69, 87, 88, 173,
    195, 218, 232, 241, 251,
    253–55, 265, 270–74
  cheap, 273–74
  elegant and more expensive,
    270–71
  moderate, 272

relatively inexpensive, 273
  tipping in, 27
Riario, Cardinal, 77, 78, 79
Riario family, 77
Richard Ginori, 282
Richelieu, Armand–Jean du
    Plessis, Cardinal, 104
Rienzo, Cola di, 41, 116, 123,
    183, 264
La Rinascente, 30
Rioni, 154–55, 156
Ripando, Jacopo, 169
Ristorante La Gensola, 241
Ristorante Pierluigi, 273
Roberto Boccalini, 282
Rodd, Lord Rennel, 95
Romana, Francesca, 137
Roman Curia, 68
Romanelli, 165
Roman Empire, 3, 36–39, 49–
    50, 109, 110–13, 154,
    164, 173–74
Roman Forum, 15–16, 36, 43,
    88, 110, 111, 112, 128,
    133, 246, 278
Roman Senate, 126, 261
Romulus, 35, 110, 205
Rosa, Ercole, 225
Rosati, 275–76
Rossi, G. A. di, 179
Rossi, Giangiacomo di, 157
Rossi, Pellegrino, 78
Roxy, 281
Ruggeri, 72
Rush hours, 22

Saba, Saint, 53
Sac Joli, 280
Sack of Rome, 42, 133
Sadoleto, Jacopo, 166–65
Saffi, 42
St. John the Lateran Basilica,
    189, 229
St. Peter's Basilica, 83, 94, 102,
    128, 174, 189, 229
Sala Accademia di Via dei
    Greci, 14
Sala del Mappamondo, 18

Index

Salmoni Albertischi family, 54–55

Salustri, Carlo Alberto (known as Trilussa), 214

Salvator Mundi International Hospital, 31

Salvi, Nicolò, 157

Sanctis, Francisco de, 56

Sandwiches, 24, 26

Sangallo, Antonio da, the Younger, 84, 93, 101, 102, 103, 176

Sanguigni family, 70, 165

Santa Brigida, 276

Santacroce, Antonio, 148

Santacroce, Prospero, 148

Santacroce family, 148

Sant'Eustachio, 276

Santini e Dominici, 280

Saracens, 234

Sassi family, 193

Sauros, 261

Savelli, Pandolfo, 127

Savelli family, 81, 82, 130

Scaevola, 213–14

Scala Santa (Vatican), 62

Scapucci family, 158–59

Scarpetta, Giovambattista (called Titta), 237

Septimulenus, 225

Sermoneta, Sicciolante da, 176

Severan Marbles, 252

Severus, Alexander, Roman emperor, 120

Severus, Septimius, Roman emperor, 112, 256, 261

Sfondrati, Cardinal, 228

Sforza, Caterina, 68

Shelley, Percy Bysshe, 253

Shoes:
  shopping for, 279–80
  walking, 8

Shopping, 12, 29–31, 235, 279–82
  for antiques, 30, 82, 95, 160, 174

for books, 157, 282

at Campo dei Fiori market, 67, 70–73

for drawings and prints, 157, 282

for gifts and household items, 281–82

hours for, 12, 30–31

for jewelry, 79

for leather goods and shoes, 279–80

for men's clothing, 280–81

for postcards, 282

for women's clothing, 281

Siesta, 12

Signs, 53, 54

Sisters of the Immaculate Conception, 277

S.I.T.A., 21

Sixtus IV, Pope, 50–51, 53, 57, 65, 66, 74, 148, 159, 174, 177, 206, 221

Sixtus V, Pope, 121

Skin, 280

Snacks, 23, 24

Sosius, C., 132

Spada, Bernardino, Cardinal, 59, 60, 62

Spada, Virgilio, 188

Spada family, 58

Spark, Muriel, 186–87

Stadium of Domitian, 165

Stamps, buying, 28

Stazione Termini, 20–21, 22

S.T.E.F.E.R., 21

Strabo, 49

Subways, 21, 22–23, 69

Suetonius, 220

Summer Festival, 14

Supermarkets, 235

Swimming pools, 15

Symon, Arthur, 176

Symphorosa, Saint, 53

"Talking statues," 196–97

La Tana di Noantri, 272

Tanino Crisci, 280

Tarquinius Priscus, king of Rome, 35, 110
Tarquins, 148, 153–54, 207, 214
Tassi, Agostino, 172
Tasso, Torquato, 186, 198
Taverna Giulia, 271
Taxis, 19, 21–22
  tipping in, 27
La Tazza d'Oro, 276
Teatro Apollo (Teatro di Tor di Nona), 170
Teatro di Marcello, *see* Theater of Marcellus
Teatro dell'Opera, 13
Teatro di Pompeo, 66–68, 69, 73
Telephones, 27–28
Television, news on, 13
Temperature, 7–8
Tempietto del Carmello, 268
Temple of Aesculapius, 207, 210, 211
Temple of Apollo, 106, 131–32, 133, 259
Temple of Faunus, 208
Temple of Fortuna Virilis, 121–22
Temple of Hope, 125–26
Temple of Janus, 125–26, 132
Temple of Juno, 260–61
Temple of Juno Sospita, 125–26
Temple of Jupiter, 208
Temple of Jupiter Capitolinus, 36
Temple of Jupiter Stator, 260–61
Temple of Mars, 37
Temple of Venus and Roma, 38
Temple of Venus Victrix, 66, 73
Temple of Vesta, 121
Testa, 281
Theater of Balbus, 140
Theater of Marcellus (Teatro di Marcello), 3, 37, 109, 125, 127, 128–31, 132–33, 184, 259, 261, 265, 266

Theater of Pompey (Teatro di Pompeo), 66–68, 69, 73
Theater ushers, tipping of, 27
Theodoric, 68
Thermae of Agrippa, 154
Thermae of Diocletian, 38
Throne rooms, 147
Thurston, 55
Tiberinus, king of Etruscans, 204
Tiber Island, 130, 203, 204, 205, 207–13, 215, 257
Tiber River, 51, 120, 177, 204–7, 213
  bridges across, 50–53, 122–23, 129, 143, 204, 205, 212–14, 257
  embankment of, 52, 97, 206, 250
  flooding of, 51, 140, 154, 159, 206, 249–50
Tiburtius, 228
Ticket agencies, 13
Tipping, 27
Titian, 17, 62
Titus, Roman emperor, 256, 261, 263
Tolomei family, 220, 237
Torre della Contessa, 208, 209
Torre della Scimmia, 157–59
Tosca (Verdi), 134
Totila, 148–49
Tours, 15
Tradate, 280
Traffic, 32
Trains, 19–21
  from airports into city, 19–20
Trajan, Roman emperor, 38, 51, 155
Transportation, 19–23
  from airports, 19–20
  buses, 20, 21, 22
  subways, 21, 22–23, 69
  trains, 19–21
Trapessi, Pietro (Metastasio), 81
Trastevere, 4–5, 20, 50, 51–52, 84, 97, 129, 130, 143, 203–4, 207, 213–41, 245, 257

Index

Trasteverini, 214
Trattoria Armando, 273
Trattoria–Pizzeria da Mario, 274
Traveler's checks, 29
Tre G, 13
Tre Scalini, 276
Tribune of Roman republic, 77
Trilussa (Carlo Alberto Salustri), 214
Triumphal Arch of Titus, 38
Trompe l'oeil painting, 168, 195, 61–62
Trovaroma, 13
Turci, Pietro, 193
Turtle Fountain, 144, 145–46

Uffizi, 261
Urban I, Pope, 228
Urban II, Pope, 127, 208
Urban VIII, Pope, 192

Valentine, Saint, 120
Valentinian, Roman emperor, 52
Valentino's Boutique, 281
Valerianus, 227–28
Valerii family, 227
Vallicelliana Library, 189
Value Added Tax (I.V.A.), 29
Valvassari, Gabrieli, 224, 239
Vanita, 281
Vanni, Raphael, 176
Vanozza, 101
Vanvitelli, Luigi, 157, 230
Vasari, Giorgio, 78, 80, 86–87, 101, 169
Vatican, 28, 43, 62, 65, 74, 77, 78, 80, 92, 101, 102, 105, 154, 155, 157, 174, 181, 197, 223, 247, 251
  papal audiences at, 15
  pilgrims to, 50, 55–56, 109, 114, 123, 154, 161, 162, 174, 227, 240
  see also Catholic Church; Papal Court

Vatican Museums, 16, 160, 236
Vecchia Roma, 135, 271
Vegetables, 25, 26
Velabrum, 110–12
Venerable English College, 83
Verdi, Giuseppe, 134, 170
Vertecchi, 282
Vespasian, Roman emperor, 208, 220, 261, 263
Vespasiani, 220
Via degli Acquasparta, 165–67
Via Anicia, 220–24
Via dell'Arco della Pace, 175–76
Via dell Arco dei Tolomei, 218–20
Via del Babuino, 95, 160
Via dei Balestrari, 64–65, 76
Via dei Banchi Vecchi, 88
Via della Barchetta, 84
Via del Biscione, 69–70
Via Caetani, 142–45
Via Capo di Ferro, 57–59
Via dei Cappellari, 79–81, 92
Via Catalana, 256–57
Via del Corallo, 191–92
Via dei Coronari, 95, 160, 172, 173–75
Via de Delfini, 140
Via dei Falegnami, 146–47
Via del Foro Olitorio, 125
Via de' Funari, 142–46
Via dei Genovesi, 221, 235
Via dei Gigli d'Oro, 161
Via Giulia, 58–59, 60, 80, 81, 92–98, 160
Via del Governo Vecchio, 187, 188, 189–96, 199
Via di Grotta Pinta, 69
Via Lancellotti, 170–72
Via della Luce, 236, 237–39
Via della Lungaretta, 240–41
Via della Madonna dell'Orto, 224–25
Via della Maschera d'Oro, 167–70
Via del Mascherone, 98–105

Via di Monserrato, 80, 83–88, 89–90, 160, 169
Via Montanara, 133
Via di Monte Fiore, 240
Via di Monte Giordano, 181–87, 191
Via di Montoro, 81–83
Via degli Orsini, 187
Via dell'Orso, 159–64
Via della Pace, 179–81
Via del Pellegrino, 76, 79, 81, 88, 89–90, 91
Via dei Pettinari, 53–55
Via di Ponte Rotto, 122–23
Via del Portico d'Ottavia, 257–67
Via dei Portoghesi, 156–59
Via Recta, 173–74
Via della Reginella, 266
Via dei Salumi, 236–37
Via di S. Maria de Calderari, 255
Via di S. Michele, 227
Via dei Soldati, 163, 164–65
Via del Teatro di Marcello, 123–33, 137
Via del Tempio, 257
Via Titta Scarpetta, 237
Via dei Tre Archi, 167
Via del Velabro, 110–17
Via Veneto, 97
Vicolo dell'Atleta, 235–36
Vicolo del Bollo, 81
Vicolo del Buco, 239
Vicolo dei Cenci, 251–53
Vicolo del Gallo, 79–80
Vicolo della Madonnella, 58
Vicolo del Montaccio, 183
Vicolo Monte dei Cenci, 252, 253–55
Vicolo di S. Maria in Cappella, 234

Vicolo di S. Simone, 167, 170
Vicolo dei Tabacchi, 222
Victor III, Pope, 208
Victor Emmanuel I, king of Italy, 42, 43
Victor Emmanuel III, king of Italy, 43
Vignola, Giacomo da (Giocomo Barozzi), 17, 58, 79, 101, 142, 223
Villa Borghese, 16–17
Villa Caprarola, 101
De La Ville–InterContinental, 278–79
Villa de' Medici, 168
Villus, Andreas, 138
Virgil, 118, 206
Visas, 7
Visigoths, 113
Viterbo, Antonio da, 230
Vitigis the Goth, 49
Vitruvius, 129
Volpetti's, 156
Voltaire (François–Marie Arouet), 63
Volterra, Francesco da, 170, 223

Waiblinger, William Frederick, 99
Wardrobe, 7–8, 33
Wine, 26
Women's clothing, shopping for, 281
World War II, 43, 54, 56, 90, 130, 172, 218, 250, 256, 257, 260

Zola, Emile, 136
Zuccari, Frederico, 224

THE HENRY HOLT WALKS SERIES
For people who want to *learn* when they travel, not just see.

Look for these other exciting volumes in Henry Holt's best-selling Walks series:

PARISWALKS, Revised Edition, by Alison and Sonia Landes
Five intimate walking tours through the most historic quarters of the City of Light.
288 pages, photos, maps $12.95 Paper

LONDONWALKS, Revised Edition, by Anton Powell
Five historic walks through old London, one brand-new for this edition.
272 pages, photos, maps $12.95 Paper

VENICEWALKS by Chas Carner and Alessandro Giannatasio
Four enchanting tours through one of the most perfect walking environments the world has to offer.
240 pages, photos, maps $12.95 Paper

FLORENCEWALKS, Revised Edition, by Anne Holler
Four intimate walks through this exquisite medieval city, exploring its world-famous art and architecture.
240 pages, photos, maps $12.95 Paper

VIENNAWALKS, Revised Edition, by J. Sydney Jones
Four walking tours that reveal the homes of Beethoven, Freud, and the Habsburg monarchy.
304 pages, photos, maps $12.95 Paper

RUSSIAWALKS by David and Valeria Matlock
Seven intimate tours—four in Moscow and three in Leningrad—that explore the hidden treasures of these enigmatic cities.
304 pages, photos, maps $12.95 Paper

NEW YORKWALKS by The 92nd Street Y, edited by Batia Plotch
One of the city's most visible cultural and literary institutions guides you through six historic neighborhoods in New York.
336 pages, photos, maps $12.95 Paper

BARCELONAWALKS by George Semler
Five walking tours through Spain's cultural and artistic center—synonymous with such names as Gaudí, Miró, and Picasso.
272 pages, photos, maps $12.95 Paper

JERUSALEMWALKS, Revised Edition, by Nitza Rosovsky
Six intimate walks that allow the mystery and magic of this city to unfold.
304 pages, photos, maps $14.95 Paper

BEIJINGWALKS by Don J. Cohn and Zhang Jingqing
Six intimate walking tours of the most historic quarters of this politically and culturally complex city.
272 pages, photos, maps $15.95 Paper.

BERLINWALKS by Peter Fritzsche and Karen Hewitt
Four walking tours through this exuberant and colorful city exploring its culture and history.
256 pages, photos, maps $14.95 Paper

MADRIDWALKS by George Semler
Five extraordinary walking tours that uncover the many architectural treasures and historical secrets of this glorious city.
284 pages, photos, maps $14.95 Paper

PRAGUEWALKS by Ivana Edwards
Five walking tours through a magical city that has been described as a museum in which people live and work, for nowhere are sights ancient and beautiful as concentrated as they are here.
288 pages, photos, maps $14.95 Paper

Available at your local bookseller or from Special Sales Department, Henry Holt and Company, 115 West 18th Street,

New York, New York 10011 (212) 886-9200. Please add $2.00 for postage and handling, plus $.50 for each additional item ordered. (New York residents, please add applicable state and local sales tax.) Please allow 4–6 weeks for delivery. Prices and availability are subject to change.